D0832944

THEORY AND PRACTICE

180
ROT

© 1977 by Martinus Nijhoff. The Hague, The Netherlands
All rights reserved, including the right to translate or to
reproduce this book or parts thereof in any form

ISBN 90 247 2004 4

SET IN ISRAEL BY ISRATYPESET, JERUSALEM

PRINTED IN THE NETHERLANDS

CONTENTS

CONTENTS

PART ONE

TRANSFORMATIONS OF CONCEPTS

I. TYPES OF KNOWING

A

In this examination of the nature of the relationship between thought and action, between theory and practice, we assume at the very outset that thought and action represent different ways of approaching the world, different modes of relating to it. Both thought and action exhibit phases that need to be explained if we are to arrive at any conclusion concerning the character of these relations, their inter-connection and their differences, whether rooted in the full or in the relative independence of each.

A discussion of the meaning of these two relations, however, is confronted with a number of interpretations. The contents of the concepts involved lend themselves to many meanings: To determine these it will be necessary to devote the first part of this study to tracing the historical development of the nature of theory, on the one hand, and that of practice, on the other. Such an examination may provide us with a number of distinctions which will stand us in good stead when we come to consider the positive concept of the nature of theory and practice. We now turn to some of the discussions that have taken place in the development of philosophical thought concerning the nature of these two elements.

B

The inquiry into the nature of theory and practice and the distinctions between these two spheres occupied a prominent place in Greek philosophy. Indeed, the terminology that characterizes this subject was given to us by the Greek philosophers.

The Greek θεωρία (theoria) is derived from the root θεωρέω (theoreo) which means to see, to regard. The word in the various European languages that corresponds to the Greek term 'theory' contains the element of 'seeing'. The Latin *speculatio*, for instance, has retained the meaning of 'sight' or 'vision', and *contemplatio*, the

3

meaning of 'viewing'. The element of sight or vision is always found in
the terminological evolution of this Greek term.* Current usage tends
to confuse such terms as 'theoretical', 'speculative', 'reflective', 'academic', in designating that aspect of discourse which is regarded for its
own sake from the standpoint of the viewer.

C

In coming now to the consideration of the specific meanings of the
concept 'theory' we must first indicate the characteristics of that
mode or type of seeing that constitutes theory as seeing *par excellence*. We shall have occasion to note a number of features that have
been suggested for characterizing this type of seeing.

In pre-Socratic philosophy we find an intimation of a connecting
link between theory as 'vision' and as 'a turning to the gods', although
it is possible to dispute this connection from the standpoint of ety-
mology. Some scholars, however, regard the relationship as well
founded.[1] Pythagoras says that it is theory, in the sense of active
viewing, that enables us to assimilate to the divine[2] or to strive toward
an *imitatio dei*. This would indicate a connection between 'theory'
and 'divinity' apart from any etymological considerations.

In the course of time this connection between theory and human
aspiration became more and more prominent, human aspiration being
made identical with well-being insofar as the individual is able to free
himself from the drudgery of daily life. This connection between the
significance of theory and the peculiar value inherent within it also
appears in the systems of Plato and Aristotle, the difference being that
what had been timidly expressed in pre-Socratic philosophy is set
forth with greater conviction in the Platonic and Aristotelian sources.
However, we must look further and seek to discover the specific connection between the nature of theory and that of the objects to which
it refers, that is, the nature of these objects in terms of reality.

D

In his *Metaphysics,* Aristotle states that we consider the masterworkers in each craft to be more honorable and wiser than the manual

---

* In Hebrew the corresponding term is *iyyun;* its root meaning is 'vision' – not in the sense
   of the act of seeing, but rather referring to the organ of vision, the eye, despite the fact
   that its original sense is 'devotion'.

workers because the former know the causes of the things that are done.[3] With these words Aristotle wishes to indicate that there is a connection between the intentionality of knowledge and the causes of things that are done. The essence of knowledge does not reside in the haphazard subjects of chance but in the realm of causes. The significance attached to causes in the sphere of possible subjects of discourse accounts for the significance of knowledge respecting causes. In this connection Aristotle states that the masterworkers are wiser not because they know how to act but because they have a knowledge of causes. Aristotle uses the term knowledge in its broad sense, which includes its relation to causes. This emphasis on causes as distinct from the procedure involved in activity itself confers a superior status on those who have a knowledge of the causes. A knowledge of causes is not activity: It is knowledge and always remains such. It is possible to perform an act, but insofar as this act involves a knowledge of causes we cannot speak of performance or execution. In this discourse, emphasis already is being placed on the status of knowledge as wisdom, because it lies in the very nature of objects as causes that wisdom should be directed to them. In this case, the object is not completely severed from the sphere of action; it is attached to this sphere, for it deals with the causes of things that are done. But insofar as there is a difference between causes and things, the intentionality toward causes places the relationship of intentionality to knowledge on a higher plane than that occupied by the relationship inherent in the doing of things.

A closer examination of Aristotle's argument reveals an additional factor. The cognitive activity referring to the knowledge of causes is the knowledge of that which is most knowable and superior to any other knowledge precisely because it deals with causes.[4] This statement does not characterize the nature of these causes but merely defines them as the causes of things that are done and not the things done themselves. It does, however, point out the significance that adheres to knowledge of the sphere of causes, since such knowledge is more instructive than preoccupation with things done themselves. Perhaps a better way to put it is that the idea of the most knowable is a greater and more instructive knowledge; its meaning in this context is that the knowledge of causes is more extensive than is the reference of the things done. The knowledge of causes could be more fruitful and could lead us into doing various things and not only some definite thing or things that we are accustomed to do as the result of skills acquired through experience, repetition, or habit. This may be illustrated by an example taken from daily life. When I repair a table, I am inclined to repeat the identical process adopted on previous occasions; but when I know the causes — that is, have a knowledge of dimension, weight, and pressure — I can evolve models for tables that need to be repaired and I am not obliged to repeat all over again the same operations used previously.

Another characteristic emerges from Aristotle's exposition. When we speak of the knowledge of causes, we refer to a sphere of knowledge which is superior to one that requires only skill and knowledge derived from experience and custom. Knowledge that pertains to a sphere that is superior by virtue of its nature and level of instruction is not mere knowledge alone since it adheres to a sphere that yields useful results. It is also knowledge of that which we are supposed to know. By virtue of these aspects, in the nature of the theoretical-speculative relationship theory becomes the highest type of knowledge.

In his characterization of theory, Aristotle accorded to theory a preferential status because of the nature of the sphere of objects (causes) to which it refers and because this sphere serves no other end outside itself. A knowledge of causes is fruitful but it is also knowledge in itself, knowledge for its own sake. The status of causes is one that exists for its own sake and not for something outside itself. Aristotle's argument thus amounts to what may be called an independent teleology of theory. Since the sphere of the objects of theory exists for its own sake, then theory, which refers to the sphere of objects, also exists for itself or for the knowledge of objects. Theory, in its intentionality to these objects, does not exist for anything outside itself.

Aristotle contends, in other words, that the theoretical sphere is sufficient unto itself (autarchy) and exists as such from the standpoint of the objects, on the one hand, and the relation of seeing directed to the objects, on the other. But insofar as the theoretical intentionality of these objects is a conscious one, theory is not a passive awareness of objects but an activity. Aristotle thus attempts to combine two aspects in this notion: In the theoretical relation we encounter the ultimate sphere of objects, but we do not remain there in a passive state of rest. Constant activity is required in order to reach this point and make of it a theoretical encounter. This emphasis on the active element in theory, the prominence given to the activity inherent within it, enables Aristotle not only to find a place for theory on the ladder of knowledge but also to give it an ethical status, since such a status is in Aristotle's view dependent on activity and not on a state of protracted passivity. Aristotle therefore combines theory, viewed as

self-contained thought, with activity,[5] and regards these two aspects
as characteristic of it.

E

We have seen above that theory is taken to be cognitive intentionality
with respect to causes. It is possible to understand causes in their
neutral sense, causes in the broadest sense of this term, including the
causes of things done. It follows that the concept of causes rests on
theory as intentionality toward the status of the object regarded as an
object of knowledge. The inner nature of this object has as yet not
been determined, nor the place it occupies in the scale of reality. This
further step is taken by Aristotle in his characterization of theory.
One of the reasons that prompted him to take this step is to be found
in the thought emphasized above — namely, that theory is a closed
circle wherein knowledge in its cognitive aspect is combined with the
object of knowledge on its own level. This fusion appears in the Pytha-
gorean dictum mentioned above and is expressed by Plato in *Phaedrus*
where it is conceived as a relationship between the cosmic status of
objects and the intentionality of knowledge or the soul toward this
object. This fusion, according to Plato, rests on the fact that there is a
mutual dependence between the soul's understanding of itself and the
relationship to the whole world: "And do you think that you can
know the nature of the soul intelligently without knowing the nature
of the whole [world]?"[6] If we understand the knowledge whereby
the soul knows itself as one of the expressions of the knowledge of the
object to be known, then such knowledge is not to be divorced from
the knowledge of the nature of the cosmos. We might say that there is
a cosmic coordinate to knowledge wherein the soul knows itself.

The cosmic status of knowledge which, in Plato's words, appears in
combination with the soul's knowledge of itself is also emphasized by
Aristotle in another form. Metaphysics, as the foremost among the
sciences, is concerned with things that exist separately and are immov-
able.[7] The cosmic status of the objects of knowledge *par excellence,*
knowledge that is metaphysical from the standpoint of the sphere to
which it pertains and theoretical from the standpoint of its inner
nature, is evident from the fact that the objects of this knowledge are
not affected by change: they are eternal. We began our inquiry with a
consideration of the connection between theory and causes; it now
remains for us to consider the connection between theory in the
highest sense of the term, which is the theory of metaphysics, and the

causes that are separate from things that are mutable and not subject
to change. The cosmic status of an object of theoretical knowledge
appears as the highest status of beings dealt with by theory, that is,
the uppermost rung on the scale of reality. In this context Aristotle
adds that all causes — that is, first causes — must necessarily be eternal, especially those causes that have a divine element insofar as such
an element can be detected by us. These words of Aristotle must here
be understood as an attempt on his part to indicate the presence of
eternal causes in the movements of the heavenly bodies.[8] He therefore
places emphasis not only on the status of the objects of knowledge as
causes, but also on the status of these objects as beings *par excellence*,
that is, as eternal beings. If theory is another aspect of the nature of
objects as objects and beings, it is represented to us as in a circle
including theory, as the intentionality of knowledge, on the one hand,
and the axis of the object and the being of theory on the other. This
circle is stressed by Aristotle, who states that the highest science —
that is, metaphysics as science and theory as the nature of metaphysical knowledge — must necessarily be considered as the highest
genus of objects and of beings.[9] The object as the highest being raises
theory to the level of the highest knowledge and this knowledge must
in turn necessarily refer to the object in its capacity as the highest
being.

We are confronted once more with the element of correlation or the
circle in its ethical aspect. The status of an object and of a being
confers ethical significance upon the knowledge that is directed to it,
and the knowledge directed to that which is an object of a being *par·
excellence* becomes the goal of man. Thinking *qua* thinking, says
Aristotle, is concerned with the object that is best in itself. In other
words, this thinking which is thinking in the highest sense of the term
is concerned with that which is best in itself, and such thinking deals
with that which is best in its fullest sense. Thought thinks itself
because it shares the nature of the object of thought. From this Aristotle concludes that the theoretical act is the most pleasurable and the
most excellent.[10] If we introduce the concept of the divine object
into this discourse, as Aristotle does in this context, theory acquires a
divine status which is an attribute of its objects.

This basic position concerning the nature of theory can be summed
up by saying that in theory we are confronted with a symmetrical
relationship of the intentionality of knowledge and the status of the
object of this intentionality. Theory presents us with the double
quality of the object as object *per se* of knowledge and as being *per se*
on the scale of beings. As a result of this symmetrical relation between

the two aspects of theory, the existential value of the object is at the same time an ethical value. Theory possesses ethical value because it is at the apex of man's knowledge and because it deals with things that are at the apex of being and of the good.

This analysis would be incomplete if it failed to note that Aristotle used the concept of theory not only in the special sense described above, but in its wider sense as the sum-total of knowledge concerning the sphere or the subject as such. He thus states that the task of science is to reduce all things to some kind of theory, and therefore he speaks of the theory of plants and the processes of nutrition.[11] In other words, theory is learning *überhaupt*. We note in this connection that Aristotle's discussion contains an intimation of the manifold meanings of the term 'theory' as used by him, as well as an indication of its future development after it had freed itself from dependence on the distinctive spheres of eternal or divine causes.

F

Accompanying any inquiry into the nature of theory must be a discussion of the nature of the act or the nature of the sphere of acts. We must at the outset bear in mind the fact that the discussion of the nature of the act emerges as a result of the threefold division of 'knowledge', that is, the act is represented from the view of the character of knowledge inherent within it. This is, of course, not knowledge referring to theory for without knowledge an act can neither exist nor be realized, and without relation to knowledge we are not in a position to characterize the various types of acts. We find one definite type that is a type of active knowledge; it is according to this type that the sphere of the act is characterized, together with its subordinate realms or subsidiary branches. The Greek conception recognizes two spheres of acts, or two areas of knowledge that are related to these two spheres: activity and productivity.

The discussion found in Diogenes Laertius in the name of Plato helps to clarify this subject. Here we read that the construction of houses, for example, and the art of shipbuilding are of the productive type of act, for it is possible to view the finished products. But the art of politics, along with the art of playing the flute and the harp and such like, are of the practical kind, for these produce no finished product that can be contemplated but merely peform something: One plays the flute, the other the harp, and a third works for the state. Geometry, harmonics, and astronomy, on the other hand, are of the theoretical kind, for these neither perform nor produce anything. A geometrician investigates how some lines are related to others; a musician is concerned with the nature of sounds; the astronomer contemplates the stars and the universe. The sciences, then, are partly of the theoretical, partly of the practical, and partly of the productive kinds of acts.[12]

There is no need now to return to the subject of theory and the sciences of the theoretical type since this subject, being intimately connected with the nature of theory, has already been examined above. This portion of our inquiry shall be confined to the act, viewed from its practical aspect, on the one hand, and from its productive aspect, on the other.

It has been suggested that the sciences may be divided according to the following criteria: namely, in accordance with the nature of the relationship of the investigator to his particular science, and in accordance with the nature of the objects to which his activity is directed. It is clear from what has been said above that such a criterion is necessary in order to differentiate theory from action. He who contemplates theoretically does not interfere in the process of things: Theory is an activity and rests on acts as stated above. Things have a structure and this structure in its manifestation is the ground of the activity of theory. We can say that the division proposed by Plato and adhered to by Aristotle (who in this matter follows in Plato's footsteps) imparts to theory the function of presenting things as they are. From Plato's discussion, however, and from the examples he gives it is plain that in both practical and productive sciences there is interference in the process of things. They are capable of bringing about definite results, the difference between the two being dependent on the nature of the results produced. This difference may be defined as follows: We are confronted with an act or with the knowledge that produces an act, culminating in a definite deed or activity. Over against this we have an act, or the knowledge that produces an act, which results in a finished product having a physical form, like a house or a ship. Even though playing an instrument or conducting state affairs may be regarded as acts — for they entail interference in the process of things — this interference does not produce something that is separate and distinct from the activity itself. In the sphere of an act of this kind we always remain within the confines of doing.

A closer analysis of Plato's discussion reveals his preference for the kind of act and the kind of knowledge that leads to action that does not culminate in a finished product with permanent features, such as building a house or a ship. We must bear in mind what was stated above concerning the character of theory arising from the symmetry between the cognitive intentionality on the one hand, and the object of this intentionality on the other. If we apply this characterization of theory suggested by Aristotle to the subject under consideration, we can say that the act that does not produce results which are distinct from the act itself and from the doer himself remains within the sphere of the act and is a kind of withdrawal into itself — which is characteristic of theory. It is true that in playing an instrument an act of hearing tones is produced, but this act is conjoined to the act itself and accompanies the act itself: The hearing exists only as long as the act of playing continues. The fact that we here have a change, that is, an act is produced whereby an auditory phenomenon creates the distinction between action and theory, does not mean that the act gives rise to a product that is separate and distinct; the product adheres to the act and relates it, insofar as it is an interiorization within the confines of the act, to the inward character of theory.

Furthermore, if the act does not result in a distinct and separate product and remains within the limits of its sphere, then this act cannot be said to serve an end beyond itself. To serve such an end beyond itself an act requires a certain degree of separate and independent existence of the product with respect to the act that gives rise to it. The withdrawal of the act into itself brings it close to the sphere of theory which serves no end beyond itself. Here again, as we have seen above, we are confronted with the independent teleology of theory. In this case, however, we do not speak of an independent teleology of theory, but of a transfer to the sphere of action. The question of an independent teleology is one that arises in different contexts, and we shall meet it again when we come to discuss Kant's views of the ethical act as well as his views of aesthetic creation. In this connection there is an additional consideration that may be called an extension of the applicability of the character of an independent teleology beyond theory in the strict sense of this concept as knowledge. Since the question of applicability is a basic one in the classical discussions of this problem, and since the theoretical sphere is presented as one devoid of considerations of applicability, philosophical discussions in the various areas of action often betray a tendency toward a leveling of non-usefulness, as it were, so that not only the sphere of theory but all the other spheres as well will be characterized by non-usefulness.

Plato's basic views, as summarized above, are also to be found in Aristotle, who elaborates them. The central point in Plato's discussion may be described as the phenomenology of the various modes of knowledge. This characterization is given a significant turn by Aristotle. There are three things in the soul, according to Aristotle, that

control action and truth — sensation, desire, reason. Of these, sensation does not originate action: This is clear from the fact that the
lower animals have sensation but no share in action. What affirmation
and negation are in thinking, Aristotle goes on to say, pursuit and
avoidance are in desire.[13] With the new component that Aristotle
introduces into this context he not only takes note of the relationships in accordance with a criterion — namely, whether they permit
interference in the process of things or not — but goes beyond this to
point out the nature of the substratum, that is, the substratum of the
soul to which the relationship applies. This substratum is on the one
hand thinking and on the other desire. Aristotle attempts to describe
our twofold relationship to these two types of substrata. The activity
of thought is a positive activity, a determination that the substratum
of things is such and such or that it is an activity of negation; that is, a
determination that the substratum of things is not such and such.
Parallel to these tendencies of the relations of thinking we have the
tendencies of desire, which seeks to attain something or to evade
something. In the sphere of desire, wherein desire originates acts themselves, we are faced with the problem of the tendency of desire or that
of deliberation to direct it to make a choice that will prove to be a
good one. Real deliberation directs the choice of desires in such a
manner that it will try to attain superior deliberation as the true one.
In the sphere of the act, discussed by Aristotle in this context, the
element of knowledge seems to mean not only that knowledge is
needed in order to act, such as the knowledge required to produce
tones on the flute or harp, but also knowledge that directs desire into
the proper course. What is proper? This is a dianoetic determination
and does not fall within the limits of practical determination. When
Aristotle here speaks of direction by means of knowledge, he is referring to intellect and to practical intellect, at the same time naming this
genus of intellect and this genus of truth as practical.[14] We can sum
up by saying that this genus of intellect which combines proper knowledge and deliberation that is rooted in it and that directs the choice
of desire to that which is proper to be chosen is the practical intellect
which establishes the practical sphere in the limited sense of this concept. If the theoretical sphere is, in the limited sense of the term, the
sphere of knowledge of what ought to be known, then the practical
sphere is the sphere of action respecting what ought to be done.
Furthermore, in the introduction to further discussion of the subject,
Aristotle speaks of a third genus of intellect, that is, the creative
intellect, an allusion probably to what Plato called the productive act.
We shall treat this later in more detail.

It seems that we here have an additional thought concerning the ethical significance of theoretical knowledge itself. Its purpose is to stress the fact that if theoretical knowledge is to be understood as the proper end of desire, then this knowledge (to the extent that it is basically directed to truth and not to what is proper and just, that is, being the goal of desire which is the opposite of avoidance) becomes the ethical end as proper desire controlled by the knowledge of truth. This Aristotelian conception, then, gives knowledge a double superiority: (a) the element of knowledge appears in all relationships, including the relationship which is practical. Without knowledge there is no act. The ethical act is not only an act that requires knowledge; it is also subject to the principle of truth which is the principle of theoretical knowledge, and as such regulates desire which gives rise to the practical relationship; (b) knowledge contains its own justification within itself as theoretical knowledge which deals with what ought to be known, and it is also the proper and supereminent goal of desire. Proper choice is regulated by knowledge, on the one hand, and is in the last analysis directed toward it, on the other. It is clear that knowledge is a condition of an act and is, from the standpoint of theory, the end of desire. This component of knowledge, which is rooted in the sphere of action, contains the ground and reason for the numerous attempts in the history of thought to base the sphere of acts on the presupposition that it has kind of syllogistic structure such as:

I need a roof over my head.
  (In other words, a roof is a good thing and I wish to obtain it.)
A roof is on the house.
  (I.e. the operation that is completed by means of previous deliberations is the building of a house.)[15]

The characterization of the practical sphere would be incomplete if we failed to mention an additional quality that distinguishes it. All things that are to be done deal with particulars or with ultimates, that is, things we wish to obtain by directing our desire toward them.[16] In this characterization of the practical sphere we no longer think of the psychological substratum of the act or the principle that regulates the act, but are concerned with the circumstances in which the act occurs and in which we desire to carry out the task for the sake of which the act was originally initiated. These circumstances are always individual and particular. When we turn to a matter that we desire to carry out under given conditions, we require judgment, which is another aspect of deliberation. Whereas theory in the strict sense of the term is intentionality toward the eternal and immutable — and it is this status of a theoretical object that confers upon it its peculiar position — the act, that is the ethical act, is an activity within the framework of partial and changing conditions. Since this is dependent upon the nature of circumstances, we must perforce know what to choose and how to choose. From another point of view, a difference emerges between theory and act parallel to the difference between thought and deliberation or between contemplation and judgment. There is an element of knowledge in both spheres. This element deals with different matters in each of the spheres and, in accordance with the diversity of matters dealt with, there is a difference in the representation of the element of knowledge — theory and judgment that are within deliberation. To this we can add another difference previously considered, namely, that thought contains no interference because it deals with a sphere that is not subject to change, interference being the intrusion of change into things. Where there is no diversity there cannot exist logical space caused by interference. An act, however, is interference, and such interference can occur in principle in a sphere that provides room for change. This sphere is that of changing circumstances since these facilitate change, and the act must adjust itself to them. The element of judgment will be discussed later when we come to consider the act as construction as distinguished from the act that is directed to the goal of desire.

Whereas the philosophical discourse of the nature of theory is that of the relation to the universe in its totality and the sphere of objects of the universe as eternal beings, philosophic discourse in the sphere of the act deals with matters relevant to man. This thought may be expressed following Aristotle in his *Nicomachean Ethics*[17] : Theoretical discourse, which is changeless, appears as being on a cosmic level; practical discourse including ethical discourse, which resides in partial and particular circumstances, appears to be on the human level. The intentionality of theory is extensive, while the intentionality of acts is limited; this is an additional aspect of the difference between theory and act. We now turn to a clarification of 'creative' or 'constructive' knowledge.

G

We have thus far been concerned with the nature of the act and have treated it as ancillary to the discussion of the nature of theory. But within the sphere of the act itself Aristotle distinguishes between two

realms, the realm of operational knowledge and that of executive
knowledge, or that of action and deed (πράξισ ... ποίησις). Let us
examine the basis on which this distinction rests.

In the chapter on intellectual virtue in the *Nicomachean Ethics,*
Aristotle attempts to clarify this point. Within the limits of intellectual virtue Aristotle makes a distinction between science as the sphere
of theory, on the one hand, and arts as practical knowledge or as a
special kind of practical knowledge, on the other. Science deals with
necessary and eternal distinctions. It is not necessary to elaborate this
point, for we have already dealt with it in connection with our discussion of the nature of the theoretical sphere. According to Aristotle,
the arts deal with change and with that which is subject to change.
However, this sphere includes things that are done. As an example of
an activity that is rooted in an intellectual ability to make something
Aristotle cites architecture. Art is concerned with the formation of
things in order that they may exist, that is, with bringing things into
the world. This refers to the production of things whose source is in
the maker and not in the thing made. To say that the source of things
that are made is within the things themselves means that these things
have an inner source, in which case it is possible to relegate them to
the sphere of necessity. But insofar as things made have their source in
the 'maker', it is plain that they belong to the realm of things that
could possibly exist or could possibly not exist. The decision in favor
of possible existence as against nonexistence depends on the maker
and not on the things themselves.[18]

In this characterization of the sphere of making or the sphere of the
arts Aristotle does not place the emphasis on the finished product, as
we found in the passage of Plato quoted by Diogenes Laertius. It is
true that this passage discusses the product with reference to the doer
or maker, but its main point is to distinguish between the maker and
the separate, distinct nature of the product after it had been produced. Aristotle, however, places the emphasis on the relation
between the maker and the product, apart from the question of
whether the finished product is distinct from the maker or not. The
fact is that the thing produced is dependent on the maker since he is
the original source of the production. This dependence is not removed
even after the product is finished and has an independent existence of
its own. We also find Aristotle quoting the example of architecture,
using words similar to those of Plato in speaking of the construction
of houses or ships. We see that Aristotle, just as Plato, recognizes the
connection between the act and the intellectual element, the source of
the act being the intellectual state of the doer, a state that finds its

expression in the planning of the architectonic project. From this point of view doing entails deliberation.

Over against this doing as the production of things in order to bring them into being, Aristotle places practical wisdom. Practical wisdom does not belong in the sphere of science, for it is not concerned with things that are eternal and immutable. From this point of view it is similar to the wisdom implicit in an opus such as an architectonic work. Practical wisdom produces things that could possibly exist and that could possibly not exist, for their existence depends on the direction given by practical wisdom or in this case by the doer. But whereas the opus produced refers to things that one wishes to produce, such as architecture, practical wisdom refers to things that are good or bad with respect to man or that are done for his sake. Practical wisdom, just as poetic wisdom, engenders things or acts; it can be poetic as well as intellectual. But whereas poetic wisdom produces works whose end lies outside themselves, practical wisdom cannot produce works of this sort, since a good activity is its own end. The difference between ethical acts and poetic acts is one within the common genus of intentionality toward things that could possibly exist and those that could not. From this point of view there is a difference between the theoretical sphere, on the one hand, and the sphere of ethical acts and the sphere of poetic acts on the other. In the common sphere of actions and deeds there is a difference with respect to ends. The characterization of this difference clearly depends on Aristotle's view that the good deed is an end in itself. Being an end in itself, theory becomes the good deed *par excellence,* an aspect that we have already considered in another connection.

Plato makes a distinction between works that are separate from the doer and works that are not separate from the doer. Aristotle likewise adheres to this distinction but gives it a somewhat new turn by holding that a work that is separate from the doer, being a work of art, serves an end beyond itself. By virture of the fact that it is separate from the doer it creates the conditions whereby it serves an end beyond itself — just as a house is the condition whereby it may be used for dwellings and these dwellings within the house are in turn different from the house itself, the house being at most the condition for dwellings within it. But insofar as the work is not separate from the doer, this condition, as Plato points out, contains the possiblity of defining it as work that is an end in itself: the end of the ethical or the political act is contained within itself. As an example of an act that is an end in itself Aristotle cites that of Pericles — a statesman who could see what was good for man and who could therefore determine ethical ends. We can say that poetic knowledge deals with the means that lead to an end but is indifferent to ultimate ends. In the example cited it does not matter whether the dwellings are an ultimate end or not; it is sufficient that they are viewed as ends with respect to the house. From Aristotle's remarks we gather that there are several interrelated points of view whose correlation reveals all the various distinctions suggested by them.

This conception can be summed up by indicating the three points of view involved:

a. The first point of view is that of the activity implicit in each of the spheres discussed:

The activity of the theoretical sphere is *vision* or theory.

The activity of the practical sphere is *action,* e.g. the act of extending aid to one's fellowman.

The activity of the poetic sphere is *production,* e.g. the making of jugs.

b. The second point of view concerns the distinction between the three spheres and is of the type of knowledge implied or inherent in each of the three spheres. From this point of view we may say:

In the theoretical sphere the type of knowledge is *science.*

In the sphere of the ethical act the type of knowledge is *deliberation.*

In the poetic sphere the type of knowledge implied is *ability, dexterity,* or *skill.*

c. In addition all these aspects are discussed by Aristotle from the standpoint of the degree of achievement or accomplishment attained in each of the spheres. According to this it is clear that in the theoretical sphere the end attained is happiness, the highest end and the one accompanied by the most intense activity, that is, theoretical activity. This highest end can be attained only insofar as man possesses in himself the divine element.[19]

In the sphere of the act, that is the ethical act, the end sought is that of the righteous life, a life in which we know what is the proper and what is not the proper object of desire.

But in the sphere of poetic activity the end to be attained is that of welfare, such as adequate dwellings, comforts, and so forth. This can be made clear by the following outline:

	Theoretical sphere	Practical sphere	Poetic sphere
1. activity	viewing	act	doing
2. type of knowledge	science	deliberation	skill
3. end attained	happiness	proper life	welfare

This sketch requires an additional observation. Aristotle remained true to his basic distinction between eternality and mutability, a distinction which is at the basis of the distinction between the theoretical sphere on the one hand, and the practical sphere together with its provinces on the other. But from the standpoint of the element of knowledge involved in each sphere and from the standpoint of the end attained we find: (a) that in every sphere there is an element of knowledge; (b) that the sphere of knowledge *par excellence* is the sphere of the end *par excellence*. From this it is evident that Aristotle gave preference to the cognitive element both from the operational and from the teleological point of view.

From this analysis the following may be deduced: (a) the difference between theory, on the one hand, and the ethical and poetic act on the other, holds true because theory does not interfere in the process of things but only contemplates them; the ethical as well as the poetic act, however, interfere in the process of things; (b) despite these distinctions between knowledge and act there is a common sphere of knowledge in which the distinction between theory, ethical act, and poetic act applies; (c) from a teleological point of view there is an affinity between theory and the ethical act in that both spheres are concerned with ends in themselves. The poetic sphere, however, is concerned with providing the means for an end that transcends them.

NOTES

1 Consult F. Boll, *Vita Contemplativa* (Heidelberg: 1922), and J. Ritter, "Die Lehre vom Ursprung und Sinn der Theorie bei Aristoteles," in *Arbeitsgemeinschaft für Forschung des Landes Nordrhein-Westfalen, Geisteswissenschaften,* I (1953), pp. 32ff.

2 On this subject, consult W. K. C. Guthrie, "The Earlier Pre-Socratics and the Pythagoreans," in *A History of Greek Philosophy* (Cambridge: 1962), Vol. I, pp. 211ff.

3 *Metaphysics,* 981a-b.

4 *Metaphysics,* 982b.

5 *Politics,* 1325b.

6 *Phaedrus,* St. 270. Quoted from Jowett's translation of *The Dialogues of Plato* (Oxford: 1931), Vol. I, p. 479.

7 *Metaphysics,* 1026a.

8 *Metaphysics,* 1026a.

9 *Metaphysics,* 1026a.

10 *Metaphysics,* 1072b.

11 *Metaphysics,* 20, A.539; 14, B.653.

12 *Lives of Eminent Philosophers,* III:84, in *The Loeb Classical Library,* with an English translation by R. D. Hicks (Cambridge, Mass., and London: 1942), Vol. I, pp. 350-51.

13 *Nicomachean Ethics,* 1138b ff.

14 *Nicomachean Ethics,* 1139a.

15 See *Nicomachean Ethics,* 1143a, and the analysis in H. Siebeck, *Geschichte der Psychologie,* I/2 (Gotha: 1884), pp. 225ff.

16 *Nicomachean Ethics,* 1143a.

17 *Nicomachean Ethics,* 1141a.

18 *Nicomachean Ethics,* 1139b; see also *Metaphysics,* 1025b, and *On Heaven,* III, 306.

19 *Nicomachean Ethics,* 1177b.

II. ECHOING THE CLASSICAL DISTINCTIONS

A

The basic concepts found in medieval philosophy relative to the characterization of the sphere of theory and that of practice were derived from Greek philosophy, especially from Aristotle. According to these streams of thought, theory is concerned with the cognition of reality, the practical act with directing the will toward that which it considers proper, while the fundamental principle of the poetic act is to give form to the sensible or material sphere. These observations of the attempts of medieval philosophy to clarify the concepts dealt with here are not made merely for the sake of completing the historical development of these concepts but rather to gain some insight into their nature. Even some of the blurred distinctions of the medieval philosophers, especially in the sphere of the act, will prove to be of value for the proper understanding of the concepts current in our day.

B

Several observations should be made at the outset concerning the sphere of theory. When in the continuation of the Aristotelian tradition the Greek concept 'theoretical' gave way to the Latin 'speculative', Albertus Magnus introduced the thought that cognition is speculative when it is caused by a thing (*causata a re*) and is practical when it is itself the cause of a thing (*causa rei*). In other words, knowledge is speculative when it abstracts the finding from the things themselves (*a rebus*) and is practical when it gives to things their form (*ad rebus*).[1] This notion of the nature of an abstracting cognition finds its expression in the widespread term *informatio,* one of whose meanings — namely, the imprint of a form on matter — is a drawing forth of the form (*forma*) of things by the understanding of the spirit.

This emphasis on the aspect of "drawing forth" or abstraction implicit in speculative cognition, in contradistinction to the aspect of molding or imparting form implicit in practical knowledge, reveals an additional aspect that is not without significance for the systematic treatment of the question we are considering, namely: If speculative cognition is caused by things themselves, then it contains a certain degree of receptivity compared to practical knowledge which actively confers form on things. The element of receptivity appears in every discourse concerning the nature of theory. A definite aspect of receptivity is to be found in viewing itself and in the viewing of immutable things disclosed to us. This aspect of receptivity or absorption appears with even greater force in the thought of the Middle Ages when God was conceived as an object *par excellence,* the most sublime object of speculative vision. Over against a God that is considered as object there is little room for action or for any manipulation whatever, in which case the height of cognition is the stand taken with respect to the divine object. True, there is some activity that leads to this height, for it is not given of itself in a sudden flash of illumination. But this activity remains in the preparatory stage of viewing in which the element of receptivity predominates over that of activity.[2] This characteristic aspect of speculation is seen even more clearly when speculation is united with an ecstatic vision or an ecstatic attitude. This aspect of the receptive character of vision — the highest and the most excellent of all degrees of knowledge wherein the object as it is in reality is disclosed to us — is found in various stages of development in doctrines concerning the nature of intuition, even when it is not in conjunction with contemplation (intuition literally means 'contemplation') that is directed specifically to the divine object. The term 'intuition' was used by Descartes to indicate an illumination in the sphere of reason,[3] but the original meaning of this term refers to an absorbing contemplation of the divine object and as such is clearly related to the character of cognition or theroretical knowledge which we have been attempting to clarify.

This attitude concerning the aspect of receptivity within theory or speculation was influenced by the confluence of mystical streams with the Aristotelian trend, a fusion which placed greater emphasis on the receptive element inherent in theory and speculation. The saying[4] that there is a viewing in non-viewing meant to emphasize the attitude to the unseen, since this attitude is a definite genus of vision that has no expression and no possibility of assuming a conceptual-analytical character. It is clear that in this character of speculative viewing we find the cognitive and systematic roots of all the negative theology of the Middle Ages which, for epistemological and religious reasons, insisted on emphasizing the gulf that separates God from man and thus on the impossibility of describing the nature of God by using positive attributes. The absence of this positive element is similar to the absence of form in knowledge. We here return to Aristotle's characterization of knowledge as a knowledge of form or the abstraction of form from things. With respect to the divine object there is a wisdom that is not dependent on abstracting form, *nulla formis sapientia,* as Bonaventura stated. This is mentioned here in order to stress the development of the concept of the nature of theoretical knowledge when this knowledge is absorbed in a religious or a mystical context and when this absorption (whether as a result of it or as a condition for it) is based on the active receptivity of speculative knowledge. The importance of this subject with reference to the concept 'speculation' will emerge later when we consider Hegel's contribution to the clarification of the concepts we have been considering.

This notion concerning the special nature of speculation has undergone a terminological development. Speculation is based on the true possession of the divine object in or by means of knowledge. Hence, it is complete 'possession' — no longer a striving toward an end but the taking of a position with respect to an end. The position thus assumed is not a passive one. This gives rise to an element of action within the intellectual position. But since the element of striving or a rational impetus is absent, we do not have here a cognitive process but a possession that is within knowledge. Related to this distinction is the terminological distinction between the two degrees of the capacity of cognizance: *ratio,* which is a striving that seeks to discover the truth, and *intellectus,* which is an inner penetration into the truth.[5] These terms, taken from Thomas Aquinas, are of course echoes of the distinction made by Plato and prepare the ground for important systematic distinctions, such as the Kantian distinction between the understanding and reason and its subsequent development in modern philosophy. The possession of happiness as the ethical end of *speculative* knowledge is a distinction between the degrees of understanding that makes it possible to view happiness as the apex of speculation and include it in the intellect, in the terminological sense of this concept.

C

Refinements of this distinction appear in the various systems of medieval philosophy. We must first consider a thought whose roots go back to a period prior to that of the Middle Ages, namely, that there is a definite type of knowledge of the general principles of ethics, such as the principle "it is bad to steal." This does not refer to the aspect of the ethical act itself which is, according to Aristotle's description, always an act that refers to definite circumstances and hence to fragmentary, changing conditions, but rather to a relationship that exists between man as the agent of knowledge and the principles of ethical conduct. The latter are, from this point of view, general principles and thus cannot be reduced to their dependence on changing circumstances. This type of knowledge, which is different from Aristotle's practical wisdom because of its character as knowledge and because its object is the knowledge of principles, is called συνδέρεσις (synderesis).[6] The systematic importance of this thought concerning the nature of knowledge that concerns the sphere of ethical principles consists in the fact that we here have an additional manifestation of the tendency to find a place for knowledge not only in the sphere of knowledge, that is, the sphere of theoretical or speculative knowledge, but also in the sphere of ethics.

The significance of the element of knowledge in the practical sphere also appears in an additional distinction found in the philosophy of the Middle Ages or in some of its schools. In this connection we must note the term *discretio,* which refers to the activity of reason or that of the understanding or to the ethical conduct produced by this activity. This aspect, like the cognitive and the contemplative, determines what is good and what is bad, a kind of theoretical determination in that it does not regard one content as superior to another. The determination is from this point of view only a proposition concerning the content of the subjects discussed. Thus we can only assume a descriptive or declaratory attitude when we assert that one action is profitable or another harmful, without having this determinant itself give rise to a definite act one way or another.

Over against this distinguishing or differentiating attitude we have *deliberatio,* which is an act that leads us to the recognition of the need to behave thus or thus, an act that influences the will and directs it. Such an act is in this influenced by the theoretical aspect of the content, but insofar as it is the aspect that regulates the will it is not identical with the differentiating activity. In this aspect, then, the emphasis is on a cognitive direction, and in the case of deliberation that leads to cognition the emphasis is on the character of will.[7]

D

In the previous section we spoke of the two cognitive aspects within

the sphere of the ethical act, the level of the knowledge of principles
of ethics and the level of the aspects of knowledge that are the conditions for the ethical direction of the will. Herein arose a theoretical or,
more exactly, an intellectual tendency in the ethical sphere, and
attempts to draw subtle distinctions between the theoretical and practical spheres could no longer be made unambiguously. Since we are
here concerned with a clarification of the origins of medieval philosophical ideas and not with a clarification of historical systems, it may
be relevant to consider the opposite tendency, namely, the tendency
to stress the place occupied by the will in the theoretical or intellectual sphere.

The intellectual trend in philosophy that confers a superior status
to the intellect as against the will found a place for the will for the
simple reason that the will is present wherever there is a separation
between man and object. When there is complete harmony between
the two, there is no room for the will since there is no object to be
desired but one to be actively possessed.* This tendency points to a
component of the will in the possession of the object. For when I
possess an object in the highest degree of the knowledge of the object,
a kind of a sanction or authorization is included that proceeds from
this object. In dealing with the object I confirm it and this confirmation is again a kind of an element of the will. Hence, this will is not
an incentive to desire but a motive that affirms it: Implicit in every
desire there is a definite component of affirmation of the object we
desire to attain. The voluntaristic tendency in the philosophy of the
Middle Ages emphasized this component of the will in knowledge by
insisting that the intellect has only a hypothetical status and it is not
within the intellect's power to elicit the will's consent. Such consent is
the act of the will *par excellence,* for consent has to do with giving an
impetus to cognition to make a decision in a given direction by rejecting another direction. In other words, consent can only come from
the sources of the will itself since to give consent necessarily presupposes, in principle, the possibility also of not giving consent. The
impelling force that has within it the possibility to will as well as the
possibility not to will can of itself decide on the direction of the will.
The voluntaristic direction is to be regarded as a reaction to the tendency that confers a superior position to the intellect, but the analysis
of the intellectual activity in its totality — that is, an activity in which
there is content and also judgment in terms of giving assent to them —
makes possible the reaction against the intellectualistic tendency
which presents this analysis out of itself.

* See the above discussion of degrees of understanding.

E

Greek philosophy made a distinction between theory and practice parallel or in conjunction with the distinction between kinds of knowledge, theoretical and practical knowledge or theoretical and practical wisdom. One of the conspicuous features in the discussions of this subject by medieval philosophers is the strong emphasis given to this insight which is now presented in its various aspects, the principal aspect being the division of the sciences in the different spheres.

We must not fail to note at the outset that we meet with something reminiscent of the classical division when we examine the various spheres of activity in limited relationship to the 'faculties of the soul' which are the bearers or the producers of this activity. Thus, for example, we find in Jehuda Halevi: When the rational soul directs its activity to the study of the sciences, this activity is called theoretical knowledge, and when it is directed to the subjugation of the animal faculties, this activity is called control and it itself is called practical knowledge.[8] The faculties of the soul here referred to are the intellectual faculties, on the one hand, and the appetitive faculties on the other. The spheres of theory and practice revolve around the growth of the intellectual faculty of the soul and the overcoming of the blind, animal desires of the appetitive soul. To the extent that we can speak in this context of the faculties of the soul we can speak of giving direction to these faculties — the rational soul needs development and care, a fact that is not stressed in the passage from Jehuda Halevi, whereas the appetitive soul, which is characterized negatively as an animal soul, needs to be overcome or restrained. These are to a certain extent opposed to the cultivation that is part of the legitimate development of the intellectual activity. At any rate, the prominence given to the psychological aspect that is at the basis of the division of the spheres, as well as the distinction between the various modes of relationship with respect to the psychological aspect, should be emphasized if we are to gain a proper understanding of the fundamental principles that prevailed in the various schools of thought we have considered.

The division of the sciences that appeared in many works of the Middle Ages went back to the basic division proposed by Aristotle between the theoretical, the practical, and the artistic. Some subdivisions, however, were added and some distinctions were more or less blurred, and for this reason they deserve a closer examination.[9]

The distinction between the practical element and the poetic element is here not drawn as sharply as it was by Aristotle in the *Nico-*

machean Ethics. The distinction is blurred, or at least a definite terminological inexactitude had set in, between the direction toward the act and that toward the work. Thus, for example, we find Maimonides using the term *malahi* or *malahti*[10] to indicate the entire sphere of the act without pointing out at the very outset the difference between "practice" and *poiesis.* But it seemed more important to try to establish the connection between the practical direction and what was now called the 'useful' direction. With the prominence given to the useful aspect we find sciences, such as geometry for example, that could be divided into the theoretical branch and the practical or useful branch. From then on the distinction between the theoretical and the practical increased not only because the practical meant the 'ethical' but because it meant everything concerned with the act, whether in an ethical direction or in the direction of an activity with respect to matter, including useful activity. The appearance of the element of applicability as a concomitant element of theory or science and not as an element residing in an area separated from the element of theory or science had to be made prominent. In other words, we can say that the distinction between the theoretical and the practical meant what is now customarily designated as the distinction between abstract and concrete. When we speak then of practical or applied geometry in this sense, it is clear that what is meant is not the form of the square but this form as it is impressed on matter, for example on wood. To apply the word 'useful' to a practical occupation was, as we shall see later, one of Francis Bacon's most significant contributions to the subject under discussion.

Furthermore, we have already seen in Aristotle's system that theory has a special object that is peculiar to it, namely, the eternal object, the eternal or divine causes. This aspect of Aristotle's discussion receives additional significance when the subject of God is treated in accordance with the tradition of the monotheistic religions. Henceforth it was possible to argue that God is a special object in whom there is a fusion of the theoretical view, which makes distinctions among the conditions of things, and the ethical view, which is concerned with the norms of conduct. However, the sphere of the arts or *poiesis,* in the exact sense of this concept, is the sphere which is sometimes translated in Latin as *mechanica,* the sphere of human activity that has nothing in common with the level of God's existence.* The next step is to enlist the combined spheres of the artistic,

* This matter implies the distinction between *agere* and *facere.* The product of the activity in *agere* is within ourselves; the work of the activity in *facere* is in the determined products, having an artistic and technical character.

the useful, or the mechanical in the interest of man's needs, a subject which occupies a central place in Bacon's discussions.

The outline of some of the discussions of the medieval philosophers would appear then as follows:

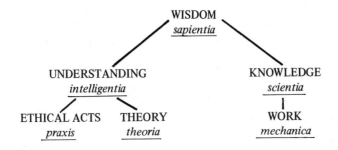

When Aristotle speaks of the practical sphere as the sphere that is concerned with man, he places the emphasis on man in his capacity as the director of his desires. Now in speaking of man with respect to the aggregate of operations, the first and foremost consideration is given to man's daily needs, and the chief emphasis is placed on the union between the welfare that man seeks and the cultivation of those human needs that are subsumed under this general heading of welfare. In the course of generations, especially in Marx's treatment of the concept of *praxis*, the attempt was made to return to the ethical meaning of practice, but not to the ethical meaning divorced from the concern for human welfare. In this matter also the connecting link to Bacon's system is evident, and it is to this subject that we now turn.

NOTES

1 On this subject see L. Kerstiens, "Die Lehre von der theoretischen Erkenntnis in der lateinischen Tradition," in *Philosophisches Jahrbuch der Görres-Gesellschaft*, LXVI (1958), p. 394.

2 See the Introduction to the *Guide of the Perplexed*.

3 *Regulae ad directionem ingenii*, III.

4 Of Gregory of Nyssa.

5 See on this subject P. Rousselot, S. J., *The Intellectualism of Saint Thomas*, translated with a Foreword by James E. O'Mahony (New York: 1935), p. 66.

6 On this subject see Überweg's *Grundriss der Geschichte der Philosophie* (Basel-Stuttgart: 1961), Part II, pp. 415-16.

7 Cf. J. Ebner, "Die Erkenntnislehre Richards von St. Viktor," in *Beiträge für Geschichte der Philosophie des Mittelalters*, XIX/4 (Münster: 1917), pp. 35ff.

8 *The Kuzari*, V, 12.
9 Consult Dominicus Gundissalinus, *De divisionae philosophiae,* edited by L. Bauer (Münster: 1903); see also H. A. Wolfson, "The Classification of Sciences in Medieval Jewish Philosophy," in *Hebrew Union College Jubilee Volume 1875-1925* (Cincinnati: 1925).
10 *Milot Hahigayon,* 14.

III. CRAFTSMANSHIP AS KNOWLEDGE

A

Despite the innovations introduced by medieval thinkers in this matter concerning the distinction between theory and practice it may be said that by and large they adhered to the classical tradition of placing theory above practice. This also applies to those philosophical tendencies in the Middle Ages that stressed the element of the will in contrast to theory or cognition. The position of theory, however, was not impaired despite the various interpretations proposed with respect to its inner nature. This problem underwent a change in Bacon's conception, a change which had a considerable influence on the various approaches to the problem concerning the distinction between theory and practice and the scale of preferences to which these approaches were attached.

We have already noted the distinction between *praxis,* which is concerned with the regulation of desire, and *poiesis,* which is concerned with the attainment of man's welfare through the satisfaction of his needs. The distinction between these two branches of practical activity was to a certain extent blurred during the Middle Ages. Eventually a point was reached where an attempt was made to identify practice, which is concerned with the good, with *poiesis,* which is concerned with human welfare. This fusion, which is found in Bacon's system, was not reached accidentally but was the result of a process of systematic development. This theme will now engage our attention.[1]

B

Before we discuss some of the details connected with the basic trend of Bacon's system, we must bear in mind the fact that Bacon was not entirely free of the Aristotelian and scholastic tradition despite his severe strictures against it. A number of traditional concepts are to be found in his teachings, and these must be considered if we are to understand the significance of the innovation he introduced.

29

1. In his discussion of the division of the sciences Bacon follows the division that is essentially more Platonic than Aristotelian or is, at least, a mixture of the two — the division into logic, ethics, and politics.[2]

2. Relative to this division Bacon also points out the connections that exist between the spheres of science and the faculties of the soul. In this matter he states that there is a doctrine concerning the intellect (most excellent King) and a doctrine concerning the will of man, two doctrines that are related to one another as twins by birth.[3] We here find the connecting link between the spheres of occupation or doctrines and the faculties of the soul, as well as the parallel between these spheres and the faculties of the soul. Using the traditional division of the sciences, Bacon goes on to say that logic discourses of the understanding and reason, ethics of the will, and appetite and affections of the soul. From this it follows that logic produces determinations and ethics produces actions.[4] In speaking of determinations in this context the reference is, of course, to determinations or propositions of the understanding, for example, those that relate a predicate to a subject. Such a relationship does not fall within the limits of an act but rather of a determination on the level of rational discourse.

3. But when Bacon discusses the nature of contemplation he no doubt has in mind the traditional approach with the classical description of contemplation as an independent, self-contained activity. Bacon disagrees with this classical description of contemplation as self-contained and as casting neither light nor heat on society. To emphasize his disagreement with this conception of contemplation — which is a kind of parallel to the idea of God thinking Himself in the divine sphere — Bacon, basing his view on biblical rather than Aristotelian sources, states that God knows no contemplation of this kind. We must here bear in mind that phase of Bacon's argument which regards the character of religion as different from that of contemplation, which contents itself with philosophic meditation. Religious existence has rules of conduct for daily life: It is not a closed circle of meditation divorced from society and daily social conduct.[5] From this point of view the religious life appears as an ideal model for that which theoretical cognition was meant to be, namely, knowledge that influences the conduct of everyday life. It is evident that with this argument Bacon desired to deprive theoretical cognition of the character that was given to it in the Aristotelian tradition. He endeavored to present cognition as a directing influence in man's daily life and not as merely theoretical in the classical sense of the term.

C

This emphasis on the character of cognition as not merely theoretical but as having a direct bearing on daily life is related to an important conception in Bacon's system, the distinction between two kinds of experimentation and the significance of experimentation within the framework of cognition. The emphasis on the element of experimentation is closely related to the argument that the kind of contemplation which is of no consequence in the actual conduct of daily life is the contemplation that is reserved for the gods and the angels but which has not been vouchsafed to man in his actual existence.[6] Bacon presents two arguments: first, that religions based on the ideal of divine imitation contain an element of active realization in the course of life; and second, that it is not for man to make himself like the gods since what has been given to them has not been given to him.

The view that human conduct belongs to the sphere of daily life and is hence an active behavior leads Bacon to the argument in favor of the central position occupied by experimentation in scientific knowledge. All industry in experimenting began with proposing that the one who experiments should keep before him certain definite works to be accomplished and pursue them with eagerness.[7] This is a significant point, for it is clear that theory concerned with reality in general is no longer being discussed. Rather the subject is cognitive operations involving experimentation directed to partial and definite ends. If we recall the classical distinction between theory as being concerned with the world as a whole and the act as belonging solely to the human realm, we can say that Bacon's restriction of cognition to parts and not to the whole compels us to conceive cognition in relation to the human sphere alone and not to the world in its totality. In other words, according to the Aristotelian conception, theory was directed to the whole of reality and the ethical act was directed to the human sphere; whereas according to the new conception, cognition belongs to the human sphere and is severed from relationship to the entire sphere. The involvement of cognition in experimentation is that which elicits these partial, human aspects.

We cannot speak of experimentation without first pointing out the difference between experiments of light (*experimenta lucifera*) and experiments of fruit (*experimenta fructifera*). Our interest here lies in the latter, for even though the former bears certain analogies to the divine sphere — analogies suggested by Bacon not without a tinge of irony — we do not find in the *experimenta fructifera* (that is, in those experiments which yield results) an imitation of that divine procedure

which in its first day's work created light only and assigned to it one
entire day, a day on which God produced no material work, proceeding to that on the days following.[8] When we speak of experiments of
fruit we are not concerned with the illumination of facts by contem-
plating them but rather with definite actual results. We indicate the
connection that exists between cognition that interferes in the process
of things by producing results and experiments as a means to this
cognition or as actually realizing it.

Another characteristic underlies the distinction between the two
kinds of experiments: the *experimenta lucifera* are those experiments
that manifest causes and axioms,[9] and these contain at most an attitude over against facts but are unable to aid us in the application of
that which we gain from the experiments. It may be said that when we
turn to causes we are turning to the conditions of occurrences and not
to the results that flow from these occurrences; when we turn to
axioms or first principles we turn to the suppositions of deliberation
and argumentation and not to the consequences that result from
these. The *experimenta fructifera,* however, are deliberations directed
to results, and of them Bacon says that they have one admirable
property, namely, that they never miss or fail to attain their end.[10]
These experiments are initiated regardless of results and not for the
purpose of producing any particular effect; if the result is reached
then the question is answered, and to the extent that the question is
answered the result is attained. This is also the case when the result
turns out to be the opposite of what was expected. The purpose is not
to ascertain the significance of the experiments of light since axioms,
when properly derived, endow the deed with instrumentality. The
importance of experimentation in a cognitive noninstrumental direction is that it finds its justification in instrumental and applicable
results. When we speak of 'experiments' we mean 'operations'. This
itself constitutes a value whether the operation of the experiment
takes place in the direction of experiments of light or those of fruit.
But in the totality of modes of experiments preference is given to the
latter.

                                    D

The appearance of the element of experimentation in the sphere of
cognition lends itself to generalization because of the emphasis given
to the significance of operation in the human sphere. The question
revolves around man's good. We must recall in this connection our

discussion of the classical view, namely, that theory is there thought of as a kind of activity and perhaps even as the highest activity. We have seen that a certain dialectic occurs in the description of theory as operation, for theory is activity restricted to possession and cannot by its very nature be productive, creative activity. This activity is distinguished by a dialectic that describes the contemplative activity as one that ends in immersion; this active immersion makes the cognitive ideal a mystical ideal. Even Bacon speaks of the active good in connection with the character of men as mortals and as creatures at the mercy of fortune. It follows that if he speaks of the operative phase of man and of the good within this activity, he does not think of this good as including the imitation of God. This good expresses the human position. To the extent that there is a desire to be liberated from the toils of time and make our existence more secure, this desire achieves realization in our acts and deeds.[11] We may even say that it is precisely in these deeds that we are redeemed from time, a liberation that is not effected by virtue of theory which in the classical conception is represented as the imitation of God and hence as touching the divine, eternal sphere. The activity, when it operates in the sphere of deeds as a human ideal, is the human good. It cannot have a fixed, permanent position that is not subject to change. On the contrary, the excellence of the active good is manifest in man's fondness for heterogeneity. If we look at the matter from the nominal side alone, we can say that Bacon identifies the good with activity, as does also the classical view, and speaks of activity directed to results and not to the contemplation of immutable reality. Bacon speaks of an activity that is not a permanent condition but which consists of permanent occurrences on the human plane, the multifarious preoccupations and their objects. If cognition is an activity it can be one not because of the constant effort that accompanies it, as taught by the classical tradition, but because of the constant intentionality toward results through interference. This intervention is concerned with introducing changes in the process of things and in the affairs of daily life, including the sphere of human society.

E

The Aristotelian conception which, as we have seen, determined the criteria of distinguishing the various occupations and their order of preferences assigned the arts or crafts to the sphere of ethical activity. Aristotle clearly gave priority to ethical activity over the arts, one of

the reasons for this preference being the affinity between the ethical
act and the theoretical activity, for both are ends in themselves. In the
critical change introduced by Bacon we witness the preference given
to art or mechanical art, as he calls it; we also witness — and this is of
decisive importance — how mechanical art is made the model of
human conduct. When Bacon argues against the traditional pattern of
the natural sciences, he maintains that these sciences remain stationary
and even retrograde. However, in the mechanical arts, which are
founded on nature and the light of experience, we see the contrary
happen, for these, containing within them a breath of life, are continually thriving and growing.[12] If the decisive point is no longer to be
found in the closed, self-contained goal but in the notion of an uninterrupted progress or, in other words, if the critical point now resides
in the operations of reality and not in contemplation as possession,
then the scales are turned in favor of the mechanical arts. Eternal
possession is no longer the human ideal or the model of human conduct; unceasing innovation is now the archetype of proper human
endeavor. It is evident that such conduct does not rest on theory but
on the nature of experimentation, that is, on the experimental contact
with nature. From now on we can hold fast to the basic manifestations of the ideal of the mechanical arts insofar as this ideal is rooted
in the nature of knowledge itself.

This central thought is to be found in one of Bacon's aphorisms
defining nature and the human sphere: "Human knowledge and
human power meet in one; for where the cause is not known the
effect cannot be produced. Nature to be commanded must be obeyed;
and that which in contemplation is as the cause is in operation as the
rule."[13] How are we to understand this basic notion of the meeting of
knowledge and power? The understanding of this notion plainly
depends on the meaning of 'power', which may be defined as the
ability to produce effects within nature by means of an activity
directed by human knowledge of nature. The power to produce
effects within nature is tantamount to the domination of nature. Such
an activity is possible through the knowledge of nature; then it is
possible through the discovery of the chain of cause and effect in
nature, a knowledge of which enables us, if we know the cause, to
anticipate the effect and hasten the production of the cause. This
notion can be formulated by saying that the cause, which is a cognitive determination, is converted by us into an operational rule of
action and procedure. It is evident that what Bacon here had in mind
was the notion of active knowledge for producing effects that would
flow from the presuppositions from which we proceeded at the outset.

Returning to what has been said above concerning the two kinds of experiments, namely, that those which deal with light are for the sake of those that deal with fruit: The real meaning of the experiments of light is the discernment of the causes of phenomena and their corresponding axioms on the level of logic, so to speak, parallel to causes on the level of physics. But since knowledge is no longer an end in itself, the end being fructification or giving an impetus to effects, it may be said that knowledge meets with power. We must here keep in mind that Bacon does not say that knowledge is identical with power but only that the two meet. Or, in less metaphorical language, knowledge is the condition for the domination of nature. This aspect of domination as production directed in accordance with rules of effects brings the end of knowledge closer to the character and rhythm of mechanical art. Mechanical art, which, according to Aristotle, is in the sphere of poetic or productive knowledge (as the expression is translated in this connection), is the perfect model for the end of knowledge. From the negative point of view, however, it is clear that since human knowledge and human power actually meet and become one, action fails because of the absence of a knowledge of causes.

Emphasis upon the character of knowledge as a producer of causes leads us to a further consideration. When we speak of the effects of causes, effects that occur in accordance with our knowledge of the rules of action, we have not yet defined the nature of the end of action from the standpoint of its content. The content differs from the level of effect, for the latter is a functional and not a theoretical level. Here Bacon states that the end, from the standpoint of content, is no mere felicity of speculation but the real business and fortunes of the human race and of the power of operation.[14] It follows that the power of operation, which is the other aspect of knowledge, is directed to human welfare, which is the end of daily human conduct. In this manner the difference is determined between speculation, in the classical sense of this term, and the real ends of the human race. This is now determined in connection with knowledge, on the one hand, and in connection with the domination of nature on the other. Analyzing Bacon's thought in this matter and seeing it against the background of the discussions of theory and practice, it becomes evident that since in the classical view the ideal of knowledge is the ideal of theory, this ideal itself is taken as the end of human endeavor. But since in Bacon the ideal of knowledge is the ideal of the knowledge of cause and effect and since knowledge is the condition for the operation of effects in the interest of human welfare, then the human ideal is no longer the ideal of knowledge but rather that of human welfare, an ideal that acquires real support through knowledge. In Aristotle's conception poetic knowledge is concerned with the satisfaction of wants, and this, in turn, becomes in Bacon's conception the end of knowledge in its totality. Poetic knowledge becomes knowledge *par excellence,* and the ideal of welfare becomes the ideal *par excellence* — and these two aspects are presented to us as a combined whole.

The manner in which Bacon combines knowledge with welfare is clearly expressed in his words concerning the utopian goal of mankind — this goal being the knowledge of causes and secret motions of things and the enlarging of the bounds of the human empire in order to effect all things possible.[15] The idea of "the human empire" is here connected with the knowledge of causes and with the operational effect that produces these causes. In the classical conception the artistic knowledge that produces effects is restricted to completed works, such as houses or ships. Bacon is no longer dealing with finished works produced by an activity that proceeds from knowledge. Knowledge as such is directed to the world in its totality. Man's domination of the world is the goal, a domination that stems from knowledge. Such domination cannot be restricted to finished products for it keeps increasing with the growth of knowledge. The continuous expansion of knowledge is a symptom of its vitality, and the domination that stems from it is further proof of this vitality. If to this domination, which in the original sense of this term is the ability to operate, we add the specific end of human welfare, then this end cannot be realized in a completed work. Bacon, unlike Aristotle, does not speak of welfare in connection with man's definite needs, such as dwellings, but in connection with the broad expanse of knowledge of nature. Operational knowledge increases the limits of welfare, and with the expansion of this knowledge the content of welfare itself changes. The welfare of which Bacon speaks is that of the human empire and not of the satisfaction of man's needs. This brings us to the discussion of the place that nature as an object of knowledge occupies in Bacon's conception.

F

Dominion over nature means the dominion over nature as a whole; the steps in this process depend on the corresponding means. This dominion is one by right or divine right conferred upon man. We must bear in mind that the operation of this human ability or the ideal of knowledge in terms of craft is no longer confined to this or that portion of material existence that men have parcelled out for themselves according to their strength or needs or in order to exploit some hidden vein of a secluded province. This is the way the classical conception regards a work and the knowledge that leads to it. Over against this we find a change in Bacon's conception: nature in its totality becomes the arena of human activity. The poetic ideal is conceived as related to a whole and not as a fragment. In the classical tradition the whole was regarded as an object of theoretical knowledge. We clearly see that the sphere which because of its totality was an object of theory now became an object of human dominion and of knowledge that is no longer theoretical. The intentionality toward the whole and not toward the part bears an ethical character just as the intentionality toward the whole in the classic tradition had essentially theoretical significance, which was in accordance with the nature of relationship on the one hand and the nature of the whole on the other. In Bacon's conception ethical status is given to the poetic knowledge modelled after the pattern of the mechanical arts, because this knowledge embodies man's ability and because the object — nature in its broad expanse — confers an ethical status on the relationships to it. But this relationship is now cognitive-domineering and not cognitive-contemplative.[16]

In Bacon's conception, theory is reduced to knowledge, knowledge to progressive effects, and these in turn to the desire for welfare to be realized in the sphere of nature in its totality. We find here the three elements of the classical division of knowledge. In Bacon's view, however, there occurs what may be called an adjustment of theory to ethics and an adjustment of ethics to welfare which is attained through craft. In this manner the ideal of craft prescribes the character of the ideals in the other spheres. We here see the harmony of Bacon's conception in that this conception does not leave the different spheres of relationships and their objects in their original state one beside the other. It arranges them in such a way that they are helpful to one another and make for the implementation of knowledge. It finally points the way to the human ideal of the empire of man in or over against nature. Whereas we find in the classical tradition that a superior status is given more or less to the theoretical-cognitive even in the practical spheres, in Bacon's conception we have the element of the superiority of the poetic over the various cognitive spheres. This superiority expresses itself in the fact that craft is closer to man's goal than is cognition, and cognition itself is but a means for an end that is not cognitive. The classical argument that theoretical knowledge is an end in itself, and hence deserves to be not only an actualization of knowledge but also an ethical end, is now negated both as a systematic and as an ethical basis. To extend man's dominion and the power of the human race throughout the entire universe — this is man's noblest aspiration.[17]

Bacon's conception exerted a powerful influence on the formation of modern ideas concerning the nature of knowledge and the deed and the relations between them. Our analysis of it brings us to a discussion of Kant's conception. Here also we shall find a limitation of the significance of knowledge, but one that takes a different direction than that proposed by Bacon.

NOTES

1 References to Bacon's works are to J. M. Robertson's edition of *The Philosophical Works of Francis Bacon* (London: 1905).
2 *Novum Organum*, CXXVII, p. 299; *De Augmentis Scientiarum*, p. 499.
3 *De Augmentis Scientiarum*, p. 499.
4 *De Augmentis Scientiarum*, p. 499.
5 *De Augmentis Scientiarum*, p. 565.
6 *De Augmentis Scientiarum*, p. 565.
7 *The Great Instauration*, p. 245.
8 *The Great Instauration*, p. 245.
9 *Novum Organum*, XCIX, p. 289.
10 *Novum Organum*, XCIX, p. 289.
11 *Of the Proficience and Advancement of Learning, Divine and Human*, p. 137.
12 *Novum Organum*, LXXIV, p. 277.
13 *Novum Organum*, III, p. 259.
14 *The Great Instauration*, p. 253.
15 *The New Atlantis*, p. 727.
16 *Novum Organum*, CXXIX, p. 300.
17 *Novum Organum*, CCXIX, p. 300.

IV. REASON AND ITS REALIZATION

A

In coming to the consideration of the place occupied by the concepts of 'theory' and 'practice' in Kant's system, we must bear in mind that these concepts have many meanings. To find the common thread that runs through the various meanings given to these concepts by Kant we must collect the different formulations that occur in his system and seek to interpret them in the light of a common pattern.

Kant gives a very broad interpretation to the concept 'practical' when he states: "Transcendental philosophy is therefore a philosophy of pure and merely speculative reason. All that is practical, so far as it contains motives, relates to feelings, and these belong to the empirical sources of knowledge."[1] Had Kant been consistent in his terminology, he would have found no place for practical reason as pure reason, for pure reason produces deeds and assumes general laws of conduct which is ethical since general practical rules apply to it. In this context the criterion of 'practical' resides in the fact that there is a motive. This factor is taken by Kant as bound up with feelings and in general to the sources of empirical knowledge, and these are neither pure reason nor on the level of practical reason, which is by definition pure and nonempirical. Hence, we cannot regard the statement in the *Critique of Pure Reason* as relevant to our discussion, and we must therefore turn to other formulations given by Kant.

To help clarify the problem it may be profitable to examine Kant's *Logik,* although this work is based on lectures that were given by Kant and not revised by the author himself. Propositions or 'practical' judgments are here described by Kant as making a judgment on an action whereby, as a necessary condition for the object, the object becomes possible.[2] It should be noted in this connection that the sphere of practical propositions is specifically related to the ethical sphere. We refer to the practical sphere in which it is possible for objects to exist, that is, the sphere in which action produces objects. Actions and objects spoken of here in a general way are neutral determinations

from an ethical point of view. Using classical terminology, we might
say that the definition of the practical sphere in this context refers to
the correlation or the absence of distinctions between the practical
element and the poetic element. Kant, unlike the Greek philosophers,
does not make a distinction between these two elements in his definition. In the neutral sphere of the definition of practical relationship
we find another definition given by Kant according to which practice,
in its broadest sense, is the intentionality toward an end. In this context Kant adds certain qualities to the general character of practice in
its relation to ends. Not every preoccupation with an end, he states,
falls within the bounds of practice but only that which can be
regarded as an undertaking based on definite general principles of
procedure, principles that we ourselves imagine.[3] It should be pointed
out that this definition does not speak of the creation of a possibility
simply for the existence of objects, but speaks explicitly of the relationship to ends. This relationship is not an accidental one but a
relationship that has elements based on general principles of human
conduct. Kant here assumes that there are rules in conformity to
which we are related to objects, and in such a case the objects are
ends. Here again we are unable to understand this definition of relationships as practical, that is, as applied primarily to the ethical
sphere, for the ethical sphere, according to Kant, is not concerned
with relations to ends and with pursuits that lead to their attainment
but rather with freedom and general conduct based on causation
derived from freedom.

Just as the practical sphere is presented by Kant in a neutral light
from the standpoint of ethics, so also theory is similarly presented.
Theoretical judgments or propositions refer to the object, and they
determine that which applies to the object and that which does not
apply to it, or what belongs to the object and what does not belong to
it.[4] In other words, we may say that the theoretical propositions, in
the neutral sense of the term, are descriptive propositions. Kant's aim
with respect to the neutral character of theory is obvious in another
determination that deserves our attention. Kant believes that the
aggregate of rules and even of practical rules is theory when these rules
are considered as principles. If we do this, we abstract for the sake of
the rules from the manifold of conditions those conditions which exert a
necessary influence on the rules with respect to their use in reality or
with respect to their application.[5] In this statement Kant gives theory
a broad interpretation: He identifies it with a general and abstract
determination; he reduces theory to its opposite, to actual use or
application. Kant uses the term 'theory' in this case in the same neu-

tral sense in which it gained currency in later generations and became part of the methodological terminology of our time.

Theory considered as an abstraction of conditions that are necessary with respect to use gives rise to the question of applicability. If we inquire about use with respect to theory in this sense, we find an identity in use between the sphere to which theory applies and the sphere of practice. The use is practice, or the sphere of use is the sphere of practice. By positing useful knowledge as practical knowledge Kant thus inclines to the same confusion of terms that we have already found in some of the philosophical tendencies of the Middle Ages. His tendency to identify practice with useful activity or with the sphere to which this activity applies is evident in his well-known assertion that it is not the fault of theory when it fails to be useful for practice; the fault in such a case is that there is not enough theory that one could have learned from experience.[6] It follows then that in order to be able to establish the applicability of theory that is general and abstract in accordance with its nature we must add data to theory to facilitate the passage from the abstract and general to the conditions from which they were abstracted. This abstraction is made in order to establish theory at the very outset. Since there is an unavoidable hiatus here between the abstraction and the sphere from which we abstract and to which we return in the application, we are obliged to make proper and deliberate use of our faculty of judgment, a faculty that is essentially concerned with the application of theory to data. Kant characteristically stresses the significance of the faculty of judgment and states that the *Aktus der Urteilskraft* (act of judgment) must also be employed, for it is with the help of the *Aktus* that the practical man (*der Praktiker*) distinguishes whether a given case is subsumed under the rule or not.[7] It is impossible that rules should always be given to guide the power of judgment, and if such rules were available, the question of the applicability of the rules — which are of necessity abstract with respect to definite circumstances and conditions — would also be raised concerning the faculty of judgment. If this were not so, we would find ourselves in a maze of an infinite series of rules. Kant avoids this difficulty by relying on a 'faculty' and not on an 'aggregate of rules' in accordance with the definition he gives of 'judgment' in the *Critique of Pure Reason*: "the faculty of subsuming under rules, that is, of distinguishing whether something does or does not stand under a given rule (*casus datae legis*)."[8] The question of the relationship of rules abstracted for definite conditions and circumstances was the subject of classical and medieval discussion. To find agreement and harmony with special conditions in the sphere of the ethical act was the concern of the judgment called *prudentia.*

B

Thus far we have seen that no status has been assigned to the ethical act within the practical sphere. But this phase alone in Kant's scattered discussions does not exhaust his conception. The following words in Kant's *Critique of Practical Reason* are a fitting introduction to this part of our analysis:

Propositions called 'practical' in mathematics or natural science should properly be called 'technical', for in these fields it is not a question of determining the will; they only indicate the manifold of a possible action which is adequate to bring about a certain effect, and are therefore just as theoretical as any proposition which asserts a connection between cause and effect. Whoever chooses the latter must also choose the former.[9]

It is clear from this passage that Kant's use of the term 'practical' is confined to the ethical sphere *par excellence* and that what is here called 'technical' corresponds to what was called 'useful' or considered as belonging to application in the previous context. The point around which Kant's distinction between the technical and the ethical now revolves is that of the 'determination of the will'. With respect to mathematics and natural science there is no room for the determination of the will. Therefore, these discussions take place outside the sphere pertaining to the practical sphere in the ethical sense of this term. From this point of view Kant returns to the classical teachings which designated that as an ethical act and assigned it to the will. The classical doctrines, however, did not recognize a pure will but only a will that is appetitive; that is, the classical doctrines placed ethics on the level of empirical conduct, whereas Kant placed it on the level of conduct – that is, the will itself as the determination through freedom – this being a cause or the motive unto itself. Despite this difference between Kant and the ancients, we may say that Kant transplants to his system the classical distinction and the classical characterization of the ethical act. Concerning the matter of applicability or the matter that is now called technical, again in the language of classical concepts, we find ourselves in the realm of determinations that define the state and condition of things. When we speak of the relation of cause to effect or the relation of effect to cause, we are speaking of the state of things and making a judgment with respect to this state. But when we speak of a matter that belongs to practice *par excellence,* the will arises before us as a pivotal center of relationships; what is presented to us is not a proposition of its operation but a motive that impels it or, in Kant's language, a factor that determines the will. We are not speaking of causal relations but of the causation of the will. It may be concluded from what has been said above that the term 'technical' is closely related to the theoretical sphere, whereas the practical sphere is distinct from both the theoretical and the technical spheres.

C

We have now entered the ethical sphere as the practical sphere proper. Because of the distinctive ethical element in the practical sphere Kant states that all knowledge that contains an imperative is 'practical'.[10] If the emphasis in the previous discussion was placed on the deter- mination of the will, it has now shifted to the imperative. Hence, in dealing with the imperative we are concerned with a content that has a determining relation to the will and for this reason we speak of a content or a cognition whose character is practical. We must bear in mind that Kant does not speak here simply of a motive but of a 'cognition' — that is, he employs the language of Greek philosophy which in relation to ethics speaks of a kind of knowledge and does not deal with ethics as if it were outside the spheres of knowledge. Against this character of ethical knowledge or the practical sphere Kant states that cognitions are theoretical for they do not assert what ought or should be but simply the state of things; these cognitions are therefore not an object as action but an object as reality.[11] To this charac- teristic of the theoretical sphere there adheres an additional charac- teristic of the practical-ethical sphere which is nothing more than an explanation of what has been said. The ethical sphere involves action because the content that activates and determines the will is a content that motivates action.[12] But the imperative, being the content that activates the will, is related to the ought or, seen from another point of view, the imperative is the operational translation of the ought. Over against this view of the correlation between the imperative and the ought, which is concerned with the theoretical judgment, is the proposition regarding the state of things as they are. This proposition is therefore concerned with reality and not with the sphere beyond reality from the standpoint of content, that is, the sphere of the ought. Nevertheless, we must again emphasize what may be called 'the intellectual component' in the ethical sphere, for Kant speaks of prac- tical knowledge and not only of practical conduct. He can speak of practical 'knowledge' because he is discussing a content which is the ought and its translation to the imperative. Since there is an element of content in the ethical sphere, this content has to be known on the level of the ought as determining the will, the will being connected with the ought. We can thus speak of practical knowledge but not of a feeling, or of conduct only on a visible, empirical level.

Kant characterizes the nature of the imperative by describing it as a 'proposition' or a 'judgment'.[13] This formal character of the nature of the imperative implies the intellectual component in the imperative. Furthermore, an imperative is a proposition or judgment that asserts a free, possible action whereby a definite end is to be realized.[14] The prominence given to this quality of the imperative directs our attention to the connection between the imperative as a content and as a free activity. When we are motivated by an imperative, we are not motivated by stimuli of reality which are factual stimuli. Our response to these stimuli is causal, that is, the response is an effect and the stimulus a cause. An imperative that is an expression of the regulative status of the ought carries us beyond causal determination. Thus, in the very response to an imperative of the ought we act in a free manner. An action is free, from a negative point of view, when it is not the effect of a cause and, from a positive point of view, when it is determined by a knowledge of the content of the ought. Kant adds the connection that exists between action and the realization of the end. This must be understood to mean that when we act as a result of our being determined in our actions by means of a content of the ought — that is from a subjective point of view — or from the standpoint of what is opposite us and in front of us, we act in order to carry out the ought. From this point of view the ought is the goal of the act insofar as the determination motivates the will that realizes the ought. We must keep in mind what has been said above concerning the sphere of the act as a sphere of action directed toward an end, namely, that the sphere of the act is neutral from the standpoint of ethics. Kant sets up this neutral description of the act as pointing to the realization of the end, but through the ethical quality of the act he indicates that the ethical ought can also be an end of acts. When he treats of practical cognitions pertaining to imperatives Kant refers not only to the difference between practical and theoretical cognitions but also to the opposition between them.

D

Kant takes a further step in clarifying the nature of the sphere of the act as distinct from the nature of the sphere of theory. Practical cognitions, he says, are cognitions containing reasons for 'possible imperatives' and they stand in opposition to 'speculative' cognitions.[15] If we look more closely at this description we find two levels from the standpoint of the spheres of acts and of ethics. The first level is that of the imperatives themselves, the level consisting of Kant's maxims, for example, the rule that we should act in such a way that the guiding rule of our actions could become a universal law. In addition there is a second level of reasons for these imperatives, for example — and here we are obliged to interpret Kant's words — the reason in the comparison between the general character of ethics and the general character of the knowledge of nature. If there is a general character to ethics, then one of its expressions is to be found in the ethical law. The ethical law, in its status as a law, is a reason for an imperative and not the imperative itself. The analogy between the rational component of a law of nature and the rational component of a law of ethics is a reason for the status of the imperative, which is rooted in a law of ethics. From the standpoint of the level of the 'content' of the imperative, as distinct from the level of the content of knowledge based on nature, Kant speaks of the opposition between the practical and the theoretical. But when he ascends to the level of 'reasons' of the ethical imperative, he points out the opposition between the practical and the speculative spheres. Here he falls back on one of the terms given to the theoretical sphere in the European tradition, giving to the term 'speculative' a meaning that differs from the term 'theoretical': The theoretical sphere is the sphere of propositions having a content that deals with reality (the state of things being such and such) whereas the speculative sphere is the sphere of pure reason unrelated to reality. The speculative sphere is placed above the sphere of propositions concerning reality and, from this point of view, is parallel to the reasons of the imperative in the sphere of ethics.[16] Kant's argument in this matter can be outlined as follows:

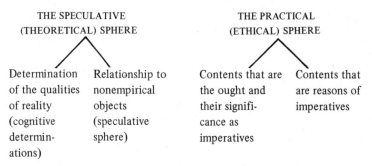

THE SPECULATIVE (THEORETICAL) SPHERE		THE PRACTICAL (ETHICAL) SPHERE	
Determination of the qualities of reality (cognitive determinations)	Relationship to nonempirical objects (speculative sphere)	Contents that are the ought and their significance as imperatives	Contents that are reasons of imperatives

Kant was not consistent in his use of the term 'speculative'; a confusion is at times evident in his descriptions. He wished to rescue, as it
were, the status of the speculative sphere by maintaining that speculation deals with nonempirical objects, objects of pure reason or ideas.
He relegates this sphere, from the viewpoint of speculation, to the
larger area of knowledge by saying that the contents of 'conception' in
general are not those of 'knowledge' in the empirical sense of this term
— that is, they are not contents of the knowledge of nature. The
principles of Kant's system reveal that those contents that are the
objects of speculation on the conceptual level also have a status on the
level of practical reason, although Kant here makes a distinction
between objects that are postulates of ethics itself (God and immortality) and a content that is a presupposition of ethics, that is, freedom.[17]   It can be said that freedom, which is the object of the
speculative conception, is the reason for the ethical imperative. This
accounts for the parallelism between the speculative sphere of reason
in the perspective of conception and the sphere of reasons for the
imperative in the perspective of ethics. The link that connects the
level of reasons of the ethical imperative with the speculative level is
found in the following passage by Kant: "Theoretical knowledge is
speculative if it concerns an object, or those concepts of an object,
which cannot be reached in any experience. It is so named to distinguish it from *the knowledge of nature,* which concerns only those
objects or predicates of objects which can be given in a possible
experience."[18]   The link that connects the level of speculation with
the level of reasons of the ethical imperative is to be found in the fact
that the reasons of the ethical imperative cannot be in the sphere of
possible experience.[19]   The sphere of ethics thus posits what may be
called the nonempirical realization of speculation. In the area of
knowledge no such realization takes place while in the area of ethics a
realization such as this is postulated on the level of imperatives and *a
fortiori* on the level of reasons for imperatives.

    Here again we must note the similarity between the tendency of
Kant's doctrine and that of the classical teachings. The classical view
regarded the highest point of theory (in Greek) and the highest point
of speculation (in Latin) to be also the highest point of the act. In
Kant, the term 'theory' can no longer be understood as if it had in
itself an ethical status. On the contrary — and here we find the roots
of the notion of the primacy of practical reason[20] — Kant points out
areas of speculation that have no realization in the sphere of knowledge but only in the sphere of ethics, that is to say, ethics depends on
contents that are not contents of knowledge but are at most its regu-

lative maxims. Kant does not examine speculation from the standpoint of its value as 'operation' but rather as use (which is for him a
problematical value): Since there is no realization for specualtion in
the sphere of knowledge, speculation cannot serve as a guide for
knowledge, for such a guide is by the same token also an ethical ideal.
Furthermore, we see that in the classical tradition the difference
between theory and speculation was at bottom a linguistic one based
on the distinction between the Greek (*theoria*) and the Latin (*speculatio*). Kant goes back to this linguistic-historical distinction and
incorporates it in his system. Theory is knowledge, that is, theory is
the cognitive relationship whose object is in the sphere of experience.
Speculation, however, is the conception that is related to objects that
could not possibly exist in the sphere of experience but whose existence is possible in the sphere of ethics, which by definition is not in
the sphere of experience.

It seems that this matter receives its final formulation in Kant's
words, namely, that speculative cognitions are always theoretical
cognitions, but not every theoretical cognition is a speculative cognition.[21] The reason for this statement is the fact that every speculative cognition, that is, a rational conception concerned with
nonempirical objects, falls within the bounds of a proposition and
insofar as it is a proposition it describes the condition of things as
being such and such. This proposition also contains a theoretical
element since the criterion of theoretical propositions is, as has been
stated, that they are propositions about the condition of things as
they are. Since speculative statements have the peculiar characteristic
of being propositions about the condition of things that are not in the
sphere of experience, they have an additional element which distinguishes them from the theoretical sphere. Hence, every speculative
proposition is theoretical but not every theoretical proposition is
speculative. Since we attribute an additional element to the speculative sphere as over against the theoretical sphere, we can say that the
latter may be considered from another point of view to be also a
practical sphere, that is, it is practical when we regard the speculative
level from the standpoint of imperatives.[22] In this case the speculative
level includes the reasons for imperatives. Both on the level of the
imperatives and on the level of reasons for the imperatives, then, we
find a cognitive element; but from the fact that such an element exists
it does not follow that there is a blurring of boundaries between the
cognitive sphere *par excellence,* the sphere of knowledge that refers to
experience, and the speculative sphere and ethics. These are the
spheres that contain relations beyond sensible experience (specu-

lation) and actualization in the sphere that is beyond sensible experience (ethics). Ethics is not actualized on the level of speculation but on the level of freedom, which is the level of reason and not of experience. The sphere of abstract generality, taken out from circumstances and conditions, is significant where applicability, use *in actu,* and so forth are concerned. Kant sometimes refers to speculation also in this sphere of abstract generality, in which case the speculative conception stands opposed to concrete knowledge.[23] If we place the speculative conception on the level of abstraction, we can say that speculative knowledge is the knowledge from which no rules of conduct can be derived and in which there are no reasons for imperatives.[24] In this description of speculation as generality Kant perhaps tended to characterize speculation beyond its systematic meaning as a rational level, capable of being actualized in the sphere of the imperative and in the sphere of ethics in the systematic sense of this concept. It is interesting that in this discussion in which Kant reduces speculation to abstract generality, speculation remains on the level of descriptive propositions as it were, a level to which Kant assigns many judgments found in theology.[25]

Speculation, in the systematic sense of this term as a rational conception without actualization in the sphere of possible experience, is represented by theology. Theology is one of the speculative disciplines. But with regard to the character of speculation as a general, abstract realm of discourse, theology has no such systematic meaning. Kant may here be more inclined to give a popular description of theology without any reference to its systematic status. This part of our analysis may be summed up as follows:

1. Kant posits the intellectual element in the sphere of ethics following the classical tradition. Therefore one cannot argue that Kant reduces ethics only to the component of will or only to the component of decision.

2. The connection on the intellectual level between the aspect of knowledge and that of ethics does not mean the identity of the aspects. Theory is not an ethical ideal in Kant's system. The separation between knowledge and ethics is expressed by attributing theory to knowledge in the empirical sense of this concept and by separating speculation from theory.

3. Although Kant assigns the theoretical element to experience and empirical reality, he does not reduce empirical knowledge to a functional aspect after the pattern of the mechanical arts as occurred in Bacon's system. Kant's innovation in this matter was to emphasize the element of 'act' within such knowledge. This act, however, is not

mechanical and is not directed to a mechanical end; it is an act that consists, in its very creation, of the possibility of knowledge, the act that lies in spontaneity and not in the mechanical end — a distinction that enables us to understand the difference between the attitudes of Bacon and Kant.

4. To the knowledge of nature Kant does not append the conquest of nature as an end. In Kant's view the knowledge of nature finds its justification within itself and not in the human end of establishing the empire of man as we find in Bacon. One might say that the end in the 'knowledge of nature' is analogous to the end in 'theory' in the classical sense of this concept. It is an end in itself and needs no justification through the realization of widening man's dominion or contributing to the increase of his power. The reduction of knowledge to empirical knowledge or the elimination of the contemplative ideal of knowledge that we find in Kant's system does not induce him to make knowledge subservient to a technical-artistic end. This is true despite the fact that Kant recognized a definite connection between his approach and that of Bacon.[26] Kant, however, does not criticize speculation for standing aloof from life as did Bacon; he criticizes it in the terminological sense of the concept of critique he employed, namely, that it was not subject to realization in the sphere of empirical objects. Kant could not say, as did Bacon, that contemplation is not worthy of being the most excellent and the most noble of human ends in a positive sense or that action *par excellence* is that action which increases man's dominion over existence. He argues that contemplation is not a realizable end. Knowledge of the datum in the "fruitful depth of experience" either fails to raise the question as to the end to be attained or it is an end unto itself.

E

If we return to the basic thought of classical philosophy we may say that the most conspicuous manifestation of reason is to be found in speculation. The Latin term *speculatio* is used deliberately so as not to depart from Kantian usage. The above analysis noted that Kant established a parallelism between the expression of reason in the speculative sphere as the theoretical sphere of propositions and the ethical sphere as the sphere of imperatives. The critical change introduced by Kant's conception with respect to the systematic tendency of Greek philosophy was to regard not the sphere of knowledge, but the ethical sphere as the highest expression of reason; knowledge only applies to the sensuous given and requires forms of intuition as the medium for its accomplishment. This line of thought in Kant's conception, which we shall now examine, may be described as putting ethics in the place that the ancients assigned to theory or speculation. From this it is clear that knowledge cannot be made man's ideal; if there is a human ideal it must fall in the sphere of ethics as the sphere of acts directed by the will, which in turn is directed by the imperatives of the ought.

On the speculative level there are no objects that correspond to reason. It is hence not actualized on the level of objects but on the level of acts. Kant therefore understands the essence of pure reason from its practical aspect. The definite expression of pure reason is that is in its essence practical is found in the universal ethical law which reason gives to man.[27] Pure reason is taken by Kant to be the sum-total of attitudes that flow from it, a sum-total that is actualized only in the sphere in which reason is not basically dependent on its cor-related objects. In other words, this sum-total is actualized in the sphere of ethics. in which reason itself creates its own objectivity by prescribing to reason the direction of the acts. Reason as an indepen-dent source of attitudes is, then, reason as freedom. This is actualized in the ethical law and in the sphere of ethics as the sphere of acts which are not subject to the laws of nature. Kant himself, who gives practical reason primacy over theoretical reason,[28] sums up the meaning of this thought when he argues that the ethical sphere deals with the existence of objects that the theoretical sphere is unable to resolve, such as the existence of God and immortality of the soul. But it seems that we here have a condensation of Kant's thought which he himself made current. The point that Kant is really making is that practical reason is reason *par excellence,* that is, it is not only that the existence of some objects belong to practical reason and cannot be decided by theoretical reason, but also that practical reason has no need at all for a correlate. It is really the manifestation of the laws that reason itself legislates that constitutes its actualization, outside of which there is no actualization whatever. Whereas classical philosophy pointed to the relationship of reason to eternal objects and attributed the peculiar excellence of theoretical reason to the fact that it made these highest objects manifest, Kant placed pure reason on the highest level because it has no need of objects at all. Pure reason has no need even of eternal objects; even if it needed them it could not attain them. The systematic conclusion that may be drawn from these considerations is that ethics is the practical sphere in the absolute sense of this concept and the philosophy of ethics is practical philo-sophy κατ ἐξοχήν (kat exochen).[29]

As long as we do not consider the practical sphere in the strict sense of this term — the absolute sense as it is called by Kant — theory is confronted with the question of its application with respect to circumstances and conditions. The question of application arises because of the separation between a sphere of abstract rules and circumstances that are fragmentary and particular. With respect to application in this sense, Kant advances the argument that (*a*) it is an inescapable problem; (*b*) since it is a problem that cannot be avoided, theory will always have to be constructed as an aggregate of rules, so that it could be applied to the sphere to which it refers. Thus, if there is a problem with respect to an application of theory, then it is theory that is at fault. The moment that the matter is transferred to the sphere of ethics as the practical sphere *par excellence,* the problem of application ceases to exist. This is the result of the status of practical reason which derives its use from this status and whose application is dependent upon nothing beyond it or upon anything to correspond to it on the level of reality where the objects are correlates of the theoretical intentionality. This is unambiguously expressed by Kant when he states that it is only in a theory based on the concept of duty that the anxiety concerning the empty ideality of this concept ceases to exist altogether.[30] For duty is the obligation which the moral law imposes on the will, the determination of the will by means of the moral law. Duty is therefore the point in which the rational element coincides with the path of action. Duty is in and of itself reason and its actualization, although not an actualization of a correlated datum placed over against reason but an actualization that springs from reason itself. This thought is expressed by Kant in his elaboration of this theme by his use of one of the methodological terms of his system, the term *Kanon:* "I understand by a canon the sum-total of the *a priori* principles of the correct employment of certain faculties of knowledge"[31] — that is, a canon refers to the manner of the application of a faculty of knowledge. This application, however, is not accidental in the manner that some hypothesis or other can be said to be accidental in finding its application in the empirical sphere. The application in which a canon is concerned is *a priori,* that is, it is inherent in the very nature of the faculty involved. Kant therefore says that the canon as the sum-total of the principles of application cannot be used with respect to speculative pure reason, for we possess no rules according to which such reason might be applied to objects that correspond to it.[32] This canon, however, is to be found on the level of practical reason, where the value of practice is based wholly on its congruity to the theory on which it rests. Everything is lost if the empirical conditions, that is, the accidental conditions, for the operation and actualization of the law are made the conditions of the law itself.[33]

With respect to the ethical law there is no problem of a diminution of theory which makes for a difficulty in application, for in the sphere we find that theory is identical with the conditions of its consummation. Moreover, we find in this sphere an identity of theory with the sphere in which reason as the source of ethics safeguards the validity of the ethical law. From this point of view the question of the relation between theory and practice arises only with respect to rules of knowledge and not to rules of ethical conduct. Kant could no longer maintain that speculative knowledge is the ethical end, but he attempts to demonstrate that ethical conduct actualizes that which is not capable of actualization in the speculative sphere of conception. The intentionality of reason is its actualization when we are dealing with the sphere of ethics. The other necessary conclusion that can be drawn is that there is no longer any need for the faculty of judgment or *prudentia* in order to apply the ethical law, since such application of the law is inherent in the nature of this law. The knowledge of the ethical law is in and of itself the knowledge of the imperative character of this law which, in turn, subjects the will to the content of the law — a subjection that is expressed in the response to a duty. This thought finds expression in Kant's conception that the ethical law itself creates the incentive to which it bows, namely, respect for the law.

To emphasize the concrete meaning of this thought Kant asserts that a violation of duty has a direct effect on the human spirit, an effect unrelated to the negative consequences that flow from such a violation. This is evident from the fact that when a man violates his duty he despises himself and feels guilty.[34] This direct feeling that attends the failure to do one's duty is, then, for Kant a negative attestation of the binding character of the direct determination by means of practical reason. It leads him to the critical systematic conclusion that here there is clear proof that whatever is proper for theory in the sphere of ethics must of necessity also be valid with respect to practice.[35] This direct path to actualization or this direct influence of practical reason on our *Gemüt* points to the fact that the sphere of ethics is a self-contained sphere whose basic conditions are also its actualizations realized. The sphere of theory was regarded in ancient philosophy as a self-contained sphere because man's highest ability was theoretical contemplation, an ability parallel to the level of eternal objects. This meeting between the highest point of the soul with that of reality made the theoretical sphere balanced and hence self-contained. In other words, this conception no longer contained any power beyond that of theory or any level beyond that of eternal objects. Theory was self-contained because it did not employ, and was not able to employ, any end outside itself. Kant considered the sphere of the ethical act as self-contained because this sphere is built wholly on a continuous, uninterrupted transition from the sum-total of laws to the application of these laws. The sphere of ethics is self-contained because it is self-sufficient in every respect; because of this self-sufficiency the ethical sphere does not run the risk of being an empty ideality. In short, we can say that there is no danger of empty ideality since the problem has found its solution in the autarky of the ethical sphere.

It is here that we find the roots of Kant's doctrine concerning the nature of formal ethics for, as he himself states, there is a connection between the autonomy of the will that expresses the character of practical reason and the very nature of the sphere of ethics.[36] Hence, there is no need for material principles of conduct since these would make ethics dependent on changing conditions and circumstances. In addition, there is no possibility for material principles, because at the very outset the sphere of ethics was placed by Kant on a level of reason that actualizes itself and is not dependent on actualization by means of material or objective factors outside itself. Kant therefore points out that the sphere of ethics is one in which an identity exists between theory and practice. Perhaps the designation of the ethical sphere as the sphere of *absolute* practice is to indicate that phase of ethical practice which, insofar as it is practical, is by the same token also theoretical. This union of theory and practice in the sphere of ethics is attained by Kant by placing the ethical sphere outside the accidental and empirical conditions of conduct. Here may be found one of the roots of Marx's conception of the union of theory and practice, except that this union does not exist, according to Marx, on the plane of pure reason alone: Its actualization must arise out of the sources of pure reason within man's historical and empirical existence.*

The difference between the tendency of Kant's treatment of this question and that of Bacon's treatment becomes clearer when we examine the context in which this question is discussed by Kant. The passages relied upon for this analysis are taken in part from a work whose ultimate concern is the possibility of creating a world-state

---

*Of this, more further on. This does not mean to say that Marx was aware of this connection with Kant's doctrine.

composed of many nations. A notion such as this is rooted in the nature of the ethical sphere and is, according to Kant's presuppositions, a valid notion from the theoretical point of view. Thus, Kant also believes that even from the cosmopolitan standpoint the assertion holds true, that what is valid for theory on grounds of reason is also valid for practice.[37] Kant's purpose here is not to extend the dominion of man over the universe, but rather to establish cooperation among men, a cooperation based on the idea of the essential unity of mankind. Basically this is an ethical idea or, to express it differently, one of the meanings of the universality of the ethical law.

F

Our analysis of the differences between modern and classical conceptions relative to our subject would be incomplete if we failed to consider another additional phase, Kant's dependence on the classical term *contemplatio,* apparently derived from the Latin *cum templum* and thus having some connection with the temple or sanctuary. If the scholars are justified in relating the term $\theta\epsilon\omega\rho\iota\alpha$ (theoria) to the divine sphere $\theta\epsilon\omega\varsigma$ (theos) there is again a correlation between contemplation and the sphere of holiness.

One of the characteristics of theory or contemplation is that it is not subservient to an end outside itself, its end being inherent within it. Thus in Kant's system the term *Kontemplation* is superseded by the term *Beobachtung,* now transferred from the theoretical-cognitive sphere to the artistic sphere. A judgment of taste is one concerning the esthetic value of the artistic work: "The judgment of taste is merely 'contemplative' that is, it is a judgment which, indifferent as regards the being of an object, compares its character with the feeling of pleasure and pain."[38] This programmatic statement needs to be examined and some features noted that are pertinent to our discussion.

A. The first question discussed here is that of contemplation in the artistic work. The simple aspect of observing, or viewing, which is one of the forms of contact between the observer and the artistic product, is here raised to the level of a principle. We have not only 'viewing' in the visual sense of this concept but 'contemplation', that is, viewing attended by pleasure.

B. Classical tradition speaks of contemplation that does not serve an end beyond itself. In the present context the question arises: Which end can possibly arise in connection with an artistic work? Here we

note that Kant was affected by a consideration which can be formulated as follows: In order that something might be useful it is necessary that it exist, that it be part of that existence to which uses apply,
attached to existence as the sum-total of time and space, or to reality
as an aggregate of relations within time and space. A thing that is not
useful — that is, a thing whose end lies outside itself — can be so if it is
not placed in the sum-total of time and space; being cut off from
reality in time and space is the condition of the ideality of the object
involved. Being cut off means indifference as to whether the object
exists or does not exist in the aggregate of relations in time and space.
Thus there is no possibility of speaking of an object from the standpoint of an end outside itself, that is, from the standpoint of use.

C. In classical philosophy an object of contemplation exists outside of time and space because of its eternality, that is, because the
order of its reality is different from empirical reality. In Kant's
conception the esthetic object lies beyond the sphere of reality
because only an object of knowledge can be in empirical reality, that
is, in time and space. Since there is no other object for knowledge,
then if there is an object beyond reality, it is, being an object, not in
reality, and from the standpoint of our relations to it we are indifferent to its position as real. The meeting ground between the level of
this object and our relations to it is in the esthetic contemplation.

D. In the classical tradition contemplation was accompanied by
the highest pleasure, as stressed by both Plato and Aristotle. Kant also
combines esthetic contemplation with pleasure, but he conceives this
pleasure as standing by itself and not accompanying contemplation in
the nature of an object that is eternal. Since the object has this status,
it confers upon the contemplation of it the highest emotional or
pleasurable quality. Kant, then, did not do away with the classical
connection between contemplation and pleasure, but merely trans-
planted it to the esthetic sphere, and what remained is attached to this
status of the object on the esthetic level. Pleasure itself is no longer an
end byt the very content of the judgment of taste. From this point of
view, and also from the standpoint of the return to use of terms that
we have considered earlier, we can say that Kant severed the combination of the concepts, theory-speculation-contemplation. He
assigned 'theory' to empirical knowledge, raised 'speculation' above
this knowledge in general or intimated its connection with pure
reason, and placed 'contemplation' in a sphere it had not occupied,
the sphere of the artistic object.

Kant speaks of propositions (*Aussagen*), sentences, or judgments
(*Sätze*). Theoretical propositions deal with things as they are, practical

propositions with imperatives or with what ought to be. Connected with this subject is the distinction between the theoretical and the practical, as well as the distinction between the theoretical and the speculative. This separation between theory and speculation turns up again in Hegel's system. However, it is clear in Hegel's work that both the theoretical and the practical spheres are partial spheres and as such there is no affinity between them, nor between the practical sphere and the rational or speculative sphere. We shall now turn to a consideration of this subject.

NOTES

1 *Critique of Pure Reason*, B29. Quoted from N. Kemp Smith's translation (London: 1950), p. 61.

2 *Immanuel Kant's Logik*, §32, in W. Kinkel's edition (Leipzig: 1920), pp. 120-121.

3 *Über den Gemeinspruch: Das Mag in der Theorie richtig sein, taugt aber nicht für die Praxis (1793)*, in Cassirer's edition of Kant's *Werke* (Berlin: 1914), Vol. VI, p. 357 (hereafter=*Gemeinspruch*).

4 *Logik*, §32, p. 120.

5 *Gemeinspruch*, p. 357.

6 *Gemeinspruch*, p. 357.

7 *Gemeinspruch*, p. 357.

8 *Critique of Pure Reason*, B171, p. 177.

9 *Remark II*, §3. Quoted from L. White Beck's translation (New York: 1956), p. 25, note 1.

10 *Logik*, p. 96.

11 *Logik*, p. 96.

12 *Logik*, p. 96.

13 *Logik*, p. 96.

14 *Logik*, p. 96.

15 *Logik*, p. 96.

16 *Logik*, p. 96.

17 See the Introduction to L. White Beck's translation of the *Critique of Practical Reason*, pp. 3ff.

18 *Critique of Pure Reason*, B662, p. 527.

19 On this subject see Nathan Rotenstreich, *Experience and Its Systematization, Studies in Kant* (The Hague: 1965), p. 111.

20 Rotenstreich, *Experience and Its Systematization ...*, p. 111.

21 Rotenstreich, *Experience and Its Systematization ...*, p. 111.

22 Rotenstreich, *Experience and Its Systematization ...*, p. 111.

23 Rotenstreich, *Experience and Its Systematization ...*, p. 111.

24 Rotenstreich, *Experience and Its Systematization ...*, p. 96.

25 Rotenstreich, *Experience and Its Systematization* . . ., p. 96.
26 *Critique of Pure Reason*, BXII.
27 *Critique of Practical Reason*, §7, Corollary, p. 32.
28 Rotenstreich, *Experience and Its Systematization* . . ., p. 99.
29 *Logik*, pp. 96-97.
30 *Gemeinspruch*, p. 359.
31 *Critique of Pure Reason*, B824, p. 630.
32 *Critique of Pure Reason*, B824, p. 630.
33 *Gemeinspruch*, p. 399.
34 *Gemeinspruch*, p. 371.
35 *Gemeinspruch*, p. 371.
36 *Critique of Practical Reason*, p. 41.
37 *Gemeinspruch*, p. 398.
38 *Critique of Judgment*, §5. Quoted from J.H. Bernard's translation (London: 1914), p. 53.

V. THEORY, PRAXIS, AND SPECULATION

A

In the classical conception, which served as a point of departure for our inquiry, the concept 'theory' occupied a central position. Over the course of centuries this concept was translated by the Latin *speculatio*. We have noted Kant's attempt to distinguish between the meanings of the theoretical sphere and those of the speculative sphere; as a result of these distinctions he was able to make several suggestions concerning the nature of the speculative sphere which, however, need not concern us at this point.

In turning to an analysis of Hegel's conception with respect to the relationship between the theoretical sphere and the practical sphere and to the relationship between these two spheres and the speculative sphere, we must first note the fact that Hegel clearly distinguished between the theoretical, on the one hand, and the speculative, on the other. This distinction and the superior status given to the speculative sphere over against the theoretical sphere constitute the critical innovation of the Hegelian conception, its systematic value and historical influence.

B

We shall begin our inquiry with the attempt to isolate the various factors that characterize the theoretical sphere and the practical sphere. Generally speaking, we can say that despite the introduction of a number of innovations and refinements, Hegel in this characterization follows in the footsteps of the Greek philosophical tradition and the systems dependent upon this tradition.

Concerning the theoretical sphere Hegel states in one of his early writings that the theoretical faculty begins with something that exists and makes it a representation.[1] The nature of the theoretical is such that it is dependent on the existent-given. In this matter Hegel follows the characterization suggested by Albertus Magnus, namely, that the cause of the stimulation of the theoretical faculty is in things themselves. The innovation of the theoretical faculty is to transform reality into representation, that is, to give the reality, which is beyond the understanding, a status within the sphere of the understanding. The expression of the theoretical faculty is representation, and representation is the content of the understanding. The representation is the expression for the operations of the understanding, but what the representation imagines is not created by the understanding itself but is a presentation of the object that is outside the understanding. Over against this characterization of the theoretical faculty Hegel places the character of the practical faculty which in his view begins with the inner determination — that is, the practical faculty is not dependent on anything existing outside the understanding or the spirit.[2] Here again Hegel follows Albertus' notion of the act whose cause is in the understanding, adding only that this inner determination of the understanding or of the spirit is 'decision' or 'resolution' (*Vorsatz*). We here meet with the transition from the inner determination to the outer; this transition is called transaction or activity (*Wandeln*).[3] In this characterization Hegel sets forth a kind of phenomenology of the act, stressing the internal aspect of decision that belongs to the inner sphere and thus regarding the act as the bridge to the outside. There is an inner aspect of this bridge that pertains to decision alone and there is an overt act within the confines of the transitional link between the inner and outer levels, that is, manifest reality. Here is a nuance of the classical insight according to which the theoretical sphere begins in the object and the ethical sphere with the act. These words are not meant by Hegel simply as a characterization of the ethical act; he is dealing with the act in its totality, and for the nature of the ethical act *par excellence* an additional characterization is required.

A somewhat different nuance appears in another discussion by Hegel concerning the nature of the practical sphere. The activity described above as forming an intermediate link between the inner and outer spheres now serves as the middle term of a syllogism which was also present in classical thought. One part of the syllogism is the universal element or the idea, an idea that resides in the inner recesses of the spirit. The other part of this syllogism is in its externality in general, that is, matter pertains to the external world or, to use Hegel's language, matter is objective. The activity is the means that translates the universal and the internal into objectivity.[4] In this description we see the identity proposed by Hegel between externality and objectivity, objectivity in this case being understood by Hegel in the traditional sense of this concept as the sum-total of given objects and not in the peculiar sense used in his system as universal existence replete with concepts.

This characterization of the act is supplemented by Hegel in another passage by an element connected with the position of the goal or end in the existing aggregate of the act. In the act, Hegel says, man has an end (*Zweck*). The function of the activity (*Handlung*) consists in this: that the content which is the end, that is, the content which is that of the understanding or the content considered as representation, is to be deprived of the form of representation; and the function of the act is to have the content of the end or goal, which is on the subjective level, cease to be merely subjective and take on an objective reality (*Dasein*). The end imagined by us is transferred by means of the act to the sphere of external reality.[5]

C

We notice that the difference between the theoretical and the practical spheres depends to a large extent on the different tendencies involved. When the tendency is in the direction that proceeds from things to spirit, we speak of the theoretical sphere; and when it proceeds from spirit to things, we speak of the practical sphere. This circumstance leads to a different formulation when we introduce two additional concepts in our discussion, the concepts of 'intelligence' and 'will'. Intelligence is generally understood to be a faculty of knowledge. From this point of view Hegel states that spirit in the form of subjectivity is intelligence, that is, spirit as a faculty of knowledge turns external reality around and converts it into the inner content of the understanding.[6] A kind of subjectivization of reality or of objects is here to be found in the theoretical sphere. The will, however, is understood to serve basically as a motive for acts or, more precisely, the will is the spirit in the form of objectivity, raising the inner content of the spirit to the level of reality of objects. The will, then, is spirit striving toward objectivity.[7] These features of the theoretical and of the practical sphere may be outlined as follows:

Theoretical Sphere	*Practical Sphere*
faculty: knowledge or intelligence	*faculty*: the will
direction: from things to spirit	*direction*: from spirit to things

These descriptions, although variously formulated, follow the

general lines of classical thought, as we have seen. We have stressed
them as being of systematic significance, for they contribute to the
understanding of some of Hegel's basic views. For a deeper understanding of Hegel's system itself we must now turn to a discussion of
one of the characteristics he ascribes to the practical sphere.

In our previous discussion we were concerned with the description
of the act, particularly with the nature of the act as a translation of
the inner content to the level of external existence. This must be
supplemented by the observation that the act introduces into reality a
factor previously not found there. To take a simple example: I set out
on a trip to a distant part, and in so doing I introduce my presence
into given reality in a place I had not been before. This constitutes a
translation of direction (itinerary) to the sphere of objects (bodily
presence in a new place). A change has thus been introduced into
reality as it is by an act of removal or, in Hegel's language, the *Aufheben* of externality as directly given. The appearance of the external
sphere undergoes a change; things assume a different context and are
differently arranged from what they were in their original state.[8] At
first Hegel was concerned with characterizing the act from the standpoint of its roots in the inner spirit and in the translation of the inner
spirit to the outer sphere. His concern now is with the act from the
standpoint of the change that the act introduces into the context of
reality as it is and the subsequent enrichment of this context through
the presence of a new element hitherto absent. The change of the
given by a new given is called by Hegel removal or cancellation (*Aufheben*), an important concept for the inner tendency of his system.
An element of interference present in the act is here prominent —
which is to be expected. However, it is also evident that the act raises
the given reality from the level of the given directly to a new level
which was not a level of reality prior to the occurrence of the act. It
seems that Hegel had good reason for using in this context such a
heavily-laden word as *Aufheben*. By introducing into reality a factor
that was hitherto not present, the act negates that reality and at the
same time removes it. Here Hegel, apparently without intent, wishes
to draw our attention to the affinity between the practical sphere and
the inner tendency of his metaphysical system according to which
reality is replete with spiritual contents. It is not universal reality that
is replete, for we are dealing with isolated novel acts and not with
reality in its totality. We find here, however, that an inner content has
been introduced within reality and with this introduction an act is
consummated that has something of the universal rhythm of removal
and elevation, that is, of *Aufheben*.

D

The act has a spontaneity of inception with respect to spirit; it also involves a change of reality brought about by the faculty of spirit. The change here consists in the negation of the real, a change that is effected by a penetration into reality and a lifting it to a new level. This is a materialization of the spiritual, although a partial one, within reality. Such a characterization of the act indicates that Hegel saw some common element between the sphere of the act and the character of spirit as a creation actualized in reality. If we keep in mind the change effected by the Kantian conception in general and the characterization of the act as ethical in particular, we may say that Hegel followed Kant in placing practice above theory. As already observed, theory is knowledge that transfers the objects to the realm of the imagination, or it is the relationship that accomplishes the subjectivization of reality. The act that materializes the objectivization of the inner has a spiritual force superior to the faculty of knowledge that accomplishes the subjectivization of the outer. We cannot say, however, that the character of spirit is exhausted by the act or by practice. The act is a part and the objectivization that proceeds from it is a part, and only where we find totality and spontaneity united in one do we have a fitting expression for reason and spirit.

We can perhaps understand the partial nature of the act as arising precisely from the circumstance that act and will are related. Change and the determination of reality belong to the act; the act molds reality by means of its content, and in so doing changes it. But to the act and to activity belong only the phase that is prior to them, that is, the inner phase in consciousness. In consciousness we find a certain content which we strive to impose upon reality by means of the act, whether this content appears as the goal of intentionality or as the imagination faced with decision. Hence, the content of the decision that motivates the act is the content that the will recognizes as its own.[9] The will is not directed to the world in its totality; it is a compressed activity or it sets in motion a compressed content, a content which we strive to make our own through actualization. This phase of the condensation of the will within an area that can be possessed by me is prominent in the teleological activity. The restriction of the will arises when I strive to attain a definite end in order to make it a part of me. For example, this happens when I seek to learn something and make it a content of my knowledge or when I strive to acquire commodities in order to own them or put them to use. The act obtrudes itself into reality, as we have seen, and imposes its content upon it. However, by a complete severance between the initiator of the act and reality we do not get to the act itself, for the initiator of the act desires, as it were, to restore to his sphere that which had been actualized by him in the context of reality. This restoration is expressed in the relations of possession or acquisition, whether it be of content with respect to knowledge or that of ownership with respect to goods. These relations of possession exist between the doer and the result of his deeds. In the sphere of the act there is an attribution of objectivity to spontaneity but it is not an attribution in which the subject returns and finds itself in the object; the subject here possesses the object. This movement from the doer as subject to reality as the aggregate of objects wherein is also placed the object that is the effect of the act and its return by way of ownership to the subject who is the doer, this rhythmic movement serves to explain Hegel's words that in the act is to be found the total movement of action, reaction, and solution.[10] Action, according to this interpretation, is the act itself; reaction is the opposition that emerges from the context of reality wherein the act converges with its producer; the solution is the act that occurs and the relation of this act to the doer through ownership. Ownership, however, refers not only to the possession of goods but also to the knowledge of the fact that the acquisition is that of the doer who is impelled by the will to act. The 'knowledge' in acquisition as belonging to the doer has a detinite cognitive or intellectual aspect that perhaps is not sufficiently stressed by Hegel. From this intellectual point of view there is some kind of connection between the effect of the act and the impulsion toward it.

The affinity of these Hegelian concepts to those of Kant is even more striking when we recall the words of Kant discussed above, that the idea of duty has a direct effect on the spirit and that the ethical sphere is hence not confronted with the question concerning application and the congruence between the idea and reality. Hegel states, again without stressing the ethical act as such, that not only does the practical 'spirit have ideas the practical spirit is *itself* the living idea. [11] We here notice a kind of union of the cognitive element, or the idea, with the operational element, or actualization. This union is embodied in what is called a practical 'spirit' and not a practical 'reason'. Following Hegel — and using Kantian terms — Erdmann describes practical reason as reason that makes laws or demands.[12]

This description of the practical spirit, in that it contains an aspect of the will, is basically similar to the tendency of Kant's view. The terminological difference between the two is explained by the fact that Hegel does not speak of 'practical reason' whereas Kant does;

instead Hegel speaks of a 'practical spirit'. This difference, as much as
it may appear to be only a terminological one, is not accidental since,
according to Kant, reason finds its appropriate expression in the
ethical act whereas it is for Hegel a faculty that is higher than the
faculty of knowledge and also that of the acts. Spirit is the actualization of reason and as actualization it is partial; in this context it is
therefore practical spirit. Since Hegel stresses this character of the
practical spirit he argues that it is chiefly free will or the will that the
spirit guides in a practical way.[13] In this question we must not over-
look a definite distinction between Hegel and Erdmann in their
respective views concerning the place occupied by the intellectual
component on the level of the act. Erdmann takes the view that
practical reason is not identical with the will alone, for we find in
practical reason, in addition to will, the component of demand as well
as that of constitution. These are not to be regarded as lacking a
connection with contents, either the contents that demand them or
the contents that constitute them on the level of reality, the level to
which, in the last analysis, the act is attached.[14] We have already
spoken of the place of the intellectual component in relation to the
problem of ownership and the knowledge of the ownership of the
results of the act to the doer. This intellectual component, which is
only implied in Hegel's words, is prominent in Erdmann's analysis;
since Erdmann follows Hegel in his basic conceptions, his words may
serve to elucidate the tendency of Hegel's system. Erdmann stresses
the intellectual component; in speaking of the theoretical component
in the sphere of the act he states that the actualization of practical
reason differs from the operation of the objective will, and that this is
so because of the structural element according to the content found in
the area of practical reason.[15] The will is the motive for independent
objectivization, but in the process of objectivization other factors are
found in addition to the will.

                                    E

The parallelism between theory and practice, which has been the
subject of our inquiry, revealed the difference between theory and
practice from the standpoint of the nature of the relationship inherent
in each of the two spheres. In this matter Hegel followed the classical
path but added some Kantian elements. Hegel does not hesitate, however, to point out the difference between theory and practice. The
final position he takes is neither with the one nor the other. The

highest attitude is that of 'speculation', a kind of cancellation or
Aufhebung of the two partial attitudes into one. From the theoretical
attitude Hegel derives, through *Aufhebung*, the relation to reality or
being; from the practical attitude he similarly derives the acquisition
of a spiritual content for reality. Since Hegel makes a terminological
distinction between theory and speculation, he also has terms for the
embodiment of his systematic attitude, which we shall now attempt to
explain.

The difference between theory and practice was based on the
nature of the relationship between the faculty and things: When the
faculty refers to given, existent things it is theoretical; when the
faculty impresses itself on given, existent things and changes them, it
is practical. In both positions there is then a decision in one definite
direction, whether it be in the direction of the things or in the direction of the faculty. It seems that the foothold that can serve as a
transition to the speculative position — which is the highest and the
one most preferred — is to be found in things, that is, the true theoretical relation is to be found where a mutual relationship actually
appears and where we still find freedom of the relationships to each
other.[16] It may be well in this connection to stress at the outset that
the question discussed is that of the true theoretical position; the
simple theoretical position, but not the true one, contains the relation
in one direction as the theoretical relation from the things to the
faculty. This position is not contained within the true theoretical
position. Such a position would be a reciprocal, two-way position —
that is, the things would refer to the faculty and the faculty would
refer to the things. In this relationship neither of the two terms
absorbs or assimilates the other; each retains its own status and yet
there is a relationship between them, just as there is an identity
between knowledge and the world (which we shall discuss later)
without one of these elements being absorbed by the other in some
totality devoid of structure or of the possibility of distinguishing
between them. Hegel, as is his custom, seeks to establish identity and
differentiation at the same time; the correlation between the two
appears to us in the speculative position. In the ordinary theoretical
position — and similarly in the ordinary practical position — there is
no identity and differentiation, nor is this possible. In each of these
two positions there is only one side. In general the second side cannot
attain a one-sided, partial position, so that we must raise to the highest
and preferred position both identity and differentiation. Expressed
differently, it can be said that in a theoretical position the knower
takes his stand over against reality; he recognizes it and what is in it.

Reality does not take a position over against the knower. In the practical position the doer impresses his signature on reality and changes it. But even here the position is from the side of the doer, and the change in reality is not a change that proceeds from its own strength but from the doer who interferes in the process of reality. The position that is closed within itself, the position that Hegel describes as being a movement within the concepts and a movement in the ego, [17] is reached neither by the ordinary theoretical nor by the practical position. Over against the separation between the subject and object there arises the speculative position whose basic principle is the identity of subject and object. [18] It is obvious that this identity is attained neither by the ordinary theoretical-cognitive position nor by the practical-ethical position in which the subject acquires for itself a part of reality, but does not achieve total identity with it. Speculation is a position that reveals unity in opposition, [19] that reveals the form of thought in all things and all objects, and in which the objects of thought as well as the objects of nature and the objects of spirit (such as the state, the law, or religion) are grasped and understood as a unity of differences.

Whereas Kant takes speculation, as we saw in the previous chapter, as referring to objects that are not realized or to the ethical sphere, Hegel takes it as referring to the totality of the world that is recognized as rational. Kant joins speculation with reason. But since reason has no actualization outside of the ethical sphere, we are bound, so to speak, to confine speculation to the sphere in which there is actualization, which is the sphere of ethics. Hegel now frees speculation from being confined to the sphere of ethics by holding that reason is actualized in the world in its totality. Its actualization consists in the fact that it does not find an appropriate object without but rather finds itself within the objects. For Kant the actualization of reason is in the ethical imperative, whereas for Hegel this actualization of reason is in the rationality of the world in its totality. Kant holds that the world in its totality is not within the confines of the possible object of knowledge. The world dwells outside the bounds of experience. It is thus a sphere of speculation viewed as knowledge that has no objects. As against this view, Hegel asserted that the world in its totality is knowable because it is the revelation of reason that knows this world. The identity of being and knowledge makes a speculative knowledge of the world possible. The division between the empirical and the non-empirical or between phenomena and things as they are thus disappears, so that it is no longer a question of theory as 'knowledge based on given nature' in Kant's language, a language also

adopted by Hegel when he characterizes the ordinary theoretical
position. Speculation is within the confines of a corresponding knowledge. An appropriate explanation is given of these words by Erdmann
— to whose analysis we referred above when we attempted to view
Hegel's position in its proper light — when he says that reason assumes
a theoretical or contemplative attitude as it approaches objects related
to it in order to find itself within them.[20] Here Erdmann indulges in
etymological interpretations of words related to *speculum* and speculation or speculative, derived from this Latin word. He takes the
meanings of this term in the strict sense of a 'reflected mirror' and
states that reason is speculative because the concept (conception)
finds itself within the object as within a mirror (*in speculo*) and knows
itself as entire reality.[21] Instead of actualization, which is not found
in Kant since in his view it was to be met within given sensuous, and
hence accidental, objects, we now have the reflection of reason in
reality. Instead of the ethical position which spoke of knowledge as
the reflection of reality within the mind, we now have Hegel's conception which speaks of the reflection of reason in reality. Reason
finds itself in reality. A certain interpretive or systematic function is
here performed by the ambiguity that adheres to the word 'concept'
(*Begriff*), which is what we conceive by the mind or by reason as well
as the object we conceive — that which is a concept in reason is a
concept as object: the object as concept is the concept that is in
reason.

From this point of view there is an additional matter to be considered in another statement by Erdmann concerning the position of
theoretical reason or speculative reason, on the one hand, and
practical or ethical reason on the other.[22] Erdmann is of the opinion
that if everything is actualized, then theoretical reason alone would
exist, for the only proper reality would be that of 'being' alone. But
since everything is not actualized — or at least we do not know the
world as a complete actualization of reason — then practical reason
exists and impregnates the given world with spiritual contents. Practical reason is then a partial attempt to actualize spirituality in reality;
morality or practicality is, as it were, the other side of the coin of
general non-congruence that exists between the rational conception
and the being of the world. Kant also was of the opinion that ethics
appears at the point where the sphere of knowledge ends; but it seems
that his human ideal is really an ethical ideal, and the inability of
knowledge to widen the horizon of ethics is to its credit and is not to
be regarded as a weakness. But in Hegel's view — and here it seems
that Erdmann properly expresses the tendency of Hegel's thought —

theoretical reason and its complete conception is the ideal. Since we conceive this conception in general, there is still room for the fragments of the spiritual impregnation in the given world, fragments that are in the limits of actualization portions of rationality the moment that the complete reflection of rationality is not conceptualized *in actu*.

The shift toward speculation and the superiority of speculation to partial knowledge, on the one hand, and the partial act on the other are here conspicuous. Over against the world in its totality one can only take the position of speculation; this speculation finds the world as the complete reflection of complete reason; it is the contemplation of reason in itself. This is found in the intellectual-rational sphere and not in the practical sphere or in the ethical sphere where reason changes given reality but does not find itself in given reality. From the standpoint of the ordinary theoretical position no superiority is to be attributed to this position over the practical position. From a certain point of view even the practical relation occupies a superior position, for this relation impregnates a partial reality with partial spirituality; but from the standpoint of speculation, in the literal and systematic sense, a decisive superiority is given to the contemplative speculative position. This is the case because within contemplation the knower finds reason in total reality as one with reason's own manifestations. Hegel's position can thus be summed up in the following basic points:

1. In classical philosophy, reason, no matter what terminology was used to designate it, was within the sphere of the knower or of the medium placed over against the phenomena of the world; in Hegel's philosophy it is the knowing instrument over against the known content. When we reach an identity of the knowing instrument with the known content (an identity of the concept from the side of reason with the concept from the side of reality) we arrive at the position of speculation as the higher and more preferred of the two positions.

2. Hegel does not adopt Kant's view of the incongruity between the complete spontaneity of reason and the status of the objects of reality. According to Kant there is a complete spontaneity of reason but it is not related to the objects of reality; and if reason is related to the objects of reality, it is not within the sphere of a complete spontaneous reason. According to Hegel, reason is complete spontaneity because its objective counterpart is also rational and not given. Instead of the relationship which is the limitation of reason to the given in Kant's view, we have the reflection of reason in being. The position reached by this reflection, and hence the position that sets in motion spontaneous reason, Hegel calls a speculative position, a position that

differs from the theoretical position which is only a partial, cognitive one.

3. Since the spontaneity of reason assures objectivity on the intellectual plane, there is no need to take refuge in Kant's suggestion concerning spontaneous reason on the ethical plane. Kant takes spontaneous reason to be creative reason, and its status is actualized in the ethical position directed by imperatives which create an additional dimension of reality alongside that of the reality of nature. Since Hegel believes that there is a creative, spontaneous reason in its embodiment in reality as a totality, there is no need to assure the actualization of reason by a creation of the ethical sphere. What Kant ascribes to reason in the ethical sphere is ascribed by Hegel to reason in the speculative sphere. Speculation is above and beyond both theory and practice.

4. In the speculative position Hegel combines the sphere of theory and of practice, but he does so without elevating either one to a preferred position of superiority. The union of the positions requires an additional position above the two ordinary ones. Hegel was faced with the problem of uniting theory and practice, and he found the solution for this problem in a supra-theoretical position, that is, in the speculative position.[23]

Marx's strictures against Hegel revolve around this point as well as his attempt to reconstruct Kant's position within the limits of Hegel's system — a subject to which we shall now turn.

NOTES

1 *Rechts-, Pflichten-und Religionslehre für die Unterklasse*, § in *Hegels Sämtliche Werke*, Vol. XXI (*Nürnberger Schriften 1808-1816*), edited by J. Hoffmeister (Leipzig: 1938), p. 141.
2 *Rechts-, Pflichten-und Religionslehre* . . . , p. 141.
3 *Rechts-, Pflichten-und Religionslehre* . . . , p. 141.
4 *Vorlesungen über die Philosophie der Geschichte*, in Glockner's edition of Hegel's *Sämtliche Werke* (hereafter *Werke*) Vol. XI (Stuttgart: 1928), p. 56.
5 *Vorlesungen über die Philosophie der Religion* in *Werke*, Vol. XV, (Stuttgart: 1928),p. 237.
6 *System der Philosophie* III, in *Werke*, Vol. X, (Stuttgart: 1929), p. 51.
7 *System der Philosophie* . . . , p. 51.
8 *Rechts-, Pflichten-und Religionslehre* . . . , §9, p. 142.
9 *Rechts-, Pflichten-und Religionslehre* . . . , p. 131.
10 *Vorlesungen über die Aesthetik*, I, in *Werke*, Vol. XII (Stuttgart: 1927), p. 297.

11 *Philsophische Encyklopädie für die Oberklasse*, § 173, in *Hegels Sämtliche Werke*, Vol. XXI, edited by J. Hoffmeister, p. 282.

12 J. E. Erdmann, *Grundriss der Psychologie* (Leipzig: 1840), p. 71. Erdmann here relies directly on Kant. He agrees with the thought that practical reason is superior to theoretical reason, but he criticizes Kant for positing these two reasons one beside the other. The union of the two reasons is to be found in speculation, as will be seen later.

13 *Philosophische Encyklopädie* . . . , § 174, p. 282.

14 Erdmann, *Grundriss der Psychologie* . . . , p. 74.

15 Erdmann, *Grundriss der Psychologie* . . . , p. 71.

16 *System der Philosophie* II, in *Werke*, Vol. IX (Stuttgart: 1929), p. 300.

17 In this connection Hegel's reflection on the nature of motion should be recalled: Motion is nothing but the eternal recurrence of identity within the differentiation and re-creation of *contractio* and *expansio*. (*Dissertatio philosophica de Orbitis Planetarum*, in *Werke*, Vol. I [Stuttgart: 1927], p. 23.) On this subject consult Hegel's *Phänomenologie des Geistes*, in *Werke*, Vol. II (Stuttgart: 1927), pp. 73, 74 and the Introduction.

18 *Differenz des Fichteschen und Schellingschen Systems der Philosophie in Beziehung auf Reinhold's Beiträge zur leichtern Übersicht des Zustandes der Philosophie zum Anfang des neunzehnten Jahrhunderts*, I (1801), in *Werke*, Vol. I (Stuttgart: 1927), pp. 34, 35, 36.

19 *Vorlesungen über die Philosophie der Religion*, I, in *Werke*, Vol. XV (Stuttgart: 1928), p. 40.

20 Erdmann, *Grundriss der Psychologie* . . . , p. 68.

21 Erdmann, *Grundriss der Psychologie* . . . , p. 74.

22 Erdmann, *Grundriss der Psychologie* . . . , p. 72.

23 Whitehead also distinguishes between speculative and theoretical reason. Speculative reason is faculty leading to new methodologies. Theoretical reason merely sums up the findings until now. See *The Function of Reason* (Princeton: 1929), pp. 30-31.

VI. HISTORY REPLACING SPECULATION

A

The union of theory and practice became a current concept as a result of the Marxian doctrine, or, rather, of a certain interpretation of that doctrine. This concept as Marx used it is far from being clear, precisely because of the widespread currency it enjoyed. Its meaning can be made clearer by recalling the connection between the Marxian and the Hegelian sets of concepts and attempting to understand the former in the light of a strict interpretation of some of the sources pertinent to the subject.

We first must indicate, from a negative point of view, that when we speak of the unity of theory and practice in Marx's system of concepts, we do not refer to theory as some kind of an intellectual pattern, hypothesis, or model which is the theoretical aspect, as it were. When such a pattern is found, we are confronted with the question of the application of this pattern to the given data of reality — a question which also arises when we interpret the given data according to the lines laid down by the hypothesis or the model which serves as a theoretical guide, as it were, in the relations between the schematic, intellectual outline and the data. In the Marxian system of concepts the question of the application of theory is not identical with the question of the relation between theory and practice. It should be stated at the outset that the question of application is a central one where the discussion is primarily concerned with the problem of interpreting the world. Where, however, the discussion is primarily concerned with the question of changing the world, in Marx's own language, it is obvious that the question of application cannot be central.

This rejected interpretation of Marx's thought compels us to return to a Kantian argument discussed above — namely, that practical reason contains within itself an imperative of conduct and that it exerts a direct influence on our behavior. It may be added that if it were not for this direct influence on conduct, practical reason would be dependent on empirical data and would thus not be pure, and ethics or ethical conduct would in principle not be possible. From this Kant draws the conclusion that there is no place in the sphere of ethics for a distinction between theory and practice, and this non-differentiation between the two led him to important systematic conclusions which we have attempted to clarify above. Practical reason as the source of imperatives and the sum-total of imperatives is then bound up with the stream of action, and thus there is no difference between it and the action produced by it. Reason is actualized from out of itself; reason thus does not give rise to the problem of application, that is, the problem of applying the system to some sphere outside of the system, a sphere of data alien to the system applied. By means of application we attempt in a case such as this to find the connection among the spheres that differ from one another. In Kant's system the question of application is made to refer to knowledge and not to ethics.

It appears that we are obliged to say that Marx, whether intentionally or not, was attracted by this Kantian thought which he either borrowed from Kant or came upon himself. He underlined the Kantian thought that the endeavor to actualize and the imperative of the actualization are inherent in the nature of the contents of reason. But, in contradistinction to Kant, he does not place practical reason over against theoretical reason. Marx treats reason as a whole, following Hegel in this respect. Furthermore, Marx does not believe that the striving for actualization is peculiar only to practical reason on the level of the ethical imperative; such striving is also an expression of reason over against the empirical existence of human beings which is, first and foremost, an historical existence. Reason is no longer actualized on its own plane but rather on the plane of existence. Thus Marx combines Kant's thought concerning the actualization of reason − and not its reflection − with Hegel's thought that reason finds its expression in institutions, namely, in the institutions of historical existence. Marx then believed, as did Kant, that there are certain contents that lead to acts. However, he understands these contents as contents of reality and not merely as formal imperatives, and he stresses the concrete causes that are used or could be used by these contents. Marx, following Hegel, attempts to give concreteness to that unity of theory and practice which, as Kant taught, is on the plane of pure ethics. Marx attempts to demonstrate this by proposing such a union on the plane of real, material existence in the economic sense of this term, a sense that is included in the concept of real existence. The arena of history is put in the place of the sphere of pure, practical reason, and this arena becomes the sphere of actualization corresponding to the imperative of reason. Marx believed that it was not only within the confines of pure reason that reason was actualized; furthermore, he maintained that actualization within pure reason was chimeric since it is not really actualization. Reason must be deliberately actualized in empirical existence and not only on the level of pure reason.[1]

B

This change that Marx introduced into the Kantian system implies a change in point of view, for Marx no longer maintained the distinction between the rational and the empirical, the most fundamental of Kant's distinctions. He wished to show that there were empirical data which, although empirical or because they were empirical, were connected to the content of the imperative and thus acquired rational meaning until the distinction between the empirical and the rational was obliterated. In this matter the highest importance is to be ascribed to the concept of need in Marx's system. Need attests to the fact that there is a gap or rift in existence, that is, there are strivings that have not yet been satisfied. But the concept of need also points to that content through whose attainment needs could be satisfied. In other words, the concept of need is a motive in real human existence. It is also a sign that indicates the transition beyond the given existence. Through satisfying the need we reach a reality where there is a created harmony between need and satisfaction. This is the case with respect to the simplest needs of life, which include, according to Marx, first and foremost food and drink, shelter, clothing, and the like. The first historical act, then, is the creation of means to satisfy these needs or the creation of material life itself. The need for food means that there is a definite need (hunger) that food can satisfy, and this holds true also for drink, shelter, and clothing. There is then a complementary relationship between a need and its fulfillment, that is, there are certain real, well-defined things, such as food, that are designed to satisfy a definite need that is directed to them. This convergence between need and the real matter required to satisfy it appears to Marx as the principle of harmony between the empirical given of the need and the real, rational content of the satisfaction of the need. It is obvious that a need can be satisfied only by means of a factor found on the level of reality. A need is a concrete motive, and it is therefore necessary that the appropriate content for the satisfaction of the need should be in the system of concrete reality in which the need is found. The need presses toward actualization, and actualization must take place on the level of the need; it is not to be assumed that a need will be on the level of empirical motives and that actualization will be on the level of pure reason divorced from actual existence. Harmony itself, the adjustment between need and reason, becomes a part of the character of rational existence. The imperative of reason is then to actualize the imperative in concrete existence; and if it is not thus actualized, a duality arises between the empirical and the rational, an anti-rationalistic duality. Furthermore, we can say that the proletariat is enslaved in that its ethical status has been violated with the consequent dissolution of the absolute ethical imperative which forbids us to use man as only a means. It is a need of the proletariat to free itself from this status and this is in and of itself the actualization of the inner content of the absolute imperative of ethics, which is the imperative of reason. From this point of view we can say that Marx, through the use of Hegelian concepts, brought Hegel down to earth. He likewise attempts to place Kant's system of concepts on a level of concreteness in a direction of actualization inherent in concretization. This is put in the place of actualization on the level of reason which is, according to Kant, real actualization. Kant took ethics to be embodied in the ethical act itself motivated by the imperative of reason; Marx saw our basic task in the realization of the content of ethics within the system of organized relations among men. This actualization is the conversion of theory to practice.

C

The prominence given to the Kantian element in Marx's system, as set forth above, is not for the purpose of tracing influences or establishing relations of historical continuity; rather it is intended to clarify the content of Marx's thinking on this subject and indicate its tendency. The change that occurred in Marxian thought, as opposed to that of Kant, is a change in the position of the actualization of reason in empirical existence. This is closely connected, as has been stated, with the removal of the duality between the rational and the empirical. This change is conditioned by the positive direction of Hegel's doctrine and by his criticism of Kant's dualism. To the extent that Kant adheres to the clarification of the relation between the ethical system and historical existence he regards ethics as the goal of history and as an end that is continually being embodied but never attained, as can be seen, for example, in the problem of world peace — an interesting example, for it is significant with respect to historical existence and with respect to the network of human relations within this existence. Universal peace is an idea that is incapable of realization, but one that man can come closer and closer to attaining.[2] It is clear that this approximation does not abolish the dualism between existence and the idea.[3] Over against this, Hegel posits the relation of identity and the relation of congruence on the basis of the identity between reason and existence, that is, the secure relation in the speculative position. The speculative position applies to the kinds of difference, whether in the area between the idea and the reality of nature or in the area between the idea and historical existence.

In this context Marx takes two diverse steps that complement one another. First, his sphere of explicit analysis is the sphere of history in which he finds the concrete actualization of reason in existence. Hegel, on the other hand, believes that the actualization takes place in history which occurs in time, and its place is not in the speculative position which contains history within it. In Hegel's system, however, history is not the exclusive sphere of actualization, for in his view every sphere and every mode of its actualization — even nature which is external to spirit — is an actualization of the spirit through externality. History, which is one of the spheres of the actualization of reason or of the spirit, is also a partial actualization of reason. But complete actualization is a concept in the speculative position which comprehends all the spheres, a comprehension that is possible only through philosophic contemplation. The philosophic synopsis, according to Hegel, is identical with speculation, and hence the appropriate expression of identity between reason and being is in the speculative position and not in any sphere whatever of existence. Marx rejects this view and seeks to establish the identity of reason and existence within the realm of existence that is regulated by reason but which does not cease to be existence despite the fact that it is saturated with reason. In the second step that Marx took he sought actualization in existence and not in reason itself. He thought he found exemplifications of such actualization in the concrete course of human existence and not in the speculative-philosophic sense of the word. The union of theory and practice in this context means, then, the position of the contents of reason as the contents of theory, that is, as the concepts in operation within existence in practice. Whereas in Hegel's view it is possible to achieve a union of theory and practice in the third position of speculation, Marx seeks this union in the practical position, which is that of history and the acts that establish history and guide it: Since history is taken as the entire sphere of reality embodying theory or reason, nature ceases to be a separate factor existing outside of the historical relation of man to the world. Nature is included in the historical relationship of man to the world, for man uses nature and its treasures in the construction of his actual historical life. Nature is therefore not a sphere apart that requires the Kantian relationship of knowledge conditioned by categories or the Hegelian relationship of viewing nature as spirit in its external dispersion. The separation of nature and ethics was part of the Kantian position and it obliged him to regard the cognitive relation that refers to nature as different from the ethical relation that flows from the sources of pure reason and is realized in pure reason. The separation between nature and history was part of the Hegelian position which saw different tendencies and different spheres of the actualization of the spirit in reality. Marx placed the relation to nature within man's historical existence and consequently he no longer advocates a dualism of nature and history, either in the Kantian or in the Hegelian sense. Kant, as is well known, adopted Leibniz's distinction between grace and nature and changed it to a distinction between ethics and nature. Marx wished to establish the non-independence of nature and this led him to regard historical practice as a general field for the embodiment of reason both in the cognitive and in the practical-ethical position. Marx, like Hegel, believed that there is no need for Kant's distinction between ethics and nature; but he criticized Hegel for having nevertheless left the spheres separated and for failing to see the need for the active realization of the ethical imperative in concrete, historical existence. In the Hegelian system we attain rational unity within the limits of the speculative position which is genuinely theoretical, and from this point of view there is no practical position, that is, no position of actualization within time. The union of theory and practice, according to Marx, rests on the prior metaphysical assumption that history can be the arena for the complete actualization of reason, taking the place in his system that speculation occupied in Hegel's system. In Hegel's view history was only one of the expressions of the spirit; whereas for Marx it could replace Hegelian speculation, because history is able to actualize the content of Kant's categorical imperative in its third formulation, namely, that man is not only a means but also an end. This being so, Marx is able to reduce reason from its position in the sphere of actualization within history to its ethical content and to subject the cognitive content of reason to the ethical content or make it a part of that content. This latter insinuation into the ethical content constitutes another interpretation of the thought discussed above, namely, that nature does not appear in Marx's system as an independent sphere of knowledge as it does in Kant's system. It has a position through the agency of man's real activity in the world, an activity that takes place in time and in history. Man's image of nature is thus part of historical existence and even the science of nature is part of this historical existence. *Pari passu* with the position of history as a sphere of total actualization we find the conception that places reason in the ethical content. Here again we are confronted with the following problem: Marx combines the Kantian with the Hegelian tendency, taking from Kant the notion that the peculiar expression of reason is ethical — that is, the intentionality to man as an end — and from Hegel the notion that the real expression of reason is to be found in existence and not only in the pure realm of reason which gives rise to ethics. The mixture of these two notions leads him to dispense with speculation and to replace it with historical actualization. We have here a kind of parallelism between the ethical meaning of reason and the actualization of this meaning in history. From this point of view the union of theory and practice is possible because an ethical content is inherent in theory and because practice means acts that establish this content in the area of historical existence. This helps to clarify Lukács' conception of the union of theory and practice as the conversion of demand into existence.[4] The union of theory and practice means, then, the actualization of the rational content in historical practice. What has now been stated in the language of systematic concepts may be put in the language of the philosophical systems: Marx endeavors to actualize Kant's demand through the union of reason and history, a union which became Hegel's speculative axis. Keeping in mind Marx's acute paraphrase, we can say that in this central point Marx does not bring Hegel down to earth but he embodies Kant's thought in a sphere suggested by Hegel.

D

We can now look back upon the design and order of our discussion of the question of theory and practice and see it in its large contours. We observed the origins of this question in Greek philosophy and noted how the distinction between theory and practice was retained despite its varied subsequent development. The character of each of the spheres as well as their order of preference underwent changes but the distinction itself remained. Hegel took the step toward a possible

removal of the distinction between the spheres by proposing the
speculative position, a proposal wherein he remained true to the
guiding principle of his system both in methodology and in content,
that is, he first established a dualism and then proceeded to derive a
unity from it that would also rise above it. In this matter — and here
we shall examine some of Marx's sources more closely — Marx's position differs from that of Hegel. Marx no longer supports Hegel's view
which holds as a matter of principle that there are different positions
or relationships of consciousness to things, a position which is both
theoretical and practical. In Marx's view the theoretical position is not
an independent one, being the expression of the fundamental practical
position. At the bottom of the division of the spheres into theoretical
and practical we find the division of labor. (The social aspect of the
division of labor is evident in the distinction between the two sexes.)
The division of labor really comes into being only when the material
labor in it appears separate from the spiritual work.[5] The creation of a
theoretical position is only a positing of a detached position, as it
were, since the detachment from social roots is only imaginary. The
theoretical position does not cease to be rooted in an existence of a
division of labor and the social relations created by it; it is also interwoven with them when this position appears as an independent
theoretical position. At this point Marx does not propose the union of
theory and practice but the dependence of the former on the latter.
Practice is here understood as occupation against a background of a
division of labor or as the creation of this division of labor itself and
its expressions in the areas of economic productivity. In Marx's
language we can say that the establishment of an independent ethical
position is a pretense and camouflage of the actual situation. It
is not the content of the theoretical position alone but the theoretical
position itself that is an ideology. If consciousness can only be conscious being, and being is the course of real life, as Marx puts it,[6] then
the theoretical position which consciousness adopts is nothing but
being in its material system when this being becomes conscious. A
closer examination of the text does not reveal that Marx advocates a
systematic position of the union of theory and practice on the level of
history as the all-inclusive level of the two positions, but rather as
stressing the primacy of practice in order to relegate theory to a
secondary position. The dependence of theory disguises its true significance as a position that is dependent on practice. History is not a
sphere of unity; it is a sphere that gives rise to the dualism that history
must overcome, the dualism between theory and practice.

E

This brings us to a consideration of the manifold meanings of practice as used by Marx, which is all the more conspicuous in view of the programmatic status he gave to this concept. In a former discussion we mentioned the blurred meanings that attended the concept of practice, since no sharp distinction was drawn between *practice* and *poiesis* as had been made in Greek philosophy. The blurred distinction arose in medieval philosophy and also played a significant part in Francis Bacon's system. The manifold meanings are seen clearly in Marx's system.

1. Marx speaks of material practice and of the practical reversal of social relations.[7] Practice is bound up with material relations and these, in turn, are connected with the rhythm of needs and their satisfaction. The concept of practice in this context has not, then, the meaning of behavior that gives shape to desire and volition, which is the meaning of this concept in Aristotle's system. The concept of practice points to actual behavior within the limits of social relationships that are attached to the material-economic system of human beings.

2. In this connection we understand the reason why practice produces social relations. Only within this system are man's needs satisfied. This practice is also the cause of social revolution for it is only by means of this factor that man's material needs could be satisfied. These material needs are satisfied by combining economic need with the actualization of the ethical imperative which assures that man has the status of an end and not merely of a means. Practice that produces material relations leads to the actualization of the ethical imperative, an actualization that is an imperative of reason on the one hand and a material need on the other. Practice is, then, a guarantee for the harmony between need and imperative. Even here Marx is inclined to give a superior status to practice over against theory, since practice is a factor that creates social relations as they are and also a factor that creates relations as they should be. In either case practice is not an operative cause with respect to man's private life, his volitions and desires, but an operative cause with respect to the communal, public sphere and to the economic, political sphere within it.

3. Thus far we have seen that the concept 'practice' designates the level of action and the content of action. In his characterization of practice, however, Marx uses language in a wider sense the moment he describes all relationships based on existence as practical relationships. A real judgment, that is a judgment based on existence, is a

practical judgment. We are concerned here not with the practical nature of the judgment but with the fact that it is based on a system of existence that serves as a background for acts produced in existence. Parallel with this linguistic usage, which tends to identify practice with existence, Marx identifies theory with abstraction. With his characteristic polemical exaggeration he speaks of 'practical' practice and — in contradistinction to it — of 'categorical' categories, which designate the sum-total of abstractions which practical practice ignores.[8] Or, to put it differently, Marx opposes the cerebral cobwebs of ideas that clutter the mind and the practical sphere, the sphere of objects. These cobwebs of the mind represent man's alienation from existence and its operations, the sphere of practice.[9] Here Marx identifies detached theory with these cobwebs of the mind, and he identifies practice with activity, on the one hand, and with existence, in which we act, on the other.

4. This composition within the concept practice — the element of action and the element of existence — serves Marx as a *terminus a quo* for a criticism of those social positions whose central point is that of the change of the character of consciousness and which distract the mind from changing the character of existence. The change of consciousness alone, one that is not conditioned by a change of existence, seems to Marx to be an attempt to attain a mystic unity of theory and practice.[10]   It is a mystic unity because it seeks to attain unity within the limits of consciousness itself. This criticism is directed by Marx against Bruno Bauer, but it could apply equally as well to Fichte, who is concerned with the changes of consciousness and its relations to the world. Marx, however, is interested in changing the world, and such a change is regarded by him as a union of theory and practice in the sphere of practice. This explains the superiority of practice over against theory, a superiority that here depends not on the position of practice as a product of theory, a position we have noted above, but on the general position of practice, which is identical with the totality of existence. In all these matters we can say that Marx does not plead for the union of theory and practice because of the one-sided nature of each of these positions when taken separately, as Hegel had argued; nor does he plead for the superiority of practice over against theory because practice attains a level that cannot be reached by theory, as Kant had argued. Marx's criticism stems from the dualism of theory and act and the dualism of theory and the totality of existence, which is at most an active and activating part within it, activating in the sense that there is an ethical content of the rational position that appears to us against the background of existence. This does not mean that

Marx's essential position — putting history in the place of speculation — is in all particulars identical with the position that does not consider practice to be one of the components of history, but rather with the position that identifies practice with the historical totality. This is the tendency indicated in Marx's words to the effect that the solution of theoretical riddles is the task of practice. Dependence on practice is limited not only to theory in the strict sense of this term as philosophical or theological theory. The organization of man's sensuality is regulated by practice, and the sensual consciousness of an idol worshipper is different from that of a Greek since his sensual or practical existence is different.[11] This explains why Marx speaks of the senses as theoretical[12] and why he restores, with a touch of irony, the original meaning of seeing-sensual to the term 'theory'.

Two additional conclusions may be drawn from this discussion. When Marx speaks of sensual practice, he is not referring to practice that fashions the sensuality, the type of practice discussed in Aristotelian philosophy and in the systems following it, but to practice as the sum-total of acts that proceed from the sensual needs of men, such as food and shelter, and all the relations, even the most complex, that are produced against the background of these needs. From this point of view the tendency to restrict the content of the concept practice is quite marked in Marx's conception.

Parallel to this — which is the other side of the coin — Marx believes that the position of independent theory and the position above it, such as the speculative approach, attest to a detachment from practice. It also attests to the fact that there are problems in the actualization of pratice from which we flee to theoretical detachment. Marx criticizes the religious position for cutting man off from his moorings in daily existence, the existence of practice, and binding him to an imaginary existence beyond. He criticizes the detached position in general, that is, the theoretical or the speculative position. Since the followers of the speculative position described their own position as detached, we can understand how Marx availed himself of this description to criticize their detachment and to disclose the practical roots of the flight from practice — for example, the discord that finds no consolation in existence and seeks it in the heavenly world beyond.[13]

In any case, we find two currents of thought in Marx: (a) one tendency speaks of the unity of theory and practice, following the classical tradition, and places this unity in the world of history; (b) the other tendency does not refer to the unity of theory and practice but to the superiority of the practical position from the standpoint of material and temporal primacy. In this context the concept 'practice' appears as the bearer of several meanings. In part these two currents of thought flow together and in part they diverge. It is obvious that the popular aspect of Marx's conceptions absorbed more of the second tendency, although current usage from time to time adopts the terminology of the first tendency.

NOTES

1 Marx-Engles, *Die deutsche Ideologie*, in Adoratskij's *Historisch-kritische Gesamtausgabe* of their works (Berlin: 1932), *Erste Abteilung*, Vol. V, pp. 17ff.
2 *Metaphysik der Sitten*, §61, edited by J. H. von Kirchmann (Leipzig: 1870), p. 195.
3 On this, see Marx's clear review of Kant in *Die deutsche Ideologie* . . . , p. 175.
4 See G. Lukács, "Rosa Luxemburg als Marxist," in *Geschichte und Klassenbewusstsein* (Berlin: 1923), p. 54.
5 *Die deutsche Ideologie* . . . , pp. 20ff.
6 *Die deutsche Ideologie* . . . , pp. 15ff.
7 *Die deutsche Ideologie* . . . , p. 27.
8 *Die heilige Familie*, in Adoratskij's *Historisch-kritische Gesamtausgabe* (Berlin: 1932), *Erste Abteilung*, Vol. III, p. 330.
9 *Die heilige Familie* . . . , p. 224.
10 *Die heilige Familie* . . . , p. 371.
11 *Ökonomisch-philosophische Manuskripte aus dem Jahre 1844*, in Adoratskij's *Historisch-kritische Gesamtausgabe* (Berlin: 1932), *Erste Abteilung*, Vol. III, p. 133.
12 *Ökonomisch-philosophische* . . . , p. 119.
13 In this matter Marx followed Feuerbach and his criticism of theory in general and of religious attitude in particular. See Nathan Rotenstreich, *Basic Problems of Marx's Philosophy* (Essay and Monograph Series of The Liberal Arts Press, Indianapolis: 1965).

VII. SYSTEMS OF THOUGHT AND THEIR CONSEQUENCES

A

The question of the relation of theory to practice has been brought into a general systematic and intellectual prominence not only by the offshoots of Marxian doctrine prevalent in our generation. Those doctrines termed 'pragmatic' also played a major role, and the connection of these 'pragmatic' doctrines to the philosophic tradition whose interrelations we have sought to clarify above are much closer than appears at first glance.

The term 'pragmatic' itself must first come under scrutiny. Kant, in several of his writings, defines it as that knowledge of the world which can be profitable not only for school but for life[1] — "life" in this context meaning ease and care, or attending to the means that lead to universal happiness. Pragmatism, then, is connected with the limited human goal of welfare and with the means that lead to it. This component is to be found in all the well-known pragmatic systems, particularly those of Peirce and Dewey, systems which also reveal unmistakable traces of Hegel's doctrine. We shall examine these systems not only to indicate their historical connections but also to acquire a deeper understanding of the concepts and the nature of their use.[2]

B

Peirce himself defines the term 'pragmatic', which he suggests is preferable to 'practicism' or 'practicalism' — terms that he associates with Kantian doctrine and which he takes as referring to the sphere of the determination of pure reason which is based on the pure will. According to Peirce, when we speak of the Kantian meaning of 'practicalism', we think of it as diametrically opposed to pragmatism. In Kant's usage, the term 'practicalism' refers to that region of thought in which no empirically directed mind is able to find solid ground under its feet; 'pragmatism', however, expresses the relationship to a definite human purpose.[3] Peirce therefore placed the concept 'pragmatism' in a teleological context and not — as Kant did — in the context of a pure source of activity. While Peirce does not here indicate his attitude to Kant with respect to the term 'pragmatism', he does indicate his attitude to Kant with respect to the manner in which he understands the term 'practicalism'.

This point of view of the relation of the system of concepts and thoughts to human ends stresses another phase of the question concerning the unity of theory and practice. This emphasis on unity has created the erroneous impression that in this fundamental point the systematic tendency of pragmatism approximates the basic tendency of Marx's doctrine. Such is not the case, however, because the concepts of theory and practice are different in the two systems. For Marx, theory — as analyzed before — is basically the ideal of the union of reason and history. In pragmatism, theory is concerned with the attitude to the conceptual systems that lead to definite effects, with drawing important conclusions and with man's relation to their causes. The essential meaning of practice in Marx's doctrine refers to the act within history and its construction, whereas in the pragmatic doctrines it refers essentially to the human goal which changes with the process of the actualization of the unity of theory and practice, which in turn is the continuous process of man's struggle to control and dominate the changing circumstances of his life. Here is an instance of various systems with different tendencies adopting identical philosophical terms, which, however, do not attest to a basic similarity in these systems.[4]

The question that arises with respect to the clarification of the nature of pragmatism is: Which human end is here the subject of discussion? Is it the end in the intellectual system itself as it moves toward unanticipated knowledge hitherto not available, or as it moves in the direction of increasing and elaborating the knowledge of things already understood or is the human end outside the system of thought, being the end of welfare or happiness, our relation to which Kant described as being characteristic of the nature of the pragmatic sphere? Different conceptions prevail in this matter even within pragmatism itself. We can understand pragmatism both as the view of the nature of the intellectual sphere and as the view of the relation between the intellectual sphere and the status of human beings in reality.[5]

This ambiguity in the understanding of the relation between thought and end is clearly stated by Peirce himself who says that thought depends on what is to be hereafter; so that thought has only a potential existence, dependent on the future thought of the community.[6] If we examine this passage more closely, we see that a thought, however formulated, always remains potential with respect to future thoughts and what it finally may come to be in a state of complete information. Since reference to 'now' and 'hereafter' has been made in the discussion, we may say that the intellectual systems themselves have a status or a perspective within time. Not only does the act of thought take place in time, but the content of thought as well is within time together with its developing nature as it moves toward the future. The development of thought is a movement of thought from the potential to the actual; the actual state is always moving forward, that is, it is placed in the future, and the thought together with its content is directed toward the future. The stream of time itself becomes the content of thought. At this point Peirce introduces the concept of 'community',[7] having in mind the thinking of the community and not of the individual. It is not clear whether he is referring to social institutions as they are, or to the subjective agreement among many people with respect to systems of thought together with the conclusions that flow from them. Although the meaning of the term 'community' in this context is not clear, we note that Peirce omits one highly important consideration in his discussion. He does not say that the movement of the system of thought from the potential to the actual means the application of thought to empirical data; the question of application does not arise in Peirce's discussion when he defines the pragmatic approach to the status of a system of thought and its nature.

Looking at the concept of 'community' in Peirce's discussion from another point of view, the same question as to his meaning arises even more clearly: Was he referring to organized social institutions, scientific or technological, or to the rational contact among groups of men engaged in a common endeavor? Peirce states that one of the most striking characteristics of the view he is setting forth — which he calls 'the new theory' — is the conception that there is an indissoluble connection between rational knowledge and the rational end. The rational knowledge here discussed, it appears, is the position of the systems of thought as conceptual systems, and the rational end is the discourse among many individuals by means of rational interchange and the rational resolution of problems that arise in this discourse. We have here a movement of thought from the potential to the actual, on the one hand, and a progressive development of the potential toward a new state of the actual, on the other. At any rate, Peirce does not here mention as a rational end man's mastery of nature, the end that was stressed by Bacon and later revived by Dewey.

C

We notice that the emphasis has been placed on the goal of thought. This aspect was placed beyond thought in the theoretical sense and became an aspect of human conduct. Peirce therefore says that whenever a man acts purposively, he acts under a belief in some experimental phenomena and consequently the sum of the experimental phenomena that a proposition implies consists of its entire bearing upon human conduct.[8]

This tends to confirm the reservation already made, namely, that Peirce is not concerned with the application of the intellectual presupposition with regard to the experiment conducted. He expressly states that the rational meaning is not in the experiment but in the experimental phenomenon. The experimental context in phenomena does not refer to any definite event in particular that happened to somebody in the dead past but to what is sure to happen to all men in the living future who shall fulfill certain conditions. When something will happen in the future, it will shatter the doubts of skeptics, like the celestial fire upon the altar of Elijah.[9] Peirce wishes to emphasize the relation to the future as a general relation, as one that makes for events which in turn produce the world in the future. These events emerge as the conclusions of an intellectual system. There is no longer a distinction between the intellectual system itself and the events produced because of the content inherent in this system. If we speak in this context of human conduct, it means that in their conduct men take into account the sum-total of phenomena that occur as a result of the movement from the potential to the actual of the intellectual system. Peirce mentions in this connection "Michelson's phenomenon," referring to the measurement of the effect of the velocity of the earth on the velocity of light. Here he attempts to combine in one general system the phenomena that actualize intellectual systems and the human conduct that is attached to these phenomena in daily life. From this point of view we can say that the human end we are considering is the end of combining ways of behavior in intellectual systems. On the other hand, it is also human conduct moving into the future. This takes into account the events which are an actualization of the conclusions of intellectual systems in the sum-total of experimental phenomena. The question still remains whether Peirce united this experimental aspect with the general human aspect, that of the human end.[10]

We are aware of the ambiguity of the term 'experimental' or 'experimental phenomenon' the moment that Peirce speaks of effects that might conceivably have sensible effects.[11] The term 'practical' equals 'sensible' and is used here to indicate what Peirce calls 'pragmatic', that is, the sum-total of human conduct that has rational ends.

At any rate, we see that in connection with pragmatism Peirce touches on two subjects which in his opinion are within the framework of the unity of theory and pragmatic practice: the intellectual effects or consequences that flow from given intellectual systems and, secondly, the effects of ways of behavior of the intellectual systems when introduced into existence and interwoven in the system of existence in which the active behavior falls. These two subjects constitute the status of the concept of end: The end of the intellectual systems is to be found in the intellectual consequences, on the one hand, and in human conduct on the other.

We can sum up this analytical discussion of the meaning of pragmatism in Peirce's view as follows:

1. The theoretical-intellectual aspect does not refer to given objects but to consequences.

2. Since given objects are replaced by consequences, two dimensions are added to the discussion of theory — the dimension of the future and that of the end.

3. In Peirce's view the intentionality to the future and to the end imbues the intellectual system with pragmatic meaning. He places the practical aspect within the limits of theory and of human conduct.

4. When Peirce speaks of an end, he does not refer to the realization of a well-defined end such as, for example, the goal of man as an end or as the end of human freedom and equality, which is at the center of Marx's conception. Peirce attaches theory to an end, the end being ethics,[12] but it may be said that this ethics faces the future, a moving, accumulative end, and is not riveted to a static principle. This relationship to the future, with respect both to thought and to conduct, leads Peirce to the statement that logic, ethics, and esthetics are all derived from one normative science.[13]

D

Whitehead in one place makes the distinction between two tendencies of reason — one tendency which is governed by the purposes of some external interest, and a second tendency which is governed by immediate satisfaction arising from the operations of reason themselves. The first is the practical tendency; the second, the tendency of the speculative reason.[14] Taking Whitehead's words as a summing-up of our discussion up to this point and as a transition to the next phase of the problem, we can say that Peirce, in his characteristic manner, endeavors to combine the inner fulfillment of the movement from the potential to the actual of an intellectual system with the outer matter that is of significance for human conduct. It seems that in Dewey's system the decision in this matter was made in favor of human conduct.

An observation must be made at the outset with respect to the concept of the 'act' in Dewey's system. To clarify this point we have selected a formulation from one of his early works where he says that what the child is after is the thing, the action.[15] Here we see that the concept 'object' or 'thing' seems to be synonymous with the concept 'activity'. The objects and the act appear to be identical, an identity that reminds us of what has been said in a prior analysis concerning one of the levels of Marx's discourse. Dewey evidently wishes to say that it is not the act itself that motivates the child but rather the achievement to which the act is directed. This achievement is in the thing or things which the child attains by means of arranging things through acts or by means of approaching existent things through acts. In addition Dewey endeavors to show that our theoretical attitude to things is not an original one; at any rate, from the standpoint of man's psychological development in time it is not a relation of contemplation but one of operation. The term 'act' is here used in the simple sense of this concept, that is, the deployment of the child's powers and the manipulation of things. No mention is here made of the relation to human ends in the sense given to the concept of pragmatism by Kant and Peirce. Dewey no doubt wished to say that if we are concerned with the level of concreteness, we can reach it by means of practical contact with things.

The contact with things, then, is a contact that is outside of the intellectual system and its inner development, this being a prominent aspect of Peirce's conception. It seems that also in ethics — and here again we rely on one of Dewey's early works — we see concreteness as bound up with the manifest world of things and, on the level of ethics, to the manifest world of acts and their effects. The effects, Dewey says, are the content of the act that is performed or executed. The results are not only significant with respect to the morality of the act, but they themselves are its moral quality.[16] Dewey appears to be saying, when we examine his words more closely, that the effects are such not only because they exert a definite influence on our evaluation of an act, that is, whether it is an act that has good effects. Furthermore, the ethical content of an act is measured solely by its effects. It is clear that we cannot speak here of the inner development of the act corresponding to the inner development of systems of thought by means of their movement from the potential to the actual. We are here dealing with the concrete effects of acts that occur within manifest reality and their effects in it. Pragmatism, then, means instrumentalism, that is, thought that perceives an ethical conduct determined in accordance with its achievements — thought in that it is concerned with things, and the act in that it produces effects. Thought is directed not to an end but to an effect. From an ethical point of view, the meaning of this transfer is that a shift has taken place from the motives that prompt the act to the consequences of the act. From this it is but a step to Bacon's system in which the mastery of the environment is not a pragmatic achievement of thought but an achievement that is identical with the ethical quality of thought. Achievement is now identical with the ethical effect, and pragmatism is consequently endowed with ethical meaning.

According to the logic of this discussion, knowledge itself is tested not by the consequences that flow from it but by practical conduct. Why not use what we know, Dewey asks, in order to regulate our practical conduct?[17] These words are meant to indicate the direction of our conduct by convictions. The test of convictions that are identical with what we know resides in the fact that they direct our conduct and make possible a continuous improvement on the level of convictions for the sake of such improvement on the level of conduct. From this it is clear that there is no cognitive element with its own rhythm nor of a movement from potential to actual which Peirce regards as the rhythm of effects on the cognitive level itself. In Dewey's view we are in a situation where the sphere of practical conduct serves as the criterion for the significance of knowledge; against this criterion there is no other. Empiricism no longer means the general empirical phenomenon of which Peirce spoke but actual conduct that serves as a criterion with respect to knowledge. The relations of knowledge tend to become relations between a definite presupposition and the verifying aspect of that presupposition. This led Dewey to suggest the transition from contemplative pleasure to manipulation and mastery[18] or, in other words, a transition from knowledge as esthetic pleasure derived from natural qualities to knowledge as a continuous means for the mastery of nature.[19] The

element of contemplation is in Kant's view attached to the sphere of
'esthetic' contemplation and this contemplation is not accompanied
by pleasure. In Dewey's system, however, the cognitive relation is
attended with pleasure, that is, there is a desire for effects in the
mastery of nature. Just as Bacon directed his argument against the
element of passivity in contemplation, which was in reality esth'etic
contemplation, in favor of an active relation and interference in nature
by combining this relation with the cognitive ideal itself, Dewey also
did so in the context of the new natural science and of the social life
built on a continuous interference in the course of things. The cognitive ideal obliges us to such interference. From the standpoint of the
status of knowledge as the expression of theory, we actually reach the
end of the road: Knowledge is no longer an end in itself. If knowledge
is thus understood, it is placed on the normative level of esthetics
alone. When it is placed on the normative level of ethics, then it must
be measured in accordance with an ethics of effects, and this will then
regulate the formulation of the cognitive ideal which is identical with
the ethical ideal of effects. Kant, if we take his doctrine as an additional point of comparison, saw the actualization of reason in the
ethical law, whereas Dewey, who was rooted in traditional philosophy
and in a certain sense pursued it to its conclusion, saw significant
actualization in the visible effects of human conduct, which is tantamount to the effects in the mastery of man's environment. In either
case we do not arrive at a general unity of theory and practice by
creating a general human world, but we conquer the environment step
by step by a process of changes in knowledge that are tested practically by their effects on the level of conduct. The environment is
created in this very process of conquest. We might say that in place of
the speculative unity of theory and practice proposed by Hegel we
have the union of fragmentary knowledge with acts, suggested by
Dewey, when the acts realize as fragments the achievements that
direct knowledge. In another passage concerning pragmatism, Dewey's
language seems to contradict the interpretation suggested above: In
this passage the act is implied in knowledge, and knowledge is not
subordinated to the act.[20] But in the very continuation of this passage
Dewey asserts that his argument has been consistent in that knowledge
once attained is the one and only means for continued improvement
and for the guidance of further experiments, and that these experiments are of the non-cognitive type.[21] These words of Dewey himself
show that he believes universal human experience to be broader than
the province of knowledge within this experience, and that the region
of knowledge is only a means for the sake of universal human experi-

ence. It may be that this general human experience is not identical with the act, but it is certainly not identical with knowledge. Dewey puts general, non-cognitive human experience in the place occupied by speculation in Hegel's philosophy where it is the highest expression of the relation of reason to the world. If we return to our previous formulation of pleasure, we can say that the general pleasure within general experience is not the pleasure that is in knowledge; it is rather a non-cognitive pleasure. Dewey does not explain the nature of this pleasure but merely emphasizes its negative aspect, in that it is beyond the sphere of knowledge.

These words do not impair the force of another statement to the effect that the process of scientific inquiry, whether mathematical or physical, is a definite aspect of practice. A scientist is first and foremost a practitioner and is constantly engaged in making practical judgments. He must make decisions as to what to do and the appropriate means to be employed for that purpose.[22] Since Dewey desires to emphasize the practical character of inquiry, he is not aware of the ambiguous nature of the concept 'practical': The important decisions with respect to method and procedure that an investigator in a laboratory is required to make appear to him to be practical. Dewey makes no distinction here between practice as the genus of acts of deliberation — deliberation doubtless being an occurrence that could happen to one and may therefore be regarded as an act that a man does — and acts on the level of human conduct directed to changing the environment in which men live by subduing it to their will and aspirations. More specifically we may say that the work done with the use of instruments on the intellectual level leads Dewey to the interpretation of the instrumentalism of that very level of thought and its procedure. The act is identical with the operations of thought itself. Nevertheless, it seems that Dewey is not satisfied with emphasizing the operational character of thought itself because he keeps saying that thought is instrumental in order to gain control over the environment.[23] Mastery of the environment, then, is the goal of thought insofar as thought takes analytical steps to reach such mastery with the means at its disposal.

Dewey sets forth two positions simultaneously — thought has a practical rhythm, and thought is the means for the act of gaining mastery over the environment. The tendency of pragmatic thought may be summed up as follows:

1. Theory itself is here understood as practice because it is a constant operational activity and because it has a manipulative tendency in the various methods it uses, such as the resolution of a

situation into its component elements and an accompanying projection of possibilities.[24]

2. Theory is not only practical; it is employed for the sake of
practice – and insofar as Dewey insists on introducing practice into
knowledge, he makes knowledge itself an instrument in the hands of
practice. Practice in turn is directed to the mastery of the environment
and its goal on the level of this mastery is to bring about a moving
equilibrium between human beings and their environment.[25] Men
dominate the existing data of the environment and then go beyond
this to conquer new data and extend their empire.

3. The test of theory is in the mastery of the environment and the
enrichment of human experience. Men live in different environments
and are engaged in securing dominion over them, and in doing so they
are affected by the very changes they themselves introduce. Beyond
change for the sake of change there breathes in this conception an
optimistic note that regards change itself as an enrichment.

4. The consideration of this element of enrichment leads us to
re-emphasize the conception that knowledge is attached to, and
intimately bound up with, the rhythm of time. Theory is not concerned with eternity but precisely with those things that are subject to
the ravages of time and change, and change, in turn, enriches man,
who is occupied with theory. It is this aspect of theory which, among
other things, confers upon it an ethical and educational meaning.
Morality is no longer interpreted as the concern with theory for the
sake of theory but with theory for the sake of acquiring mastery over
the environment and enriching men with the means toward this end. It
is therefore no accident that Dewey no longer speaks of happiness as
attending knowledge, for happiness should be directed to an existing
object and not to changing data; he speaks rather of enrichment as
being the effect directed to it when there are no fixed objects but only
acts that test intellectual presuppositions. Ethics is no longer attached
to ultimate ends or to rational sources, that is, ethics is not caused in
accordance with either Aristotle's or with Kant's conception. Both
ethics and knowledge insist on effects.

5. Insofar as the pragmatic conception continues to use the traditional terms of theory and practice, it clearly reveals its source; at the
same time, however, pragmatism has changed the classical terms to
such an extent that we may say that it has deprived the traditional
distinctions of their content and significance. This explains the
importance that is attached to pragmatism in developing the concept,
so widespread in our generation, concerning theory as hypothesis.

E

In summing up the preceding discussion, a few pertinent observations are in order regarding the meaning of the concept 'theory' as it is commonly used in present-day discussions of the nature of science or in methodological discussions of the sciences.

We may say at the outset that the prevalent concept of the nature of theory has been deprived of the unique meaning that characterized it in traditional discussions. This concept is now used as a kind of a synonym for a corresponding system of knowledge, such as the theory of numbers or the theory of relations. This concept is designated a *system* of knowledge to differentiate it from the particular knowledge of the individual. Since a concept of theory is posited on this content, the question arises: Over against what do we posit this concept in the methodological discussions, since we no longer oppose to it the concept 'practice' as was customary in classical discussions? It seems that we might say that, generally speaking, the concept of theory is placed in opposition to the concept of the empirical given with which theory is concerned or in opposition to the empirical data which with the help of theory are given a fitting and comprehensive explanation. Historical discussion and constant interest in this subject oblige us to observe that even in the speculative school we found intimations of this meaning of the concept 'theory'. Erdmann states that basically intelligence is directed to experience because it presupposes a law supported by experience, that is, by assuming an hypothesis or a number of hypotheses which are taken as theory.[26] We see in this determination one position placed over against another, the law that is the hypothesis and the experience that is concerned with affirming the hypothesis. We thus see that the theory is taken as the sum-total of hypotheses. An hypothesis, then, is a single assumption that can be verified by experience, and theory is the sum-total of those hypotheses that can also be verified by experience. Experience presents the factually given, then, to indicate to the one who holds a theory or an hypothesis the conditions laid down by him to verify his hypothesis or his theory.

This thought appears in speculative philosophy as an *obiter dictum*. It became the prototype of the modern theory on the nature of theory. This explains the three components of theory as presented, for example, by Ernst Nagel:[27]

1. The first component is "an abstract calculus that is the logical skeleton of the explanatory system, and that 'implicitly defines' the basic notions of the system."

2. The second component is "a set of rules that in effect assign an empirical content to the abstract calculus by relating it to the concrete materials of observation and experiment."

3. The third component is "an interpretation or model for the abstract calculus, which supplies some flesh for the skeletal structure in terms of more or less familiar conceptual or visualizable materials."

There are then various components in theory, and because of them theory is faced with the problem of finding an explanation; this is found in a component that is not concerned with theory but with observation known to us from a source that is not within theory itself. Theory is thus faced with a problem of interpretation, since interpretation is part of the application of theory to data. The latter are not derived from theory but are observations of some kind or another, and we thus return to our previous conclusion that the confrontation is no longer one between theory and practice but one between theory and observational data. It is evident that in this discussion concerning the essence of theory we have remained wholly within the limits of knowledge and within the limits of the problem of knowledge as a problem of the application of a presupposition to the observational given.

This conception of theory is embodied in the language prevalent in the methodological discussions which employ the terms 'theoretical entities' or 'theoretical expressions' in contradistinction or in opposition to nontheoretical entities or nontheoretical expressions. It is held that theoretical entities may be found within descriptive entities and these special entities cannot be seen, heard, or felt;[28] the reason for this is not that these expressions designate objects that are related to them by way of rational conception in the direction proposed by classical philosophy and its various schools. It is impossible to see, hear, or feel these entities because the expressions that characterize these entities have meaning only within the limits of a definite theory, and outside the limits of this theory they have no place and no meaning. The theory itself, then, confers in this case an interpretation on the entities described by the expressions found in them.[29]

We see that the prevalent concept in the methodology of science concerning the nature of theory is a concept that does not characterize the special nature of knowledge respecting objects, but characterizes the nature of a system of presuppositions that applies to data. More precisely, the concept of theoretical entities or theoretical expressions has no longer anything to do with objects with which knowledge is confronted. It is wholly concerned with emphasizing the inner structure of knowledge or the inner structure of the system of hypotheses which is autarkic within its own sphere.

Thus, with this development the classical concept of theory has reached the end of its evolution. The philosophical question we are faced with is whether the concept of theory is destined to remain stationary at the point it has reached, or whether it may be possible to imbue it with new meaning in relation to the classical tradition by taking into consideration modern developments. Can we "save the philosophical phenomenon" of theory?

NOTES

1 See, for example, *Von den verschiedenen Racen der Menschen* (1775), in G. Hartenstein's edition of Kant's *Sämtliche Werke* (Leipzig: 1867), pp. 446–47. See also the *Critique of Pure Reason,* B828.

2 Consult Morton G. White, *The Origin of Dewey's Instrumentalism* (New York: 1943).

3 "The Essentials of Pragmatism," in *The Philosophy of Peirce, Selected Writings,* edited by J. Buchler (London: 1950), p. 252 (hereafter = *Writings*).

4 For a more complete comparison with Marx, see Nathan Rotenstreich, *Basic Problems of Marx's Philosophy* (New York: 1965), pp. 51ff.

5 For an analysis, see W. B. Gallie, *Peirce and Pragmatism* (London: 1952), Ch. VII, "An Ambiguity in Peirce's Pragmatism," pp. 164ff. See also *Perspectives on Peirce, Critical Essays on Charles Sanders Peirce,* edited by Richard J. Bernstein (New Haven and London: 1965) (hereafter = *Perspectives*).

6 "Some Consequences of Four Incapacities," in *Writings . . .,* p. 250.

7 Cf. on this subject, John E. Smith, "Community and Reality," in *Perspectives . . .,* pp. 108ff. Smith justly claims that pragmatism is rationalistic.

8 "The Essentials of Pragmatism," in *Writings . . .,* p. 262.

9 "The Essentials of Pragmatism . . .," p. 261.

10 See Richard J. Bernstein, "Action, Conduct, and Self-Control," in *Perspectives . . .,* pp. 66ff.

11 "How to Make Our Ideas Clear," in *Writings . . .,* p. 31.

12 Paul Weiss, "Charles S. Peirce, Philosopher," in *Perspectives . . .,* pp. 120ff.

13 "Philosophy and the Sciences: A Classification," in *Writings . . .,* p. 71.

14 See *The Function of Reason* (Princeton: 1929), pp. 30–31.

15 *The Logic of Verification* (La Salle: 1890), p. 222. Quoted in Morton G. White, *The Origins of Dewey's Instrumentalism* (New York: 1943), p. 78.

16 *Outlines of a Critical Theory of Ethics* (Ann Arbor: 1891), pp. 8–9. Quoted in White, *The Origins . . .,* pp. 8–9.

17 *The Quest for Certainty* (London: 1930), p. 43.

18 *The Quest for Certainty . . . ,* p. 92.

19 *The Quest for Certainty . . .,* p. 98. In this transition Dewey sees the difference between the classical and the modern views.

20 "Experience, Knowledge and Value: A Rejoinder," in *The Philosophy of John Dewey,* edited by Paul A. Schilpp (Evanston-Chicago: 1939), p. 528.

21 "Experience, Knowledge and Value . . .," p. 528.
22 *Logic, The Theory of Inquiry* (New York: 1938), p. 161.
23 *Essays in Experimental Logic* (Chicago: 1916), p. 30.
24 *Essays in Experimental Logic . . .*, p. 30.
25 *Essays in Experimental Logic . . .*, p. 123.
26 J. E. Erdmann, *Grundriss der Psychologie* (Leipzig: 1840), p. 69.
27 *The Structure of Science* (London: 1961), p. 90.
28 Y. Bar-Hillel, "Neorealism vs. Positivism, A Neo-Pseudo Issue," *Proceedings* of the Israel Academy of Sciences and Humanities, Vol. II, No. 3 (Jerusalem: 1964), p. 5. The paper also includes a bibliography concerning this subject.
29 R. Carnap, "The Methodological Character of Theoretical Concepts," in *The Foundations of Science and the Concepts of Psychology and Psychoanalysis*, edited by H. Feigl and M. Scriven (Minneapolis: 1956), Minnesota Studies in the Philosophy of Science, Vol. I, pp. 38–76. Carnap here states that in the employment of theoretical concepts there is no commitment over against ontological conceptions in the traditional metaphysical meaning of this concept (p. 44).

PART TWO

UNDERSTANDING AND ACTIVITY

VIII. RESIDUES AND SEEDS

A

The purpose of the present inquiry is to find a new meaning for the concept 'theory'. If this quest proves successful, we shall then return to discussion of the relations between theory and practice and those among the various aspects of practice. But before taking up the consideration of this theme it may be best to review the essential elements of our preceding discussion so that we may find our bearings with respect to the constructive phases suggested by these elements.

Can any permanent features be discerned in the evolution of the concepts of theory and practice? The first meaning of the concept 'theory' that we encountered was that of 'seeing' or 'contemplation'. With all the different nuances attached to this concept — excluding the meaning given it in methodological discussions — it has retained this element of seeing, or rather this element of rational activity, that is not based on a progressive analysis but upon conception or perception within seeing. Seeing stands high on the scale of knowledge, and hence theory in classical philosophy is considered the height of knowledge or knowledge *par excellence*. Theory occupies this high place because of the rational effort invested in it and because of the special nature of the objects or entities to which theory refers. Theory is significant both because of its place in the scale of knowledge and because of the place occupied by its objects in the scale of objects. In this matter relating to the nature of theory, classical philosophy stresses the parallelism between the position of seeing and the position of its objects.

Implicit in this matter, as stated above, is the ethical meaning of theory as a human end, and this end is conceived as activating the best in contemplation, on the one hand, and the most distinguished relation to the objects, on the other. Intimately related to all this, of course, is the matter of the meaning of philosophy as a theoretical preoccupation *par excellence*.

Since the objects to which theory refers are not given directly,

99

theory reaches them indirectly by way of an abstracting from the data. The abstraction referred to in this context concerns the discernment of objects that are not given to and perceived by way of the senses. Theory is abstraction at its starting point in terms of its relations to the senses; it is the conceptual end as it removes itself through abstraction from the sensuous given. Abstraction then is the nature of the activity inherent in theory. Theory is detachment, on the one hand, and attainment, on the other. Yet activity is the real condition for having the attainment of theory accompanied by happiness.

While the classical conception of theory maintains a balance between theory and the entities around which it revolves, the speculative conception of theory insists on the identity between conception and the entities, or on the identity between reason and being. Identity takes the place of the balanced equilibrium — a significant change in the idealistic doctrines as over against the classical position. In the classical conception philosophy was a theoretical preoccupation. The world itself in its being is philosophic, that is, rational; this is the predominant thought in the idealistic conception of philosophy. It follows that the difference between contemplation and the entity to which it refers is only secondary or incidental up to the rational attainment of identity between reason and being. Since reason is the awareness of having reached its identity with being, the rational subject that knows itself by the same token also knows its identity with the object which is being in its totality. Being in its totality is rational being or reason *qua* being. Thus, a system of unity in the idealistic conception replaces the system of equilibrium found in Greek speculation.

What the concept 'theory' in Greek philosophy has in common with the same concept in idealistic philosophy is to be found in one circumstance of decisive importance: Theoretical contemplation does not change the face of things or entities to which it refers. In the Greek conception theoretical contemplation reveals the entities, and in the idealistic conception such contemplation finds itself within being. In both cases a limit is set to activity, for without such a limit theory would be endless; the end it reaches lies in its contact with the entities, whether such contact is effected by way of seeing or by way of identity itself. The ontological status of the entity puts an end to activity in the classical conception; the rational nature of the entity puts an end to activity in the idealistic conception. In both cases there is an activity in theory and a limit of activity that is prescribed by the nature of the object to which the theory is directed, whether it be the eternal object in the Greek conception or the rational object in the idealistic conception of the nineteenth century. Only the pragmatist conception of theory effected an essential change in this matter for it emphasized the continuous activity of knowledge and an endless activity on the correlative level of the object to which theory applies. Since theory contains an attitude with respect to the state of things as they are, we can understand the nature of practice or the nature of the act as a change in the state of things as they are or as we find them. The emphasis placed upon this factor of change and interference effected by the act is a constant element throughout the entire development undergone by the concept 'act' in the history of philosophic speculation.

Several arguments may be advanced to account for acts or for the need of acts. The defective character of reality may be said to require acts in order to remedy the defects in it, a dominant thought in Marx. It may be assumed that there are acts because there are constant human incentives that seek them, such as longing or desire, and the question arises concerning the causes that direct the acts. This was the principal line of argument employed by Aristotle and Kant. It may be assumed that the whole of reality itself changes and that man changes with it, as held in the basic tenet of pragmatist philosophy. But whatever rationale is followed, we can say that the theoretical sphere is characterized by an activity that finds its end in things, whereas the practical sphere is the sphere of interference and the introduction of changes. This sphere must then be understood as an unceasing activity that has no conclusion in an inner end such as is to be found, for example, in things as they are.

B

We have thus far dealt with one aspect of the problem before us, the aspect concerned with the evolution of the concepts under consideration and the conclusions that may be drawn from it. In the preceding discussion we distinguished an element of activity or of effort in both theoretical and practical intentionality. The fact, however, that there is an element of activity in an act is self-evident and needs no further proof. Our task is to discover the element of activity in theory as seeing and at the same time to demonstrate that this seeing is an activity and not a casual encounter.

However, it is precisely at this point that we are faced with a problematic element in the concept of theory in the traditional sense. It was still possible to maintain that theory contains an activity whereas experience is but a passive encounter, something that happens to us in our sensuous contact with the world. The peculiar characteristic of theory was that of seeing which combines the position concerning the state of things as they are as an intellectual discernment with the deliberate activity within this attainment. This fusion of activity and the unchanging state to which the activity is directed was the distinguishing characteristic of theory. But the modern concept of experience changed the face of things. If, for example, we examine the root meaning of the German word for experience, *Erfahrung*, we see that it denotes a 'ride' or 'journey'; the findings of the experience or the resultant impression is not independent of the road or 'journey' toward this impression. But it is not only the linguistic aspect of the matter that reveals an element of activity. The material and methodical aspects of experience, as this concept is treated, for example, by Bacon, clearly indicate that experience is not the absorption of impressions but an interfering activity or an activity that calls for impressions. In this matter Bacon distinguishes between experience gained accidentally from absorbing impressions we happen to receive and experiments where we are constrained to go in search of impressions.[1] The introduction of the element of activity into the sensuous contact with the world as a result of the methodological crystallization in the experiment or in experience as experiment constitutes an essential change over against the classical picture of the world, in which activity was not a characteristic of theoretical or rational attainment but was found in the original contact of the senses with the world on the level of experience. It need not be said that this aspect of activity within experience is prominent in Kant's conception, particularly in his formulation that the experiment compels nature to answer the questions put to her by the investigators.[2] The activating element in experience or, in a broader conception, the experimental contact itself contains conceptual elements *a priori*. In the procedure of experimentation *qua* a guided procedure directed toward an encounter with the world or with nature, there are *a priori* elements. The prominence given to the activating element in experience has a twofold significance with respect to the problem before us. On the one hand, it places the activity on the level of experience itself and thus relegates the activity in theory to the level of experience; on the other hand, it combines an element of practice with knowledge on the level of experience. It posits a kind of union between the cognitive element and the practical element on the cognitive level of experience, a union which differs from that proposed by the classical tradition between the element of activity and the element of knowledge. This con-

ception of the twofold nature of knowledge within its original relationship on the level of experience leaves no systematic room for the
relation between knowledge and its objects as a balanced relationship.
The ethical significance of knowledge is not in this balanced relation; *a
fortiori* no mention is here made of the relation of identity of reason
and being. The ethical aspect emerges in the empirical effects, in the
effects on the level of reality which proceed from the activity inherent
in experience and in the various levels of knowledge beginning in
experience and terminating their verification in it, that is, providing
for human welfare. The double nature of experience is the second
aspect of looking upon the world as changing, moving, and developing.
From this point of view the world does not contain beings or determined objects our relation to which guarantees the significance of
knowledge as well as the agreement or congruence of knowledge with
the world. In an ever-changing world of experience there is no longer
any room for theory as an attitude to things as they are in an immutable or eternal nature. This point was emphasized by Dewey, who
stated in one passage that there are no longer objects for modern
science to deal with, but only data.[3]

C

The primacy and the superiority of theory over against practice was
one aspect of the classical conception of the subject under discussion.
The reason for this superiority may be found in Thomas Aquinas's
discriminating formulation: Whereas there is in every act the desire to
be related to the highest entity, inherent in theory there is actual
possession of the highest entity. Theory, in which is found the object
as it is, is a state of attainment. In theory we have reached a point
beyond desire and beyond actions that are rooted in desire. To put it
somewhat differently, in practice we find ourselves in processes in
which there is a movement from the potential to the actual; in theory
we find ourselves in a state that is wholly actual. Even in Marx's view
it may be said that action is undertaken for the purpose of establishing
an identity between man and nature, an identity that does not take
place in a *status quo*. It follows then that the act is justified in that it
serves as an instrument or tool to achieve total identity. Totality is a
rational category and from this point of view may be called a speculative category.

These possibilites of establishing the superiority of theory over
against practice took the ground from under the feet of the modern

conception because no object was found that could be taken as being in a state of *in actu* altogether. Reality is conceived as a network of relations, as a network of processes that involve relations. The status of the objects of knowledge, therefore, is not enough to justify the superior status ascribed to the knowledge of these objects. Perhaps the question that must now be raised — after ascertaining the new or revised meaning of theory — is not that of the superiority of theory to practice but that of the dependence of practice on theory.

We now proceed to a clarification of these questions regarding the nature of theory and of practice and the relations between them. While our clarification will follow the traditional development of these concepts, it shall also attempt to go beyond that development.

NOTES

1 *Novum Organum*, LXXXII, p. 281.
2 *Critique of Pure Reason*, BXIII.
3 *The Quest for Certainty* (London: 1930), p. 96.

IX. THE WAYS OF THE UNDERSTANDING

A

In coming to the consideration of the nature of theory and of the nature of practice we must first determine the sphere in which it is possible to characterize these two modes of relationships to the world. Theory may be described as a special kind of knowledge or cognition; in the classical conception, the essential feature of this kind of knowledge was 'seeing'. But when we speak here of knowledge or cognition, we refer to that area of knowledge or cognition in which we shall characterize the nature of theory.

Is there any knowledge to be found in practice? Practice involves knowledge: It must at times seek knowledge as to what is to be done, the course to be pursued and the consequences likely to ensue. Practice, however, is not knowledge: It is not required to give an account of the state of things which it seeks to change. Practice arises from a definite attitude of the doer toward the world. This attitude, the attitude that seeks to give us the common ground on which theory and practice meet, is distinguished by a peculiar characteristic, namely the position of the 'understanding'. We shall now proceed to analyze the nature of the 'understanding'.

B

The position of the understanding is a peculiar position of relationship to the world. It seems that throughout this relationship we can make a kind of geometric distinction, a distinction between man as the one who activates the mode of the relationship, on the one hand, and the thing or the status of the thing to which he is related on the other. It should be emphasized that we are here dealing with the status of this thing, to which the doer is related, and not to its content — that is, we are speaking of that which stands in some relation to man, and not discussing whether the thing is a table, the heavens, an electron, or an

105

historical hero of the past. We are not referring to the nature of the
content of the relations to man but to the status of this component
within the relationship.

One who bears a relation does so within understanding and by
means of understanding, and no matter what the activities of this
relationship may be — whether thought, analysis, deliberation, orientation, or similar definite activities — they are performed in some
particular situation. It is obvious that there are differences, for
example, between the analysis of a situation consisting of various
elements and man's orientation in a field or city. In spite of these
differences — differences that entail various methodological approaches to the world or to the things to be known — all these modes
of behavior have in common an attitude of the understanding toward
things, whatever these things may be.

To this wide sphere of the understanding belongs also theory in the
classical sense of this concept as well as the basic method of modern
science, the method of construction whereby the single impression is
redeemed from its isolation and given a meaning and a place within
consciousness and experience.[1] The correlative element to the attitude
of the understanding is the element of the thing understood in its
basic meaning as that to which the understanding is related. It is
evident that the distinction between the understanding and the thing
understood is made for the purpose of analysis. It is not to be
regarded as a real separation of the two elements, for the former does
not exist without the latter to which it is related and the latter does
not occupy this status without the former for which it is intended.

A reservation should be made at this point, namely, the fact that
the sphere that we are discussing being that of the understanding
prevents us from seeing the element to which the understanding is
related as an opaque thing or as something simply given. For when we
come across something whose real meaning we fail to understand, we
call it crude and impervious. An investigator finds a potsherd in the
course of his excavations and does not know what purpose it served
nor whether it was part of a utensil or an independent object by itself.
Since he does not know these qualities of the potsherd, it appears to
him amorphous and crude. From the standpoint of the understanding
to which the potsherd refers, this piece of clay is an opaque fact. As
such it is a determination within the sphere of the understanding that
attests to the fact that the understanding has not as yet fully arrived at
the identity of the real content of the potsherd the investigator
stumbled upon. The potsherd is within the limits of the understanding, and it is within these limits that we seek to ascertain its

content and identity. From a position within the understanding we are able to establish a relationship to the elements, for these are the bearers of meaning. Paradoxically, we may say that non-understanding is itself a position within the understanding since it is within the limits of things understood, although in an inchoate state in which the qualities, relations, connections and so forth of these things have not yet been completely identified by the understanding. The absence of meaning, then, is relative with respect to the total sphere of the understanding, the sphere that also comprises elements that have no meaning. The distinction, then, between the understanding and the thing to be understood is one that is within the sphere of the understanding. Hence, any question concerning the real meaning of any particular thing whatever is one that exists within this sphere as a mode of relationship and occurs for the sake of the definite actualization of this understanding. When, for example, we ask what is this potsherd, or how does an object move, or what is the meaning of some observation, or other questions similarly formulated, it is for the purpose of the definite actualization of the understanding. The distinction here can also be formulated as one between the total relationship of asking the question and the definite question itself, the former being the relationship that seeks to arrive at the meaning and the latter a definite relationship that seeks to obtain this definite meaning of the object we happen to find or the meaning of some observation and things of a similar nature.

This matter can perhaps be summarized by saying that the body of the relationships of the understanding is a relationship that the understanding itself has established. The understanding creates within itself this difference between the total position of the understanding and the element that is understood or that is to be understood. This relationship of the understanding is an original one, and to withdraw to a position prior to it would place us in an inarticulate, speechless region inaccessible to the understanding and to meaning. Or, if we withdraw we transfer to another level the polarization of the understanding in which we discern meaning. The relation of the understanding as an original relation is one that defines the area with which we are concerned and in which definite questions are asked concerning cognition and knowledge; it is also one that clarifies the practical intentionality to things and situations. This relationship, precisely because it is an original one, is neutral with respect to the distinctions between theory and practice and with respect to the various cognitive positions, such as the position of classical theory, on the one hand, and that of the modern natural sciences on the other.

C

The aspect of the relationship between the understanding and that which is understood as an original, irreducible relationship is illustrated by language. The whole character of language resides in the fact that it is replete with meanings and it is used with a certain understanding which accompanies the awareness of these meanings. Through this operation words are uttered, heard, and understood. The understanding accompanies the meanings in language and these meanings are established as such *in actu* through speaking and utterance which constitute acts of the understanding. Since this relationship of the understanding to the thing understood is an original relationship in general and one that reveals itself in language in particular, it cannot be reduced to a simple relationship. An example of the difficulty of such a position is illustrated by the theory of meanings known as the referential theory of meaning. According to this theory the meaning of a statement is to be found in that to which this statement refers, as in the example generally given in this connection of the word "Fido," which means the dog designated by this word. According to this conception the meaning is given by the material correlative of the word (that is, the dog with respect to the name Fido). The meaning within the language, then, refers to the *designatum* on the plane of things or objects. The understanding reflects the thing on its own plane.

It seems, however, that in an essential aspect this attempt to reduce meaning to something external to it is not likely to succeed. In order to understand the meaning of a word it is essential to understand it as a sign and thus as charged with meaning. The doctrine we are discussing, however, holds that the meaning of a word is to be found only in the thing designated by it. But if we do not understand the word, we cannot understand that it is related to the thing it designates. This brings us back to the primacy of the understanding and the primacy of the relation between the understanding and the thing understood on the plane of the understanding. It may perhaps be argued that the word charged with meaning denotes a thing or an object from the standpoint of its content, as in the above example of the dog Fido, or, differently formulated, this status of the word as charged with meaning is one that is not exhausted by being related to the thing or object designated by it. The meaningful character of the word is to be found in its internal structure and is not identical with the sign of the thing alone. To be able to serve as a sign of a thing a word must be related to meanings from the very beginning, and such a

relation is one which presupposes understanding, whether the understanding is brought about by directing our gaze to the object designated by the word or to the relationships in which the word appears,
such as the words 'also', 'yes', 'no', and so forth. A version of Kant's
well-known statement about the "I think" is that, when I am related
to the world through the understanding, this relationship must
accompany all my relationships to the world. It follows then that the
content of that which is understood is not the result of a transference
of things to the plane of meaning. On the contrary, the placement of
things on the plane of meaning is an activity that presupposes an
original relationship between the understanding and the things understood. Insofar as there is understanding there are meanings to which it
refers, and insofar as there are meanings there is an understanding that
refers to them.

There are two possibilities for characterizing the nature of the
understanding. The first possibility holds that the understanding arises
in the total sphere of relationships to the world. The understanding
knows the things that confront it as a correlate. In Platonic philosophy, for example, the understanding refers to things to be understood, which in this system are called ideas; these ideas are discovered
by the understanding when it reaches the highest level corresponding
to it. Ideas as the relevant correlate of the understanding are open to
our understanding; these meanings, when attained or actively understood, are determined by us, for the understanding has exhausted
itself and reached the stage of its adequate realization. The second
possibility is associated with the fundamental tendency of Kant's
philosophy and constitutes the basis of the methodological procedure
in the modern natural sciences. According to this possibility, the
understanding imposes its apparatus on the data of the senses which it
interprets but whose real meaning it cannot fathom. There is hence no
congruence between the understanding and its objects but only a
process of creating the objects to be understood by the methods of
the understanding. The understanding is not faced with the object; the
object is constantly being created by the progressive movement of the
understanding.

The concept 'theory' in its classical sense is connected with the
conception of the understanding as the original correlation between
the understanding and that which is related to it as an object to be
understood in accordance with its original content and status. When
the correlate of the understanding is something that is to be revealed
and not created, then the understanding is on the highest plane, being
at least a kind of 'seeing'. The object to be understood on the highest

plane — as the Platonic idea — falls within the limits of that which is seen.

In the second view of understanding, things, that is, objects, appear differently. Here understanding is not confronted with a correlate that is in principle understood, but with unknown data, an x; to be understood here depends on what is imposed on this x by the understanding. The understanding is now not within the sphere of seeing but within the sphere of continuous interpretation. This interpretation is necessarily continuous because of the original alienation between the understanding — in Kantian language the system of categories — and an x that is foreign to the understanding. The understanding is thus not in a position to 'see' the object to be understood, but it can continue to propose interpretations without end. It is unable to remove the basic alienation between it and the x because the original alienation is between the level of the understanding and the level of the x. This separation of the object within a continuous process is evident from the fact that we understand the given by the way it is interwoven in a functional system, such as the system of causal relations. It is no longer ideas that we understand, as in classical philosophy, but the relations among the data, and our understanding is realized in a system of causal relations filled with data that have but one thing in common, namely, that they are all interwoven in one causal system. It is clear that when the relation of the understanding is an x, there is no possibility for theory; its place is taken by construction. Construction is always within the sphere of hypothetical knowledge which can be replaced and changed by other such knowledge. We remain within the limits of correlation between the understanding and the object that is indispensable to it. This relationship is *in actu* a relationship of constant striving to translate the x to the level of the understanding or to give it meaning.

These two approaches are to be found in the various systems of philosophy which have attempted to investigate the nature of the understanding. In conclusion we can say that for Plato understanding is an intellectual activity and therefore by the same token its material correlate, that is, the idea, has an intellectual status. In Kant's conception the understanding is also an intellectual activity but the objects to be understood have not a status analogous to that of the understanding. The understanding subdues that which is related to it by giving it fragmentary meanings that are continually being changed by the understanding.

The two conceptions can employ the same argument in their defense. According to Plato, the understanding derives its essential vigor from the circumstance that its material relation corresponds to it

at the very outset; according to Kant, the strength of the understanding resides in the circumstance that it is able to understand that
which is impervious to it at the very outset. In the Platonic conception
knowledge is obtained by "directing one's gaze"; in the Kantian
conception knowledge is the result of penetrating "the fruitful depths
of experience." In Plato's view knowledge has an end because of the
open nature of the object investigated; in Kant's view knowledge has
no end because the element attained by the understanding, the x, is
closed or opaque at the very beginning. The end of the activity of
theory as seeing lies in the nature of its correlate. Kant, however, does
not believe that the nature of the correlate can impose an end to the
activity of seeing, and instead of Plato's ideas as the correlative to
theory he posits ideas that direct knowledge to an ever-progressing
goal. Plato's conception of knowledge is the human manifestation of
the meaning of the object itself, a manifestation that is brought about
by knowledge; for Kant, knowledge is the continuous creation of
meanings within the understanding itself and by means of its own
methodological apparatus.

D

The purpose of the preceding analysis was not so much to present the
essential features of two philosophical attitudes, but rather to illustrate the inner logic that pervades each of them and so prepare the
way for raising the systematic question as to the necessity for the
existence of these two approaches. Since the modern conception of
the world is derived from science which is based on the creation of
systems of relations constructed by the understanding, there is no
longer any room in the modern conception for the classical concept of
theory. Are there still any areas of meaning to which theory can apply
if the concept 'theory' is given a definite meaning? We are inclined to
answer that there is room for theory even for modern philosophy, an
answer that requires further clarification if we are to understand it
properly. For this we must return to our analysis of the status of the
understanding in its relational nature with respect to its object. It is
apparent that in Kant's system the understanding is given a preferential status, for it applies its apparatus to the given, the x, and without it the x has no meaning whatsoever. Although Plato seems to have
felt that it was sufficient to establish a correspondence between the
understanding and the object related to it, he still confers a superior
status on the understanding.

We find that a preferential status is given to the understanding as over against the objects comprehended by it. Even when the height of knowledge is taken to be theory *qua* seeing, it is not argued that seeing is that which is seen. A distinction is made between seeing and that which is seen. This is all the more so when knowledge is interpretation and not seeing. In the system of theory there is an end to theory in that it reveals that which is understood by it as an idea. In order for theory to know that which is comprehended by it as that which is supposed to be comprehended by it − in other words, to know that it has attained the idea − it is necessary that theory *qua* understanding should understand itself. Or, comprehension should reach its connection with the correlate, the idea, that is comprehended by it. Theory knows the idea, and it knows that it knows the idea; theory therefore has knowledge of the object and knowledge of the theory as the understanding of this object. This double aspect of knowledge, then, is to be found in the nature of theory, and it is this that bestows a special status upon the understanding, no matter what systematic interpretation may be given to it. Since the understanding is not absorbed in that which is related to it, understanding constitutes an independent level and retains its character as such in Plato's system and, *a fortiori*, in that of Kant.

The absence of complete identity between the understanding and the level comprehended by it raises immanent problems for each of the philosophical systems discussed with respect to their attitude toward the understanding. The system that bases the understanding on theory is faced with the internal problem of the certitude that attends seeing − that is, whether or not seeing attains the end toward which it strives, whether or not it reveals the idea, or what is the idea whose revelation would assure theory that having attained the idea it has fully comprehended it. The understanding as theory, then, is faced with the problem of the constant verification of the distinction between the appearance of a thing and its real being. To distinguish between these two possibilities, theory requires a constant examination of the revealed object in accordance with some internal criterion. Such an examination, however, must be conducted on the level of the understanding and not on the level of the object to be comprehended. It is not the idea that conducts its own tests as to whether or not it has reached the understanding, but it is the understanding that determines whether or not it has attained its ends.

The system based on the interpretation of the nature of the understanding is faced by a problem from which it cannot escape, namely, the problem of the subjection of the *x* to the apparatus of the understanding. It must ask itself the question as to whether the given is to be subjected to method or not; it must cope constantly with the problem of verification or the problem of the application of method to the given. If it were not for application, the transition from method to method would proceed smoothly; the given could be transferred metaphorically from one dictionary to another and from one language to another and we would never reach the *designatum* of the original language. The problem of evidence serves as an index of the tension between the understanding and the object from the standpoint of a system of theory; the problem of verification and applicability is an index of the relationship between the understanding and the object according to the system of the methodological imposition of the understanding. It should be remarked that between these two approaches, that of theory and that of method, there is the approach of evidence, according to which the understanding attests in and of itself that it has attained the knowledge that corresponds to the state of things. According to the conception of evidence, the relation of the understanding to itself or the relation of the thinking entity to itself contains a guarantee for the attainment of knowledge. This guarantee cannot lie in the comparison to the idea, nor in the verification of the method used.

                                    E

It is clear that the two views concerning the fundamental nature of the understanding, which is seen either as a theory or as a system of methods, depend on the view that is taken concerning the nature of the world. The world that is rational in itself presents us with a possibility of theory; the world that is not rational in itself, or at least a world whose rationality is inaccessible to us, calls for methodological impositions.

An additional factor emerges at this point: If the world is rational in itself and the understanding of the world is theory, the distinction between theory and practice appears reasonable at first glance. An end is set to knowledge as action. An end is set to the status of that which is attained by knowledge, so that knowledge is an activity that terminates with its consummation. Practice, however, is an activity that does not terminate at the pole of its relationship to the world, since practice is not related to a complete or rational pole within itself. On the contrary, if practice refers to desire which it serves as a guide, for example, desire will never be eradicated, and thus there will always be room for the renewal of practice that refers to desire. But if the understanding is a continuous imposition of methods and the given x is never exhausted by methods, then the given x in the classical conception is parallel to desire with respect to the correlative element of practice. Knowledge is thus an unceasing activity and, if this is so, what is the difference between the sphere of knowledge and the sphere of practice?

It seems that a reservation must be made with respect to this determination. According to the methodological-functional system, which we have identified with Kant's basic approach, there is a consciousness of the limits of understanding. This consists in the fact that the understanding is aware of its immanent character, that is, it cannot eradicate the original alienation between itself and the x. The methodological process itself is endless; but with this process goes an understanding of its methodical character only, that is, a consciousness of the ultimate incongruity, negatively speaking, between it and the x to which it is directed. The methodological process is without an end because those who initiate it are always conscious of the distance that separates the process from the given. The closed nature of the process over against the given constitutes the limit of this process. The philosophic consciousness now sets a limit to a process which in itself is without an end. The understanding of the understanding in the methodological system is the understanding of the essential status of knowledge as interpretation, and not as a source. This consciousness of an essential limit placed upon the understanding leaves room for various approaches to the world, all of which posit a standpoint of the understanding — although it is not necessary that they all be approaches that translate the understanding to a cognitive-methodological process that has no end. Since the world is such that it contains an element of x, it may be possible to intervene in its process by introducing an active, changing factor. From a certain point of view we may say that a world without a rational structure in itself invites or facilitates more intervention than a world with such a structure. A rational world is complete and in no need of change; a world that is not rational is incomplete and may need to be changed. Thus, there still exists in principle the possibility for acts even in the functional approach and not only in the theoretical approach. Obviously, the direction of the acts will change in accordance with the different systems, and the technical character of the act in the functional approach will be more prominent than in the theoretical approach.

In these two systems, then, systems best represented by Plato and Kant, the understanding is taken to be superior to the thing under-

stood. The other aspect of this superiority is the consciousness of the
cognitive limit of the understanding. If it were not for the self-
consciousness of the understanding, there would be no consciousness
of the limit of the understanding over against itself. The consciousness
of limitation is one of the expressions of self-consciousness.

F

An additional consideration to be kept in mind is the fact that
theory, understanding itself, is not within the limits of theoretical
understanding in the peculiar sense of this concept, for it is neither a
seeing nor a revealing. This understanding always involves an element
of comparison between what the understanding understands in its
relation to the thing understood and what it is itself in this relation.
Consequently, the self-understanding of the functional understanding
is not itself a functional understanding, and it has no methods of
imposing relations on the x. An element of comparison is always to be
found here between the inner process of the understanding itself and
the x to which the understanding refers. This understanding cannot be
formulated with the same tools as the understanding of the given. The
understanding that applies the principle of causality to experience
does not mean that an analysis of the categories uses the principle of
causality. A limit is thus set to theory within theory and a limit to
methods within methods.

We now pass to another aspect of the nature of the understanding.
Even here no sharp distinction can be made between the various philosophical interpretations of the nature of the understanding. In every
understanding we can distinguish two strata. In the first stratum,
which is called the stratum of qualities, I make a judgment such as,
here is a red object, the electron moves in a path around the neutron,
and so on. These determinations of qualities presuppose the area of
the understanding, that is, they are determinations concerning qualities of an element that is comprehended by the understanding. The
second stratum, however, is that of generic or categorial determinations in which are made judgments such as: every understanding has a
correlate of the thing understood; every understanding refers to an
object, which may be either thing (the determination of qualities) or a
personality (also a determination of qualities), and similar determinations. The determination that creates a duality between the
understanding and that which is understood by it — no matter
whether the duality is according to the Platonic interpretation or

according to the Kantian specification — belongs to the class of the categorial determinations and not to the class of qualitative-specific determinations. Every determination of the essential limit of the understanding, that is, every determination that refers to the self-understanding of the understanding proper belongs to the stratum of categorial determinations and not to the stratum of qualitative determinations. This being the case, the self-understanding of theory does not in principle belong to the genus 'theory' itself, because theory is formulated in qualitative determinations, that is, we have before us an idea or we have before us an idea of a triangle.

With respect to the methodological conception, the understanding of methods falls within the limits of the categorial and not the qualitative determinations; it does not belong to the class of determinations, such as a is the cause of b, and b is the effect of a. The position concerning the limits of the understanding and the corresponding position concerning the correlative character of the understanding are categorial and not qualitative determinations. We can here find a certain speculative justification for the conceptions (for example, in William Stern's psychology and in Sartre's existentialist philosophy) that take the source of reflection to be in the encounter or clash between tendencies and forces. We are here concerned, however, with the consciousness that accompanies limitation, this being the manifestation *par excellence* of reflection as understanding wherein the understanding understands itself. In this very reflection in which we find the correlative character of the understanding we also find the limitations of the understanding.

The reflective understanding in which the understanding comprehends itself from the viewpoint of its characteristic correlative structure is crystallized in the distinction between subject and object. The subject is the bearer of the understanding, and the object is the crystallization of that which is understood. The reflection that presents us with the nature of the understanding also presents us with the distinction between subject and object. This distinction is also found in Plato's theoretical interpretation of the understanding where, however, the subject is the soul and the object the idea. This interpretation of the status of the subject, on the one hand, and that of the object on the other can be regarded as an interpretation which contains qualitative determinations (subject = soul; object = idea). Yet the distinction itself between subject and object falls within the limits of categorial distinctions that are not exhausted by qualitative distinctions, for the two are not identical.

In concluding this part of the analysis we may say that the various types of the understanding represented in the major philosophical systems do not belong exclusively to these systems. These two tendencies are found in what is commonly called intelligence.

Intelligence refers to the sum-total of acts of seeing the connections among phenomena that actually exist but which are not discovered by us without effort. Intelligence is apparent, for example, when a child grasps that since 2 follows upon 1, then 3 will follow upon 2, and so on, thus coming upon the principle of the sequence of numbers. Intelligence as invention, however, is apparent when we find connections previously not found, or when we combine one system with physical data. The element of discovery and the element of invention constitute the two aspects of intelligence, and these are by and large parallel to the two approaches to the nature of the understanding discussed above. In speaking of this parallelism we might point out that the very intelligence which is concerned with the clarification of the nature of intelligence contains an element of revealing that is in discovery and an element of creation that is in invention, that is, we have here a combination of approaches which are intelligence in its various aspects. We see then that a place could be found for reflection both on the level of philosophical exploration and in the employment of concepts in daily life.

NOTES

1   S.H. Bergman, *Introduction to the Theory of Knowledge* (Hebrew) (Jerusalem: 1940), p. 121.

X. DISCERNMENT

A

The conclusion arrived at in our preceding discussion was that the attitude of understanding itself, whatever its nature may be, differs from the specific methods whereby the understanding is actualized in qualitative determinations. From the categorial point of view the understanding is understood by the reflective understanding. The reflective understanding, however, is neither a theoretical under-standing, in the classical sense of this term, nor a functional-methodological understanding in the modern sense.

The understanding of the understanding — we are dealing here with discovery and not with creation and hence we find in the reflection of the understanding that refers to itself a certain aspect of 'seeing' — reveals to us distinctions inherent in the understanding, the distinctions between the understanding and that which is understood by it. The understanding understands the distinction between the under-standing which refers to that which is understood and the thing comprehended by the understanding This brings us to the next phase of our analysis: It seems that the structure of distinction is the basic structure of the understanding, no matter what its systematic inter-pretation may be. The first and foremost distinction, the prototype of all distinctions found within the limits of the categorial distinction between the understanding and its object, between subject and object, is the distinction between the understanding and that which is understood. Were it not for this prime distinction, there would be no relation of the understanding at all and, at the most, the knower would stand on the same level as the thing understood from the standpoint of position. But even according to the system of theory, the knower is on the level of the thing known from the standpoint of the content comprehended by the knower and not from the standpoint of his position; the knower understands the idea but he himself is not an idea. This is strikingly exemplified in Plato's doctrine of the soul, according to which the soul belongs to the world of ideas but is not within this world.

Further analysis of the distinction within the understanding reveals the original correlation between the understanding or the act of understanding and that which is comprehended by this act as well as the division between these two positions. The reflective understanding of the understanding indicates not only the understanding of the distinctions between the elements but also the understanding of the original relationship within for the sake of, and despite, the distinctions. The understanding of the understanding is, then, essentially synthetic, a synthesis of distinction, on the one hand, and contact, on the other. The relationship understood is synthetic and the distinction is analytic. Hence, the total understanding is a synthesis on the high plane of the synthesis and the analysis that preceded it. We must therefore attempt to emphasize the element of distinction, the recognized distinction that is absorbed in the relationship of the understanding.

B

It is thus apparent that every understanding has a distinction, not only in the categorial stratum but also in that of the qualitative determinations, to use our former terminology. Every definite understanding has a definite matter to understand — the understanding of a word, of a word designating 'table', or the connections between words or the things to which the words are in some form related. Before a thing can be understood it must first be isolated and distinguished from another thing. To understand the meaning of a 'table' it is necessary that it be set off by itself and distinguished from a 'chair' or an 'electron'. Within this understanding of the content, then, lies the distinction of the matter in question. What we do is to put the definite content 'table' in the place that the categorial stratum has set aside for that which has been comprehended by the understanding. In the place of the category of that which is understood we put a definite content — a table, an electron, or Napoleon. We understand the definite content because we understand the status of that which is understood within the relationship of the understanding; we understand the concreteness of the definite content because we understand the abstractions of that which is understood. The understanding of the content, then, presupposes the understanding of the understanding, whether this understanding on the categorial stratum is known to us or not. In an act of the qualitative understanding or in an act of a definite understanding there is an act of the understanding of the division between the broad

category of that which is understood and the definite content, thus
consummating an act of consolidating the category of what is known
with the definite content. Also on the level of the definite understanding which is formulated in qualitative determinations there is a
synthesis of the analysis, the thing understood and the definite
content, and of the synthesis, the categorial thing that is understood
which in specific instances is filled by the definite content — table,
electron, Napoleon, and so forth.

The distinction is a crystallization of the understanding and the
principal tool at its disposal reveals an additional aspect by showing
that not only do I assign a definite content to the status of a categorial
thing understood but that I also separate this content from another.
The separation of this content accompanies me in my understanding
at the same time that I understand the separated content. One of the
simplest ways of arriving at understanding is to point to an object,
'table', and to an object, 'chair' — the purpose of the pointing being to
indicate what is the object 'table' and that it is different from
the object 'chair'. If there were but one entity in the world, the act of
understanding would be exhausted by putting this content in the place
of the categorial determination of the thing understood. Since there is
more than one entity, however, the understanding of a definite object
is accomplished by distinguishing one object from another, that is, in
the stratum of the qualitative determinations we indicate a relation of
separation between the object 'table' and the object 'chair'. We may,
generally speaking, say that the moment we descend from the categorial determinations to the qualitative determinations and put 'table'
in the appropriate place of the thing understood, then we can put
'chair' in this place and not 'table'. When we put 'table' there and not
'chair' as the definite content, we remove the definite content 'table'
from the sum-total of all contents and make it conspicuous. This
content is a given distinction but it has relations with the contents from
which it has been distinguished or isolated. We are thus able to determine what a misunderstanding is, namely, unintentionally putting a
content we do not mean in the place of a content that we do mean, so
that someone else will understand that the content we have in mind is
a 'chair' when we really have in mind 'table'. A misunderstanding is
the result of putting a definite content in the place of a categorial
thing understood when this content is not designed to fill the logical
place of the categorial determination of the thing understood, a place
that is assigned to another content. It is plain, however, that a
misunderstanding is a kind of understanding, that is, it presupposes a
prior relation between the understanding and the thing understood

together with all the elements pertaining to this relation which have been discussed previously. In concluding this part of our inquiry we can say that distinction is a definite activity of the understanding, the active side of the original distinction between the understanding and its object.

Just as we found two basic systems in determining the nature of the understanding, the Platonic system and the Kantian system, so we find these same two systems when we come to the problem of determining the place of distinction in the system of understanding that corresponds to these two systems.

The Platonic system conceives the task of distinction to be that of distinguishing between the various ideas, to determine which content falls within the realm of ideas and whether every content (including that of 'dirt', the well-known example given by Plato) or only definite contents are ideas. Our task, according to Plato, is to determine what relations exist between the various ideas after they have been understood and to ascertain the relations between sensuous things and ideas in accordance with the basic distinctions between them. In this connection Plato proposes the general formulation of the participation of ideas in sensuous things or the formulation that things take part in ideas; or he suggests the method of division whereby a general idea may be broken down by means of distinctions into specific contents.

Correspondingly, in Kant's system we proceed from the basic distinction between the understanding and the sensuality. The understanding is concerned with finding the connection or, in Kantian terminology, the synthesis between these two provinces in order to make definite knowledge possible. Or we proceed from the distinction between *a priori* and *a posteriori* existence and make that the prototype of all distinctions. To make knowledge possible we must find an *a priori* method that would establish a connection between the *a priori* and the *a posteriori*, two separate areas that are divorced from one another but which need one another to make knowledge possible; without the *a priori*, the *a posteriori* can neither be known nor recognized. The structural element in discernment is found in both the Platonic and in the Kantian systems; but in accordance with the inner logic of each of these systems this element is given a peculiar interpretation and consequently a cognitive meaning.

We can therefore say that we find in the understanding definite elements which can only be regarded as revealed to us through reflection and having the inner structure of reflection. Reflection is revealed unto itself, and this is a position of understanding which is the condition for all understanding outside itself. We place reflection outside the brackets of both the classical theoretical doctrine and the modern hypothetical doctrine. We say simply that there is reflection – this is the first understanding. Consequently, this is the first discernment and this first understanding must from this point of view necessarily accompany all my subsequent understandings. We now turn to a discussion of the activity of abstraction and the part it plays in the understanding.

C

Discernment is an activity of the understanding. This aspect of the nature of the understanding will become clearer when the connection between the understanding and abstraction is examined. The status of the understanding is that of abstraction; the steps taken by abstraction are for the purpose of actualizing the understanding. The isolating process that accompanies abstraction constitutes the continuous and never-ending path toward the understanding.

When the activity of the understanding is examined in the broadest sense of this term – as a close relationship to the thing understood and as an awareness of the difference between the two in consequence of this relationship – we notice that the relation of the understanding is two-sided: There is a relation to the thing to be understood, on the one side, and a separation from it, on the other. Without the former the understanding would have no material focus or objective; without the latter there would be no understanding and the element to be understood would, at most, merely present itself and have no status. The separation of the understanding from the thing understood is the first and foremost act of abstraction.

Abstraction as an original and primary activity is an affirmation of an act of the understanding, which itself is not an element that is comprehended or understood by the act. The act can be conceived by another act, as an object of the understanding, but insofar as it is an act it is not an element conceived or understood by the act. It is an act relating to that which is conceived by it. Since the act of understanding is removed from the content to which this act is related, it is possible for the act to be related to different contents or to lie in wait for this particular content; or it may be possible for it to understand the relations that exist among the different contents to which the act applies. An act of the understanding can refer to the content 'table' or to the content 'chair'. Or it can refer to a content common to both, furniture made of wood, and refer to the material aspect of definite, isolated contents to which the act refers.

The separation of the act from the content attained by it makes it possible for the acts to be free. The knower, the performer of the acts, goes forth in search of contents. He is free with respect to the contents, and this freedom finds its most striking expression in the comprehension of various contents, in general, and contents separated from what has been attained by the act here and now, in particular. It may be said that every understanding has abstraction that removes it from the object to be understood; since it has this primary abstraction, it can be expressed in the understanding of various contents, and the contents are not abstracted without an understanding of the abstraction.

To the same degree that an act of the understanding has abstraction that removes it from the object to be understood it also has concreteness, for abstraction is a mode of relationship to the content of the thing that is understood, a content that gives concreteness to the understanding. We comprehend the concrete only because we truly comprehend it — we are able to abstract its essential qualities — for the essence of our comprehension is an act of abstraction. Since the act of understanding refers to the content of the concrete, this act refers by its very nature to the concrete. We see then that the relation between the understanding and the object comprehended by it is a relation that is synonymous with that between the abstraction and the concrete. The resulting abstraction is not empty but is a correlative member of the concretum of the thing abstracted, and the latter is related to the very concretum from which it was abstracted. We can say, therefore, that the concretum occupies the area of the abstracted thing which, in turn, is the area for the identity of the definite content which, in this case, is the concretum.

From what has thus far been set forth it follows that: (A) Abstracting is accompanied by a consciousness, whether we are actively aware of such consciousness or not, of the relation of the abstract to the abstracted concretum related to it. Color is the abstract with respect to blue, and blue is the abstract with respect to a specific blue of a particular garment, or with respect to the blue of the sky as it is perceived here and now. (B) We can therefore comprehend every concretum as a definite specification of the abstract, that is, that blue is a specification of color and the blue of the garment is a specification of blue, and so forth.

We have thus far dealt with the relation between the abstraction and the concretum as a relation that is implied in the act of the understanding in its relationship to the object understood. We have not spoken of the specific operations of abstraction, a subject that presents another aspect of the act of understanding and of the distinction within the understanding.

D

Abstraction is a cognitive-discursive activity in the literal sense of this term, being an activity that involves a going to and fro. We isolate the abstract from the given or from what is comprehended by us when we place the content 'table' or 'blue' or 'color' within a distinct conceptual area. We perform an intended act of the understanding in order to arrive at the abstract. But over against this the act of the understanding in which one understands the relation between the abstract and the concrete, the specification of the abstract, is not a discursive act. One identifies the concrete that fills the area of the abstract. When I identify the blue color of the garment as a color or as a blue color, I identify an understood content in the area of abstraction or I fill the logical space of the abstractions: color − a definite content − blue. The act of the understanding is not an act of going to and fro but one that may be called an act of 'seeing'. The understanding of concreteness in the mediation of the abstraction to which this concreteness applies is an act of the understanding that is unique. We can thus say that real understanding as the understanding of the concrete within the abstract has an element of the understanding through seeing, although not in its literal sense but as it is understood in an expression, such as "I see what you mean." This does not refer, of course, to seeing in the classical sense of the term as a theory of eternal objects, but to seeing the connection between the concrete and the abstract. It may be said that every definite understanding has a component of seeing, a component in which the process of understanding converges on a focal point, and from this point of view the process has an end, although a relative one. When I wish to understand what blue is, I can point to an object that is colored blue; when I wish to understand the status and nature of blue I point to a blue object, but I add that the blue color is a specification of the abstraction 'color' and that I can explain this specification in various ways: by finding a place for the color 'blue' within the scale of colors of the rainbow or by describing it with reference to its wave length − all in accordance with the abstractions whereby the concretum is specified. If the abstraction is physical I discourse within a context of waves; if it is an abstraction of seeing I refer to the colors of the rainbow. Even the understanding of the understanding has thus an element of seeing because it operates simultaneously in two directions, proceeding both away from the object to be understood and toward it. This movement in two directions clarifies the nature of misunderstanding, namely: a misunderstanding arises when I fail to place a concretum in the area of abstraction, for example, when I mean the color blue but point to yellow. In this case, the concretum is not the one that the act of the understanding should be directing itself to.

This relation of the understanding to the thing understood by it, or the relation of the abstract to the concretum, proceeds in two directions: from the concretum to the absract and from the abstract to the concretum. We have then a double relation of intentionality from the concretum to the abstract and from the abstract to the concretum. The complementary relations between the two acts of intentionality are not in themselves to be taken as discursive, that is, the discursive method that isolates the abstract cannot be applied to the understanding of the relation between the abstract and the concretum. We here have one of those instances on the level of the understanding and on the level of discrimination in which, not seeing the connections, we meet with an endless regression of the conception of the relations between the abstract and the concretum or the relations between the understanding and the thing understood. Even this regression cannot be understood without a definite act of the understanding which as such is not a regressive act. This is the reason why Kant, for example, felt obliged to have recourse to the faculty of judgment to reveal to us the relations of application between the system of the categories and the given. We may extend this Kantian thought and say that in the act of the understanding itself there is, in accordance with its very nature, an element which in this respect is not methodical; it is proper, then, to identify it as knowledge that involves seeing. On the other hand, if we examine additional historical relations, it seems that modern phenomenology justly places the relation of intentionality at the center of its discussion. However, it fails to give sufficient attention to the fact that there are two relations of intentionality in the understanding and that the understanding contains the congruence between these two relations in different directions — both from the thing understood to the understanding, and from the understanding to the thing understood.

One need not necessarily conclude from this that there are no acts of the understanding whose nature is not wholly regressive. A considerable part of scientific procedure is based on what may be called the transference from one language to another, for example, from the language of physical data to the language of theoretical concepts or

mathematical equations. We find a meaning or a conceptual element
making its way from one level of abstraction to another or to a corresponding level of abstraction, and we are busily engaged in turning one
abstraction into another. This may be compared to parallel columns of
synonymous words or to the compilation of a concordance of various
languages where the mutual relations can be determined without
consulting the original language we understand, the concretum that
occupies the area of abstraction. We are accustomed to these changes
because of the special symbolism of the modern sciences which are
divorced from the senses and from intuition. This method is justified
because all qualities are found in the position of transformation on the
methodological level itself and we have no need of the intentional
relation to the concretum that is in the world in which we live, which
Husserl calls the *Lebenswelt*.

Despite this, however, it seems that the fundamental relations
between the understanding and the element comprehended or understood by it are not different in their nature on the level of the understanding as a result of a change over against the level of the understanding by way of concretization. A physical model for biological
data, for example, involves a relation of intentionality to these data,
and this relation differs from the physical model proposed for these
data. In this case, as in cases of concretization, the biological data
constitute the element of the object understood and the constructed
physical model the element proposed for the understanding of these
data. These data themselves are not within the limits of the concrete
but, from the standpoint of the method of transformation, they
perform the function that is performed by the concretum with respect
to the abstract. The understanding as a translation from language to
language, then, remains within the limits of the understanding to
which the description of the nature and structure of the understanding
in general applies.

The observation that the structure of the understanding applies to
the spheres that are wholly methodological calls for a critical comment of the doctrine of speculation proposed by Hegel, according to
which the knowing subject finds himself within the known object.
Only when there is this relation of discovery do we attain — according
to Hegel — understanding *par excellence*, which is the speculative
understanding. Speculative theory teaches that there is no real difference between the abstract and the concrete and that there is no
reciprocal intentionality between the two which are, in its view,
identical. As long as there is an intentionality that is not identical, we
remain on the level of external relations between terms or on the level

which Hegel called external reflection, that is, a reflection that comprehends but does not unite opposites. Yet, it seems that there is no understanding without a certain externality of the knower who possesses understanding with respect to that which is understood by him, for the understanding is removed from the object to be understood and at the same time related to it. We cannot dispense with this reciprocal relation of separation and affinity without at the same time doing away with the understanding or without erasing the distinction between a blurred and a clear understanding. Since a relation of removal and connection exist together, an understanding of the understanding is possible in general. It is the possibility of understanding the structure of understanding, and this opens the way for a philosophy that is the formulated crystallization of the relation of the understanding or of the understanding that refers to the understanding itself. Hegel wished to change the twofold relation of intentionality into a relation of identity. He attempted to identify philosophy with reality or with a kind of embodied rationality within reality. But a rationality without a self-consciousness of rationality is defective, for there would then be at most an identity of the content of rationality with reality but not the element of the self-understanding of rationality. Hegel, however, thought that consciousness appears when reality reaches its end. A rationality that is identified with reality is incomplete and defective because it lacks the essential element of reflection, an element that is always external to the content to which it applies. Reflection is not only a knowledge and understanding of the content we know but also the knowledge of the results of our knowing, and this knowledge is not identical with the results nor absorbed by them. Reflection refers to the relation between the abstract and the concrete and to the correspondence or lack of correspondence between them; the understanding of the correspondence or lack of correspondence is not implied in the existence or non-existence of the correspondence.

E

We have examined the two aspects of understanding or discrimination that cannot be reduced to functional method, aspects that we distinguish by 'seeing', namely, the aspect of the understanding of the intentionality of the abstract to the concrete and that of understanding that the understanding itself is not exhausted by this intentionality. This two-sided intentionality goes to the abstract from the concrete and from the abstract to the concrete. We have intentionality on another level of the understanding of these relations themselves — an intentionality on the first level of the relation between the abstract and the concrete and a reflective intentionality on the level above this. On both levels we discern that understanding is through seeing.

To avoid confusion we must here bear in mind that when we speak of the relations between the abstract and the concrete we refer to relative abstraction, that is, to the sum-total of qualities in one aggregate, such as the aggregate of qualities 'table' in its relation to the aggregate of qualities 'this table', here and now. We do not refer to any other linguistic usage of the concept 'abstract', such as when we say that mathematics deals with abstract entities, for in such a case the question does not arise concerning the relationship between the mathematical entity on its level and another entity that is its concrete correlate. We are speaking of the abstract in its relation to the concrete from the standpoint of correlation, that is, its entire nature is explained by the fact that it is to be considered in a correlative system.

We can now sum up this discussion of understanding and discernment as activities of the understanding:

1. Within the limits of the relation of the understanding we indicated the ultimate elements that cannot be reduced to a functional system that is external to themselves; these elements will appear in every functional system as structural elements of the intentionality of the understanding; they are the elements of the understanding and the thing understood that appear in the systems of the understanding as elements of the abstract and the concrete.

2. Understanding is possible among these elements; these are the ultimate elements of the understanding not because of its content but because of the status of its structural components. No matter what the definite content of the understanding may be, we find these elements imbedded in the understanding.

3. The understanding of the status of these elements and the understanding of the original, essential relations between them is understanding of a unique kind; it differs from the functional knowledge of searching for systems of relations in accordance with methods or hypothetical systems. In the functional structure of knowledge we discover components that we comprehend through the understanding and that are not discursive, and understanding to which we may apply the classical term 'theory'. This is an understanding of elements and relations and not of eternal objects, and yet it has a non-functional tendency in a negative sense, a tendency which in a positive sense we

call theoretical. We now find reflection as a theoretical position or a definite tendency of such a position that is not done away with in systems of knowledge that involve a knowledge of laws and not of objects or forms.

4. The description of this special character of reflection is only the other side of the determination that reflection occupies a superior position in knowledge or in the relationship of the understanding. The understanding itself is reflection, and reflection is *a fortiori* the understanding of the understanding.

The question to be clarified now is: Do we find the theoretical element only in the structure of the understanding or can it also be found in a definite class of contents to which the understanding applies?

XI. UNDERIVABLE CONTENTS

A

Our inquiry thus far was concerned with an examination of the structure of the relationship of the understanding to itself, a structure inherent in the very nature of the understanding. The revelation of this structure is itself an understanding and is, from this point of view, a kind of knowledge or a kind of information concerning a state of affairs as it is. This knowledge, however, is of a special nature; it has no position with respect to systems of laws and is without integration or specification within these systems. This understanding and this knowledge concerning the nature of the understanding can thus be said to be a kind of seeing. Is this seeing limited to the structure or to the revealing of the members of the relationship? Are we able to indicate the kinds of content that are open to seeing, contents possessing definite meaning and not only having position such as understanding, on the one hand, and the position of that which is understood on the other?

In coming to the consideration of this subject we must recall the conclusion reached in our discussion of the development of the concept 'theory'. We saw that the position of the understanding or of the knowledge called theory is the other side of the position of the contents to which theory applies. Theory is the other side of the reality of eternal immutable objects confronting theory, which comprehends them in its own peculiar way. The correlation between the nature of the object and the nature of the intentionality toward it constitutes one of the most conspicuous characteristics of the classical conception of theory. Just as there are degrees of knowledge — theory being the highest degree — so are there degrees of reality or degrees of objects; eternal objects, ideas, forms, and God fall within the limits of the highest degree of reality or of objects.

The question with which we are now confronted is the following: Since the scientific image of the world no longer has degrees of reality and since the components of reality and its particulars form a web of

relations that occupy a common level, can there be a theoretical relation with respect to objects? Since the functional conception of the
world for one reason or another disregards areas of reality that are not
functional, such as the existence of God outside the world, it is possible to maintain that there is a cognitive-theoretical relation with
respect to this special area of reality. Over against this there is no
theoretical relation, nor is such a relation possible, with respect to
other areas of reality. Thus, the area of reality 'God', for example,
constitutes a limit for the functional cognitive approach which from
the standpoint of logic extends its network of relations to include all
areas and their ramifications and to relegate them to one region. Can
we maintain that the only way to establish a theoretical approach
within the functional approach, or in spite of it, is to combine the
functional conception of the world regarding one or more areas of
reality not to be absorbed in a system of relations? We might say that
as long as the modern conception retains a relation to God in the
Biblical sense and grants this relation a cognitive status, vestiges of the
classical conception will remain, knowingly or unknowingly. Add to
this remnant the historical development of the Biblical, religious conception which contributes to the fusion of Biblical tradition and
Greek philosophy. This amalgamation also appears in the modern
conception when we confine this conception only to the empirical
spheres, the spheres of the senses, and place beyond this sphere the
unique contact of man, including man the knower and God.

This method of rescuing the theoretical approach insists on the
unique nature of the area of God's existence and its separation from
the system of all-inclusive relations. The other method, of course, is
the pantheism of Spinoza and Hegel which does not rescue a single
area of reality from the systems of relations nor select one reality in
preference to another. This method directs knowledge to reality in its
totality − whether it introduces this total reality as God or not − by
arguing that the relation to reality in its totality gives rise to a cognitive relation that is different from the relation concerned with partial
areas of reality. The uniqueness of total reality is not such as is found
in the ordinary theistic conception; it is rather a uniqueness of content
since the content of the whole is different from that of the parts or
since the content of the world in its totality is different from that of
nature, in the physical sense of this term, or different from the content of history as a sphere of successive events that take place in time.
Total reality, then, provides a unique or special type of knowledge,
which in Spinoza's system is intuitive and in Hegel's, speculative.

B

The argument we now propose to set forth is meant to provide an additional method of safeguarding the place of theoretical relationship *par excellence* in the world of relations. We do not set aside one particular area of reality invested with a unique cognitive relation. We shall not have recourse to transcendent areas of reality, whether conceived as separate or all-inclusive, but shall attempt to show that a conception of relations presupposes or is accompanied by a special conception of special contents. These, however, are not designated as eternal objects but have a special status assigned to them that is different from that of objects that are interwoven in systems of relations. We do not maintain that there are objects with an eternal ontological status and because of this status require a special theoretical relation that refers to them. We maintain, however, that there are contents which have a special status in the system of the understanding. Because of this status a knowledge of them entails a type of knowledge which differs from that of systems of relations that keep developing *in extenso*. The classical conception identifies the ontological status of objects with their status as understanding, or it takes them to be complementary — God has a special ontological status and has, therefore, a special status in the system of the understanding. We must examine this view more closely to ascertain whether there can be a special relation from the standpoint of the understanding and to what extent this special status must necessarily entail a similar status from the standpoint of reality.

From this point of view we propose a systematic attempt based on the modern conception of the world, although we do not pretend that this basis is self-evident and altogether free of criticism. This attempt is proposed as a system of the modern world-view because in the religious or in the classical world-view a theoretical relationship arises from the inner logic of these systems. In both conceptions the ontological status of the object is the guarantee for the status of this object in its correlation understood. In the modern world-view there is no ontological guarantee for the status of the content to which the understanding refers. Herein we observe both the strength and the weakness of the proposed systematic conception.

C

The methodological point of departure of this inquiry raises the question as to the conceptual minimum crystallized in the ontological level of definite objects as eternal objects. Since a definite content is considered as eternal, it is by its very nature not derived from another content. In the classical system God, according to his meaning and ontological status, is not derivable from another content. In the religious world-view every other content depends on God and is derived from him, either by way of emanation or by way of creation. In Spinoza's view the world in its totality is eternal and hence every particular within it is a limitation or mode of the world in its totality. It is evident from these examples that non-derivability is for the classical view another aspect of eternality. If we disregard this aspect of eternality, which is an ontological aspect *par excellence,* we may say: If there are non-derivative contents we can point to a common feature between the contents in the world-view of the systems of relations and to the definite contents in the world-view of degrees of entities, which is the classical and the religious view. Things which from the standpoint of their content are an ultimate sphere not derivative from another sphere are things to which theory can be applied. We refer to ultimate contents from the phenomenological point of view and not from the ontological. Immanent contents within the limits of knowledge are given a special status because of their content and not because of their position in the scale of real entities. We must therefore conclude that contents have a component of temporality and are not eternal. Although they have a component of temporality, they occupy no position in the systems of relations, a position that would deprive them of their special meaning. We are not here advocating eternality as the overcoming of the component of time, but we hold that contents develop within time and that time is included in them, as are the contents 'world' and 'man'. Consequently, we find in these contents a propelling force that releases them from an ever-widening system of relationships, a system that contains within it the various particulars of the world, such as motion, an electron, human experience, and so forth. We are dealing then with those contents confined to spheres that have a non-derivative status, that are not eternal nor capable of having a status of eternality. The contents that we shall consider are world, man, and time.

D

First we shall consider the content of the concept 'world'. 'World' is the sum-total of objects or the sum-total of contents. In the

terminology employed in the preceding section we may say that it is
the sum-total of the correlates of the understanding. The concept
'world', however, is not exhausted by these two characteristics — that
is the sum-total of objects and of correlates. A third characteristic
must be added, namely: The world is an aggregate in which all the acts
of the understanding occur *in actu*. We cannot therefore simply say
that the world appears on the level of material correlates of acts of the
understanding or, as Husserl puts it, as an aggregate of *noemata* of the
understanding, because we know the things of the world in the world,
or to phrase it differently, our understanding is within the world just
as the things that are understood by us are also in the world. We must
therefore say that the world is the sphere of all the acts of our understanding; it is hence a content on the noetic plane and not only on the
plane of the *noema*. The world then is to be designated as an aggregate
from the standpoint of the elements that are understood and also on
the plane of the understanding. Consequently, we cannot locate it at
any one particular pole of the relation of the understanding. From this
point of view we find inadequate Kant's characterization of the world
as an idea, his view that the world is the object of every possible
experience[1] ; for we are concerned with the world not only from the
standpoint of experience that refers to data but also from the standpoint of the acts of experience. We thus cannot look upon Kant's
conception of the idea of the world as if this were nothing more than
the extension of experience. The world is the extension of the complete relationship of understanding with the two correlative poles of
this relationship, the pole of the understanding and the pole of that
which is understood. There are some additional conclusions to be
drawn from this distinction which we shall have occasion to note
below.

Having placed the content of the concept world at the two poles of
the axis (at the pole of things understood and at the pole of acts of
the understanding) — this content thus standing within and without
the distinction between the elements of which the understanding is
composed — we can say that the world as an aggregate of things,
meanings, and acts is the condition for our relationship to this or that
object, just as the world is the condition for the concentration of our
understanding upon this or that object. The content 'world' comprises, then, the level of things that are understood and also the level
of the understanding, and it is thus the aggregate in which the acts of
the understanding set bounds to those things to which these acts are
directed. On the other hand, it is for the sake of these things to which
our acts are directed that we restrict the aggregate of our acts to a

definite act in which there is a correlation between a definite understanding and a definite object of the understanding. The content
'world' exists prior to and beyond this definite correlation between
this understanding and *this* object, for both the understanding and the
world dwell in this aggregate world. The moment I discuss or analyze
the content 'world', I treat it as an object of the intentionality of my
understanding. But at the same time I know or understand that this
content does not cease being a total content, that is, a content that
comprises the component of the object understood and also the
component of the acts, insofar as I impart to it the status of the
noema or the status of an understood object by an act of intentionality of the understanding realized by me at this moment. The
content 'world' becomes the object of my understanding, but while
doing so I know or understand that it is not exhausted in this status
with respect to the act of the understanding that is directed to it. This
characteristic quality of the content 'world' does not make it the kind
of inarticulate, all-encompassing whole of which Jaspers speaks. We
can point to various well-defined aspects of this content precisely
from the standpoint of the correlative polarity of the act of the
understanding. This quality of the content, however, prevents us from
seeing it as being derivative from another content. The comprehensive
character of this content is not inarticulate but one which, from the
standpoint of the understanding and its aspects, imparts to the content
its peculiar status. We here have a dialectic of the content 'world': It is
one content among others and thus belongs to the level of understood
objects. But we know that it is not only on this level alone and that
our understanding of this content is in and of itself an understanding
of the fundamental superiority that adheres to this content.

This concept, then, represents the furthest limit of our discussion.
Corresponding to the preceding observation that there is an understanding that necessarily accompanies all our understanding there is a
world that is the sum-total of meaningful things and acts of the
understanding that necessarily accompanies all definite acts of our
understanding that are definite, limited, and refer to particular contents. The world is the ultimate horizon of the understanding. Our
definite understanding is thus accompanied by an understanding of
the limitation of the understanding, though not a limitation from the
standpoint that I cannot penetrate to the last layer of reality, a kind
of a thing-in-itself that is inaccessible to me. What is here meant is not
a limitation of layers or strata but a limitation of the horizon. We
understand within the total horizon but do not understand the total
horizon itself, and this is because our understanding here and now

limits the total horizon to that which is here and now. In understanding a definite thing we understand both the thing and the world of which it is a part. Our attitude of comprehension takes place on two levels: on the level of content of the understanding of a definite thing and on the perspective level of the understanding which reveals that a definite thing is a limitation or a fragment of the world as a total content. Two concomitant understandings, already referred to above, are combined in this focal point: "That I understand" must accompany all my understandings; its supplementary meaning is "there is a world a fragment of which I understand" accompanying all my understandings. That there is a world is not an understanding of a particular content but a categorial understanding, for I do not understand the world from the standpoint of its definite content since it is the sum-total of contents and it is this that constitutes its very content. It follows that I cannot shift this content to the level of definite contents but I see the definite contents as a condensation of this total content, just as I understand the specific understanding as the condensation of the sum-total of the understandings that have been and that will be. The world is a special content that is distinct from the contents and from this point of view permits us to conclude that the contents are bound to the content 'world' and also separated from it. The content 'world' is bound to the definite contents and also separated from them; it is a kind of transcendence within immanence, or a kind of transcendence that is forever bursting the bounds of immanence.

This brings us to another characteristic of the relation of the definite understanding to the total content of meaningful things – the world – and to the sum-total of the understandings – the world. The understanding is accompanied by a consciousness of fragmentation; this gives rise to an active rhythm of knowledge as that of a search for connections among the particulars that are known or understood by us. We accompany our active knowledge with the consciousness that this knowledge is limited. We strive to overcome this limitation by placing the particulars in an ever-widening network of relations. But the consciousness of fragmentation that impels us to seek systems of connections and relations keeps summoning up the limit of this expansive urge toward totality. This totality is never reached because it is by its very nature not translatable to the level of definite contents; it remains within the bounds of the periphery of limitation which we unceasingly attempt to overcome. From this point of view the content 'world' serves as a constant complement of fragmentation or of things understood, a complement of the meaning of fragmentation.

Since we have established a close connection between the content 'world' and the understanding as well as the thing understood, we cannot now argue from a phenomenological point of view that the world is eternal. We do not transfer the content 'world' to an ontological plane that is different from that of the acts of the understanding and its meaningful elements. Precisely because the content 'world' appears as the horizon of the understanding and of things understood and as a completion of these, being from this point of view on the same plane with acts and with the things understood, it differs from them. Since we are thus confined to a phenomenology of intentionality and cannot proceed beyond this to ontological decisions, it is enough to say that the world is the content as a totality. We need not say, or rather we have no phenomenological basis for saying, that the world is eternal with respect to the temporality of the things or the acts of the understanding that occur in time.

It is clear that the content 'world' is one that may be called spherical, that is, it designates a sphere in which other contents are found but is itself not one of them. The spherical content does not serve as a definite explanation of the contents of the sphere. It is not a kind of content 'world' that serves as a transition to contents such as 'time' and 'space' or contents such as electron, table, planets, and so forth. This content is not a formal condition of contents, such as the law of contradiction, nor a material condition of content but rather an aggregate in which we find limitations. For this reason the understanding of this special content requires an attitude of understanding and knowledge that is different from that pertaining to other contents. The spherical content is one that is understood by theoretical understanding, which is true with respect to the world as a content and with respect to other spherical contents.

E

In coming to the consideration of the specific features of the content of the concept 'man', we note two conspicuous aspects which can at first be formulated only negatively: (a) We are not concerned here with a content that is an aggregate of reality outside of time. It is obvious that real man, or individual man, is a being that dwells within time and is constantly subject to it; (b) Because of this position in time, man's nature cannot be reduced to an aggregate of theoretical qualities divorced from time, that is, we cannot say that man has an essence in which existence in time is not included. Man is not an

aggregate of qualities that can be analyzed on the level of qualities
alone. He is not a definite, self-enclosed aggregate of qualities as might
be said of a square or a triangle which can be determined by the
qualities composing them. From this point of view man cannot be an
object of theory in the classical sense of this term as referring to
objects that have an eternal status, that is, objects whose material
nature have no positive bearing to time. We may say that man as an
object of discourse is a correlate of the understanding. The meaning of
this correlate, however, must not be reduced to content alone, that is,
to the aggregate of qualities in the category of things understood as a
category designating the object that is related to the understanding.
Man is a being who rises above all attempts to have his nature reduced
to fixed qualities for he is a being who dwells within time.

It has been stated above that the world is an aggregate of acts of the
understanding and a corresponding aggregate of all meaningful objects.
Of man it may be said that he is an aggregate of his acts of the
understanding with respect to himself, and within the aggregate of the
world he is a relative aggregate involving an unending self-creation.
This creation is realized by way of a relationship of the acts of the
understanding as man understands or thinks. The world is an aggregate
of acts that occur and of emergent meanings. Man, however, is an
aggregate of acts that is constantly being created, and at the same time
man himself combines these acts into a synthesis of his own. In reality
we find the traces of this synthesis imbedded in the memory which
contains a mixture of acts and meanings from the past to the present
and an anticipation of the future with its intentionality of acts from
the present onward. Man, the creator of this synthesis of the unity of
his own understanding, is a creature whose nature is not open to
others because it is possible for them to rely only upon expressions of
man's understanding, whether these expressions take the form of
language or of acts. Our fellow-creature proceeds from the expression
to the understanding revealed in it, and he assumes a dimension of
understanding in the other because of such a dimension in himself. The
understanding is not exhausted in expression and does not remain a
treasure locked up within man himself. Man not only creates the
synthesis of the understanding in his private capacity but he also has
the consciousness of this synthesis. What has been said about the
dialectic of the understanding as having understanding and as having
the understanding of the understanding may also be said of man as
creating a synthesis of the understanding and at the same time being
conscious of its use. Man is related to the object through himself, and
the object is expressed in language and conduct. Yet man has a

consciousness that he is not altogether absorbed in the aggregate of the things to which he is related. He is not actively related to the entire aggregate of things — the world around him — because the individual is related only to segments of the world since he spends his life within limited time from which he cannot escape. In contra-distinction to the world, which is an aggregate devoid of the under-standing of the understanding, man in his fragmentation being an aggregate of limited segments possesses self-consciousness, which is also a consciousness of the synthesis of his understandings. We there-fore cannot agree with the existentialist conception that makes a distinction between essence and existence and assigns to man a status in terms of existence as over against essence. Since man is conscious of a synthesis of his understandings, he knows that this synthesis is the result of his relationship to a set of relations in which he himself is interwoven, a set of relations with society, with the world or with nature. He finds himself with a network of the material correlates of his understandings which are adopted by his own understanding but which are not identical with it.

It is impossible to reduce man's self-consciousness to the various components of his real existence here and now, an existence of sys-tems of relations, the treasures of inherited speech and similar factors that make up man's real existence. What distinguishes man is the fragmentary aggregate of acts which he combines into a set of relation-ships in which he himself is involved. If these sets of relations are taken away, an empty understanding, so to speak, will be left; but since the understanding is itself a correlate of the thing understood, it cannot remain empty. If you remove the understanding and leave the thing understood, then you also remove the status of the latter since it occupies a correlative position with respect to the understanding. Without the understanding there is no category of the thing under-stood, that is, without the relationship to the understanding man would be but a mere spectator. But man is more than a mere spec-tator. He has a dimension over against himself which is not that of his fellow creature, the dimension of his own understanding, the com-bining of acts of the understanding and a knowledge of this process. It is plain that in this discussion of man's status from the standpoint of his nature one is prone to philosophize by transferring one's own experience and understanding to the level of explaining them to one's fellow man, that is, one individual man summons another to inves-tigate in his own sphere whether the structure proposed by the one corresponds to that which is revealed to the other. From this point of view this philosophic method may be regarded as a summons to self-consciousness. Complete objectivity regarding man's nature is not possible because the limit of such objectivity is on the plane of man's understanding of himself. This self-understanding does not apply to his qualities, whether he is meek or irascible, for example, but to the meaningful components of his existence and nature. The other aspect of this limit to objectivity is the fact that no analytical approach to man, including the scientific approaches of biology, sociology, psychology, linguistics, and so forth, can singly or in combination fathom man's character. The reason for this is not, as is generally argued, that man is an anti-rational creature but, on the contrary, that he is rational — if we take rationality to be understanding and bear in mind its peculiar structure. Rational man is not exhausted in the scientific-analytical approaches because of the original synthetic nature of the rationality of the understanding and because of the basic incongruence between the method of analysis and man's synthetic nature which cannot be transferred to an aggregate of analyses. Again, in contra-distinction to existentialism, we insist on man's unique character because his real life is lived on an inner dimension and not because he is anti-rational or emotional. In regarding man as a rational creature we must distinguish between the rationality of the method of analysis and the rationality of original synthesis, the synthesis of acts of inte-gration which constitute man's nature. The distinction between these two methods may be expressed by saying that it may well be possible to analyze man and make him the subject matter of some scientific discipline. Yet this removal to the level of subject matter does not mean that man ceases to exist as subject. Man's status as the object of analytic discourse proceeds from the functional approach of resolving knowledge into sets of relations. Man in his own sight occupies a special categorial status; because of his self-consciousness he dwells in two systems, the functional and the categorial. The fusion of the various systems is the task of man who understands himself as subject and not only as the object of analytical method.

In this connection we must make some reservations with respect to Buber's doctrine of the I and Thou, which he regards as a primary relationship. We have seen that from a phenomenological point of view the primary relationship is that of man to himself. The I is an expression of an integrating activity, and this has no place in sets of relations and not even within the framework of the Thou. Further-more, the relation to the Thou *qua* Thou presupposes a relation that distinguishes the Thou as such, that is, I from the standpoint of the Thou. This discernment of the 'I of the Thou' or of the 'Thou as the I' with respect to himself is not an insight obtained in the sets of relations between the I and the Thou; it is obtained in the regression from the expressions of the Thou, for example, in language, and in conduct on the level of the Thou as the I with respect to himself.

When we speak of the primary synthetic nature of man we do not refer to syntheses within the sphere of pure acts of reason, namely, the understanding itself. One of the most important syntheses performed by man is that of attributing his body to himself. Here we have an identification of man with his body, which is an identification of consciousness as the identifying factor and of the body as the identified factor. Acts of attribution make of the body a body, or they withdraw it from the sphere of matter and make it into a body. The body is then on the plane of things that are understood, and it is on this plane that it becomes man's body. We can in justice speak of that which is identified with man as a part of man only as man. But since man identifies his body as such, we cannot say that the body is man because his existence as body depends on an act of identification which is not in itself an act that takes place on the plane of the body. Language that speaks of the body and of man as a part and a whole does not apply here. It is an analytical language which is not valid for the attribution of meaningful things to the understanding, which is an act of consciousness. The body is a body with respect to another person not because of its material structure, but because the other person discerns that someone else ascribes a body to himself and because of this attribution of the I he grows accustomed to attributing the body to himself and does not regard it as matter only. Such attribution is an expression of synthesis and, in this case, also of integration, for just as a man creates order in the totality of his acts of understanding by storing them in his memory, so does he create order among his limbs in order to appropriate them and make them his own. Because of this attribution through the understanding, man's body does not consist of components which can be studied only by the analytical method. This method is defended on the basis that it is taken only as such, with due acknowledgment of its qualitative limitation, and does not pretend to reduce the organism to mechanical and causal processes; and, even if such reduction were possible, the component of the attribution of the body to man or the component of the consciousness of such attribution would go beyond scientific statements. This component has no position within the limits of the analytical approach, for it is by its very nature a matter for synthesis that is inaccessible to analysis. The limit of analysis is not in the content but in the position of consciousness as a synthesis of the understanding.

Since the analytical approach consists of placing the object into a set of relations, such as causal relations, it is as a matter of course confined to the method of discovering sets of relations. In the matter of attributing a body to man we are dealing with a primary relation. Man is not absorbed by relations that are outside himself.

A definite analogy can here be made between the content 'world' and the content 'man'. These contents are not only the methodological substrata of interpretation; they designate spheres to which areas are related in connection with which the interpretation applies. What has been said of the world as a total sphere may be said of man as a partial-total sphere. Within the limits of our meaningful relationships we find or come across contents which we must distinguish or whose relations we must note. Such an investigation is not a methodological, functional one since the contents are not derivative from other contents, and as such the investigation may be said to be theoretical. Classical philosophy spoke of eternal objects, and being eternal they had no position with respect to other contents. A distinction may thus be made between the component of eternality and that of irreducibility. It cannot be said of man — and, to repeat, we are speaking of real man or of the individual — that he is an eternal object. We refer to man who is immersed in time and whose acts of synthesis occur in time and are related to it. The objects we find before us are in time and without position and may thus be regarded as legitimate subjects of metaphysics which is concerned with that which is primary or irreducible. The aspect of our investigation of these contents is a theoretical one, which is given a meaning different from classical theory in that it does not concern itself with eternality but approaches the classical meaning in that it is concerned with that which is not derived from another content.

We opened our discussion with an analysis of the understanding and pointed out that the understanding is not reducible to functional-methodological knowledge. Proceeding beyond the immanent aspect of the understanding we arrived at definite subjects or contents to which the understanding refers, namely, world and man. The understanding is irreducible and as such is open to theoretical knowledge. The contents 'world' and 'man' are not reducible to theoretical knowledge and as such are also open to it. All interpretation presupposes understanding, but the understanding is not a means of interpretation but its horizon. All knowledge presupposes the entire horizon of the world, and all understanding presupposes the entire horizon of the acts of the understanding, this horizon being man. We do not follow the classical view in saying that the height of knowledge is theory; we

merely say that theoretical understanding is ancillary and complementary to functional knowledge.

There is another aspect of this analogy between world and man that
is concerned with those contents that have an element of integration
or totality, whether it is the totality of the world or a partial totality,
man. In both cases we speak of an open totality: The world is an
aggregate of meaningful things and an aggregate of the acts of the
understanding, and thus, is an open aggregate; the acts of the understanding have not yet all taken place but keep occurring and as they
do so become related to meaningful things which are the correlative
members of these acts. The world is thus a totality that is forever
becoming. Man is also such an ever-growing totality within his partial
limits because he is related by way of synthesis to sets of relations and
to syntheses of himself and *pari passu* with this activity he grows and
changes. A man with these definite memories is different from one
who is without them. This difference is not apparent because it depends on an independent, inner dimension of the man with these
memories and not others. The world can be comprehended as the
aggregate of particularities of the understanding and of things understood; but we can also comprehend it as the totality of these. We can
understand man as an aggregate of particularities insofar as they
impinge upon him successively and not as a totality. The content
'world' as well as the content 'man', then, have a dimension of
particularity and totality. In this respect also there is a parallelism
between these contents which makes an analogy between the two
possible, permitting us to proceed to the third content which is 'time'.

F

The content 'time' belongs wholly within the world and is not found
outside of it, for it is a content of the data of the world and not of an
eternal being. Every determination of eternality removes the determinant to a region beyond change and consequently beyond time.
Since this inquiry proceeds from the standpoint of a non-transcendent
conception of the world, we are not concerned with theory that refers
to eternality but with one that refers to the data of reality. This
thought is clearly expressed in the fact that time, the dimension overcome by classical theory, is now posited as an object of theory in the
sense introduced here. How was this brought about? Was it accomplished by conferring on 'time' the status of a 'spherical' content?

We must first clarify the connection between the spherical contents 'world' and 'man' on the one hand, and the additional content that can serve as a spherical content in this discourse, the content of 'time', on the other. The world is an aggregate of things, an aggregate of meanings and of understandings, these understandings being acts which as such occur in time. Sometimes understanding is not present and indifference, inattention, and so forth appear. Time is the formal expression of the process indicating the succession of events. From this point of view, whatever happens in the world happens in time, whether on the level of the evolving growth of things or on the level of the occurrence of acts of the understanding that refer to meaningful things. Time is the form of events that occur in the world. Similarly with respect to man who is the synthesis of his experiences and relationships through the medium of the understanding. The experiences, the understandings, and the synthesis are all acts and as such take place in time, for time is the form of events with respect to man as it is with respect to the happenings of the world, so that the formalization of the characteristics of the world and of man constrain us to concentrate on time. Time is a content that pertains to a sphere, and this is so because of the material connection between the content 'time' and the other contents that are prior to it. We can thus say that 'time' is a kind of connecting link or *tertium comparationis* between the content 'world' and the content 'man', for it is the formal sphere of events both in the sphere of the world and in the sphere of man.

In this connection two basic determinations must be kept in mind. Present-day philosophy, nourished by the two streams of intuitionism and existentialism, tends to stress the distinction between physical time and existential time. Physical time is conceived only as the index of processes that have direction; existential time is conceived as that of experience whose focal point is the 'now' of man, the subject of experience. We should not blur this distinction between physical time, which has no connection with man as the subject of experience, and existential time, in which man lives and moves. But in spite of these differences, we must look upon time as a totality because of its nature as the form of the world and of man. This universality means that no matter what the material level of discourse may be there are always events taking place, and time is the formal expression of these events. There are events that may be measured on the physical level and others that are experienced on the existential level; but events themselves that are common to all levels also have in common the element of time.

The second systematic conclusion to be noted is bound up with the difference between time and space from the standpoint of the systematic status of these contents. Human events as acts of experiencing and as acts of understanding, as well as their synthesis, are connected with space. Thus, the meeting of one body with another takes place in space; the other body occupies a place in space; natural events take place in space. But acts of experience are not acts in space but acts in time, for it is the nature of the act *to happen* and not simply *to be*. We therefore experience in time also when the object experienced exists in space, such as the body, a fellow-creature, or a natural occurrence. In this we are only formulating more distinctly Kant's conception of the superiority of the inner sense to the outer sense or the superiority of time over space. This superiority is also valid with respect to man's attribution of a body to himself. The body occupies a place in space, but its attribution to man is an act performed by man which does not occur in space and which by its very nature does not pertain to it. We can say, in short, that when an event occurs in time, it occurs and does not exist. This leads us to the conclusion that the totality of occurrences is superior to that of being in space. From this point of view we regard time as superior to space.

Turning to features connected with 'time', what has been said of the 'world' and of 'man' is also true of 'time' — that it is an ultimate horizon of all discourse. It is the level on which and in respect to which various things are determined as well as the locus of various events. But if we wish to understand the content and not the status of time, we must first note that time is a meaningful correlate that is unique because it is something that is both present and not present. From the standpoint of its actual presence 'here' and 'now' time is not present in its totality. Furthermore, even the time of an instant is not present. What is present is a definite event 'here' and 'now' of which time is a component but which is not exhausted by time. But the meaningful relationship to time of which the instantaneous act consists emerges as a relationship by way of abstraction, as in every understanding. In the understanding of an event there is an understanding of its status in time, whether from the standpoint of the duration of the event or from the standpoint of its following upon the heels of another. The understanding of the duration of an act is important also on the level of personal time as time that is not measured, for the understanding of the duration of an event is the understanding of the event or, while experiencing, we also experience the duration of the event we are experiencing. Because of this connection to the component of time within the event, we can truthfully say to each moment, "*Verweile doch, du bist so schön.*" We understand the event from the standpoint of its content as beauty, pleasure, excitement, or we understand it as an impression of red or movement. Thus we get to know the content-element of the event and its status in time. Understanding thus has an understanding of the integration of the event with the component 'time' and also an understanding of the component 'time' within this integration.

We have thus far considered present time in the present event. But the conception of the event in its aspect of being present binds the event to the totality of time. When we understand the duration of the event, we understand it in the concepts of time which is the form of duration; we compare the duration before us with that of other events. There is no sense at all in determining an instant in time without assuming a total axis of time, and this axis is not present; but our understanding of the present requires the relationship to the axis which is not present. We understand the present as belonging to total time, and we understand it as separated from this as definite time within total time. We have here a double act of the understanding and its corresponding abstraction: The act of ascribing the fragment to total time and the act of differentiating the fragment from total time. Attributing a fragment to total time and the withdrawing of a fragment of time that has been cut off from total time — both need the act of the understanding. This act is one of discerning relations and involves the creation of syntheses of attribution and separation when these two determinations are complementary to one another.

An analogy is here found between the relation of man to his experiences and understandings and the relation of the segment to total time: Man completed the synthesis of attributing experiences and understandings to himself by a definite withdrawal from them. If it were not for such a withdrawal man would be unable to attribute to himself what he does. Thus man carries out with respect to time the act of attributing the segment to the totality of time; he also carries out the meaningful act of isolation and of relating himself to this isolated segment within time. I understand the present because of the non-present of the totality of time, and I understand the non-present of the totality of time because I direct my understanding to the present in time. The present has meaning, then, only when I relate the understanding or the intentionality to the past and to the future; I understand the meaning of the future only because I direct my understanding to the meaning of the present and the past; and I understand the meaning of the past because I place it — in terms of integration and of separation — over against the present and over against the future. Without this binding and separation the present would appear as if it were in space and not in time; similarly, the past and future would appear likewise to be in space and not in time. This is the phenomenological nature of space, namely, that it exists over against its totality even when it exists as fragments, that is, space in Euclidean geometry has three dimensions not only from the standpoint of its totality but also from the standpoint of every definite object in space. In regard to time, it must be emphasized that the present moment, insofar as it is present, does not reflect all of time, but the present situation cannot be understood without the relation of this moment to time as a whole. Hence the acts of the understanding that occur in time and are related to it always have a conception of the present. This conception is combined with an anticipation of the future and with a regression to the past. It may be said, using a play on words, that in the understanding of the present there is a direct relationship to the present and there is a presence of something that is not present, either in the direction of the past or in the direction of the future. Because of this understanding of the present by way of integration, it is clear that time is the horizon of things integrated. Time in this status corresponds to world and man in being a horizon of understanding. We find an intimation of this meaning of time in the Latin word for time, *tempus*, derived from the root τέμνω, *to cut*. Time, as we have seen, refers not only to a slice but to a totality; *to cut* has no meaning apart from its complementary relation to the whole. Since time is the ultimate horizon, it is not only a methodological means for interpretation but a level on which all interpretation is placed. This superior position of time over against every method and over against the direction of interpretation provides us with another criterion for the analogy between time and the contents world and man.

We have seen the integrative relationship to time to be the insertion of the present and the non-present and the mutual dependence of these two aspects. Another aspect of time is revealed when it is noted that time indicates both change and duration. At times we perceive and understand the one and at times the other. Changes in time we understand as a form of succession, and duration as a form of continuity. Time therefore serves as the bearer of a form of passing, on the one hand, and a form of permanency on the other. Even when we describe eternity we characterize it as a continuous duration. It is not possible to separate these two aspects of time or understand one without the other. Duration is found within change itself, just as we measure the passage of time from one event to another and not the duration of one event alone. Furthermore, we cannot reduce the aspect of present and non-present to duration and change despite the fact that there is a definite connection between the two. 'Succession' refers to the fact that the present has ceased to be the present, that is, *a* has passed, *b* has come. The aspect of non-present is intimated or implied in the aspect of succession. The union of the present and the non-present, however, is one of extension, uniting the segment (moment) with the totality (time as a whole); the union of change and duration, on the other hand, is one in depth, for it unites various aspects in fragmentation itself, the change of the fragment and its permanency. Without this union we could not characterize the fragments from the standpoint of their inner composition.

The relationship between the fragments and the whole, a relationship that we find in time, can be reduced to an analogy not only with man but also with the world. The world is the totality of things, meanings, and acts of the understanding; the particulars pertaining to these can be located only with reference to this totality. This is the meaning of the horizon, which designates the ultimate limit to which they are related. This limit is one that extends from the particular in the world and from the background of the present in time. Time, like the world, is a limit or a kind of horizon that does not designate anything beyond the level related to it. Time is nót a thing-in-itself with respect to the world, or something eternal with respect to the present background and event. Time is beyond the moment on the level where the moment also exists, as the world is beyond the particular and is also on the level where the particular exists. The analogy between the status of the content 'world' and that of the content 'time' reveals the same immanent transcendence that characterizes both world and time. An analogy thus arises between world and time since complete totality pertains to both; with reference to man, however, we speak of partial or fragmentary totality. But within the limits of this partial totality the structure of complete totality reappears. Man also is with respect to himself within the sphere of transcendent existence within immanence, for man is related to his experiences and not identical with them. This is true of his body and of his understandings — that is, he is a moving limit with respect to his own particulars, particulars that occur to him, in which he exists but by which he is not exhausted. Man is therefore a transcending being within his own immanence.

G

Our analysis of the three contents — 'world', 'man', and 'time' — leads us to the conclusion that regarding the intentionality of the understanding to its subjects the three contents are ultimate or spherical, not from an ontological but from a meaningful point of view. We find a definite structure on the level of the relation of the understanding, on the one hand, and on the level of contents, because of their status as meaningful objects, on the other. The absence of an ontological bias in this discussion is particularly evident in determining the place of the content 'time' as a spherical content. We do not define time as ontological or objective, but it is important to note that it has a structure. The three contents are ultimate contents from a structural point of view, the operational meaning of which is that the various determinations — determinations of qualities as described above — exist as a result of integration in these contents and do not transgress the bounds of the integrative status of these contents themselves.

We began by examining the structure of the understanding and then considered the status of some contents on the level of meaningful objects. The understanding as an intentional act is related to meaningful objects as its correlates. There is an intentionality that pertains to the sphere and not to this or that particular conceived by the understanding; there is also an intentionality with respect to the spherical content, or contents that have a comprehensivee status in their spheres. This means that there is not only an intentionality of the understanding over against itself, an intentionality that is essentially definite in accordance with the special status of their content. Over against these objects, which are an ultimate horizon of the intentional relation of the understanding, we take a position of knowledge that is theoretical. A symmetry is thus apparent in the basic structure of the understanding and in the basic status of the spherical objects to which the understanding is related.

The status of these contents reveals an additional characteristic when we consider that they, being ultimate, are also factual. But they are ultimate from the standpoint of the intentionality of the understanding to them, because of the special status they enjoy with respect to the understanding, and because of the inner structure of these contents that contains a component of both particularity and totality. Since the particulars are within the totality, the totality has a spherical status with respect to these particulars. We are dealing with contents that are ultimate as the correlates of the understanding and also from the standpoint of their structure in consequence of the correlation between the particulars and the totality. Here again we find a symmetry between the understanding and the essential structure of these contents. We are dealing with mundane contents that have a special structure with regard to theory or contents that elicit theory insofar as they are mundane, and not with contents within the limits of positive facticity, like a stone we stumble over or a particle in which we discern an electron. It is true that these are not contents that are within the sphere of theoretical entities that require interpretation. We are confronted with an essentially meaningful facticity. It is this correlation between facticity and meaningful objects, or between facticity and cognized objects that confers on these contents their peculiar status.

A question pertinent, although not central, to our inquiry still remains to be clarified: Whether the discernment of these ultimate contents and their changing character, which we relate to theory in the classical sense of this term, is not what is generally known in philosophical and in ordinary language as 'intuition'. The tendency to relate the acts of the understanding to acts of the intuition seems reasonable considering the linguistic affinity between $\theta\epsilon\omega\rho\acute{\iota}\alpha$ and *inituitio* (*intueri* = look, observe). We must therefore examine the difference between intuition and understanding, whose nature from the standpoint of its structure and objects we have endeavored to clarify. The matter may be put as follows:

1. When we speak of intuition we generally mean the direct perception of objects to which the perception refers. We therefore designate the nature of intuition as a simple perception removed beyond all doubt, that is, a perception that emanates from the light of reason itself.[2] We sometimes think of intuition as referring to contents that are revealed to the understanding in a direct manner as, for example, the contents of the axioms. We do not mean to assert that special meaningful objects that belong to the sphere of contents emanate from the light of the understanding. These contents are the correlates of the understanding and not emanations from it. In analyzing the inner structure of the understanding we come upon these contents; they are not revealed to us directly but understood by us through a discursive analysis of the structure of the understanding. These contents are of a special nature in that they are ultimate and not because they are revealed to us directly.

2. We therefore cannot say that these contents become manifest to the understanding in one direct, unmediated act. It is not possible for us to understand these contents directly, just as it is not possible for us to understand the structure of the understanding without a discursive position. Discursiveness has a terminal point because of the nature of the contents and not because of the nature of the understanding itself.

3. We establish a position of abstraction over against these con-

tents, an abstraction inherent in the very structure of the understanding as a correlative structure. The understanding is not absorbed
by the thing that is understood, nor do we coalesce or blend with the
contents or with the objects which we regard as ultimate. It should be
noted that the intuitional attitude is often presented as one in which
the distinction between the knower and the thing known has ceased to
exist, or as one in which the two are inseparably fused. Whereas the
conception that presents the intuition as unmediated knowledge
stresses the special character of the act, the position that presents
intuition as a total conception stresses the specific result in which
subject and object coalesce. Over against these two attitudes we posit
the theoretical attitude as one in which there is no unmediated knowledge, a position that is wholly bound up with analytic, reflective
position. We thus understand the abstracted and abstracting position
which is connected with the distinction between the understanding
and the thing understood, a distinction that prevents the coalescence
of the two terms of the correlation. Reflection, which is an analytical,
abstracted attitude, arises over against the intuition and prevents it
from becoming absorbed in the level of the object understood or of
the content attained by it. If we recall what has previously been said
concerning time, namely, that it is not a finished but an ever-growing
and developing totality — which, to a certain extent, is also true of the
content 'world' and 'man' — it will become clear that in contradistinction to the intuitive position that is characterized by totality we
are here concerned with a tendency toward totality and not with a
given totality.

We have connected the position of theory with that of reflection
and in so doing we have attempted to effect a kind of synthesis of the
classical and modern positions taken in their widest sense. The classical position is concerned with the special status of objects of knowledge and holds that knowledge is related to the nature of these
objects; the modern position starts with knowledge and places the
nature of the objects of knowledge against the background of knowledge. We are concerned with a theory that is reflective or one that is
the complementary aspect of reflection as understanding referring to
itself. In every relationship to the correlative term of the thing understood we find the understanding of the understanding. This understanding of the understanding is not suspended even when we consider
the material pole, that is, even when we direct the understanding to
that which is understood by it. Hence we cannot agree with Husserl's
analysis of the acts of the understanding concluding that the thought
of confirmation (*Bestätigung*) is necessarily suspended.[3] Thus, we

cannot speak in this connection of an 'act' in the original sense of this
term as deed or action. Husserl is evidently of the opinion that the
element of confirmation should be suspended because of his characteristic fear of the intervention of the psychological component in the
intentional relation. We, however, need not fear this danger since we
go back to the activity inherent in the understanding, an activity that
reflects the basic nature of the understanding and is not bound to the
level of the everyday human subject as a psychological subject.
Because of the intentionality on the plane of the relation to the noesis
and not only to the *noema*, to use Husserl's terminology, we cannot
dispense with the activity that discerns the relation of intentionality
to the objects of the understanding within the spheres which we seek
to clarify. Without the understanding these objects will not be revealed, and without these objects we are unable to characterize the
understanding. The essential analysis of the understanding — that is,
reflection or, more accurately, philosophical reflection — leads us to
the structure of the understanding and the poles to which it refers.
The understanding of the understanding, or reflection, brings us to an
understanding of objects as objects pertaining to spheres. In reflection we understand the difference between objects on the plane of
qualitative determinations and objects on the plane of spherical
meanings or the horizons of every understanding. Intentionality is the
total sphere of our discourse when we characterize the nature of the
understanding. This intentionality, however, acquires terminations in
that the understanding of the understanding directs the understanding
to special objects that are by nature ultimate in their meaningful
facticity. Since theory is not intuition, it requires analysis and clarification. Reflection, as the understanding of the understanding,
determines the difference between the inner structure of the understanding and the objective correlates to which the understanding
refers. The same reflection that understands the understanding also
understands the difference between itself, from the standpoint of
structure, and the object of understanding to which it is related.

Before coming to the discussion of an additional aspect of the entire
problem we are considering, the aspect connected with the clarification of the nature of the act and its relation to theory, we must
refer briefly to a problem on the level of experience which may be
able to provide empirical confirmation of the fundamental status of
the understanding as reflection. We refer to the psychopathological
phenomenon of *agnosia*, the inability to identify objects by recognition, the inability to identify an object here and now with an
object that has been seen before or, conversely, to identify an object

that is absent with one that is before us. *Agnosia* is, then, a defect in the faculty of spontaneity, a faculty that is in no way associated with the present or with the ability to distinguish among meaningful relations between the present and the non-present. Relations between the present and the non-present can be only relations understood. Instantaneous intentionality, so to speak, also exists in phenomena of *agnosia* as phenomena of attachment to an object that is present. But this intentionality does not unite different contents and establish an identity of content by means of abstracting from the present. Meaningful discernment, which is an understanding of the totality, as is clear to us in the spherical objects of the understanding, does not exist *in actu* in phenomena of *agnosia*. What is missing in *agnosia* is the totality of the understanding on the level of the object understood or the acts of the understanding which effect the integration of the given data.[4] Thus it can be said that the understanding of the understanding and its correlative relation to objects is not a matter that is in daily language termed mere abstraction. This abstraction is involved in our everyday existence; it is an active abstraction.

NOTES

1 *Critique of Pure Reason*, B633.
2 Descartes, *Regulae ad directionem ingenii* III, 5.
3 E. Husserl, *Logische Untersuchungen* (Halle a.d.S.: 1913), Vol. II, Part I, p. 379.
4 See, on this, J. M. Nielsen, *Agnosia, Apraxia, Aphasia, Their Value in Cerebral Localization* (New York – London: 1948), pp. 49 ff.

XII EVENTS AND ACTS

A

Having examined the various aspects of theory both from the standpoint of the act of the understanding and from that of the spherical contents, we now turn our attention to the nature of the act or deed. It will not be necessary here to review the characterizations found in the systems of traditional philosophy. Our purpose is to clarify the principal features of acts themselves.

1. The first component of the act or of practice is operation or use, the ability to utilize knowledge toward a specific end. In this sense we speak of a physician having a large practice, that is, he deals with many cases of illness and, in bringing his knowledge to bear upon them, extends and enriches that knowledge. With this meaning of the act in mind, we say that one must be practical, meaning that one must know how to put one's knowledge to use or know what kind of knowledge is to be employed in reaching a desired end — in short, how to act with respect to the reality that we desire to influence. An act in this sense means use in conformity with orientation in reality.

2. This leads us to a second aspect of the concept 'act' or 'acts' that is similar to the first but is nevertheless distinct from it. We speak of acts as the application of knowledge. It is not said of the physician that he has a practice because of the number of cases he is treating but because he knows how to apply his knowledge to the patients under his care. In this connection an act means the intentionality to the concrete, or attaching importance to the concrete case before us to which we apply our knowledge. We here have a manipulation of knowledge with respect to experience and a measure of instruction derived from experience. When we speak of application, we refer to the distinction between the cognitive and the operational component; knowledge is judged and valued to the extent that it is directed toward the act. We thus have a kind of professional knowledge and a knowledge of how to manipulate it, which is called practicality. This practicality also means the horizon of intentionality, that is, the sphere of

154

the concrete and of daily life to which knowledge is applied. Practicality, then, refers to the common intentionality of every day.
Conduct within reality means in this context acts or practices as an
aggregate of acts. This connection to reality appears in such terms as
fact, derived from *facere* (to do or make), *indeed, en fait, in der Tat,*
all of which have the root meaning of *to act* and also a connotation of
the extensive region of reality.

3. We have already made a distinction between the aspect of attitude which in doing or acting is that of knowledge as to how to apply
our knowledge to reality. We know, for example, the principles of
economics, but of this knowledge we apply only a segment to some
definite problem that has attracted our attention. We thus apply our
knowledge to the aspect of events or occurrences within an act, such
as that involved in healing the sick, in a political or economic undertaking, or in some daily activity. To take the simple example of
purchasing an article: The intentionality toward one thing or another
is an aspect of the operation of knowledge; purchase or acquisition,
however, is an act that actually occurs. A distinction can be made
between these two aspects of the act, that is, between the act of the
intention that is carried out and the act itself. Because of this distinction there appears in the sphere of the act or of acts the distinction
between the will and the act or the distinction between will and the
behavioral event. As long as we keep in mind the distinction between
this factor that gives rise to the act and the act itself, we can ask
ourselves the question as to what are the components of the content
that cause the act, whether they are aspirations or inclinations and
how they are related to the essence of the act performed. However, in
dealing with the act from the standpoint of its occurrence the question concerning the causative factor or the springs of action does not
arise in this context. What we have before us is a form of behavior
which in its visible manifestation is an event in the world of time and
space. An act of purchase or acquisition is, for example, an event that
takes place here and now. In short, it may be said that in the sphere of
the acts we include the acts that are performed and the events that
occur.

4. Since this aspect of the event is in the act and since the act
occurs in reality, we can say that the act introduces a change within
the context of reality in which it occurs. The act that is performed
introduces a change in the spatial condition of reality prior to the act.
When we here speak of change, however, we must distinguish between
the change that occurs on the level of the doer as performer of the act
that gives rise to the deed and the change that occurs on the level of

reality wherein the deed or the event of the deed takes place. The act that causes the deed introduces a change on the level of acts or on the level of the one who performs the deed; the condition of the doer before the act is different from his condition after the act. This change on the level of the act appears in action as the intention of the doer over against the deed or event or as his intentionality to obtain to the effect or result that the deed will or is likely to engender. The act that causes the deed is not simply an act devoid of content; it sometimes contains previous knowledge of the deed that will or may occur as, for example, the act that causes the purchase contains previous knowledge of the thing one wishes to acquire by means of the act of purchase. This brings to light another component of knowledge in the sphere of the deed, with regard to the kind of knowledge that is to be applied in a definite instance. We are concerned here with a previous knowledge of the object or of the goal we wish to reach by means of the deed we are about to perform, a knowledge that may be called anticipatory, since it is related to the performance of the deed from the standpoint of intention. It is plain that the event does not contain intention or anticipatory knowledge; only the act of the doer holds this intention or knowledge. Every deed on the level of performance and on the level of the act is an event, but not every event is performance as an act that engenders results or as knowledge of an effect or of an object to which the performance is directed. In performance, then, we find that an attitude is taken — for example, in the attitude taken in purchasing something — wherein change is introduced. In an event proper, no attitude is taken, and change merely occurs, as when a stone falls; there is a change in the situation prior to this occurrence. But the falling of the stone assumes no attitude with respect to the falling or to the data wherein it fell.

5. We see, then, that a deed entails change since it applies to reality, and this is true on the level of the doer and on the level of reality. From the standpoint of action and intention as well as from the standpoint of the occurrence, the deed constitutes an interference in the context of reality and the consequent introduction of change. The deed occurs within the regular order of reality as it is, but it introduces a change within this order by adding a fact to the context of reality that was previously not present — the fact of purchase, for example, means the transfer of a thing from the area of the shop to that of a private home. On the level of the act performed we also find in the deed an interference in the ordered arrangement of reality since the act, once performed, removes us from a state of indifference in which we desired no particular object here and now. If doing or per-

forming means the concentration of knowledge on a matter or an object, then it is similar in this respect to cognitive acts which have a cognitive intentionality to this or that object; but if doing terminates in an act which involves a change in the context of reality, such as the transfer of an article from one place to another, then such an act, however trivial the changes it effects, is different from cognitive acts whereby I discern the meanings of objects but do not posit the objects. When we say that we are practical and not theoretical or academic, we mean that we not only observe the orderly arrangements of reality and understand their meaning or that of the objects found within them but that we also desire to take a position of intervening in this orderly arrangement of reality, either by a decision to do something or by activating and applying knowledge. Because of this component of intervention inherent within the deed, we must distinguish between knowledge prior to the performance *qua* anticipatory knowledge of the goal or of the object to which our activity is directed and knowledge of the effect of our intervention on the relations that obtain in reality. In the first case we are concerned with a regulative and planning knowledge and in the second case with a discerning and differentiating knowledge of a given state of affairs. Knowledge itself does not change reality but discerns the changes that occur in it as a result of the deed. From the standpoint of doing or performing, we take a position over against reality; from the standpoint of the deed that occurs or has occurred, a trace of the deed is left in reality. In doing, a breach is made in reality; once the deed occurred, it is left in the order of reality. We thus say of deeds that something has been changed by them, just as we might say that a plan has been changed — or converted — into reality.

B

The deed that enters reality changes it by its very introduction and ensuing consequences. The very act of my walking to the shop entails a change in reality, a new element hitherto not present; an additional change is produced by the transfer of an article from one place to another. The intervention of the deed in the course of reality cannot be effected without the doer himself, for the doer is the one who directs the deed to this or that segment of reality, and he is the one who introduces the occurrence inherent in the deed into the context of reality. The doer condenses, as it were, the total reality through his intentionality to a definite segment. He thus introduces into reality a perspective that is not found in reality itself, a perspective derived from the doer's creative relationship to reality, the perspective of circumstances, condition, or situation. Situation is either that segment of reality in which the deed as an event occurs, or it is that segment which the deed intends to change. Reality itself in its totality is not a situation, but it becomes one with respect to the doer. Since the deed is preceded by anticipatory knowledge of achievement or the knowledge of the intentionality to the object, we may say that the conversion of the total reality to a situation is bound up with the anticipatory knowledge of the doer. The perspective character of the situation is another aspect of the cognitive relationship to reality which is necessary in order to perform a deed within reality. Circumstances, however, are not to be equated with fate, which must be taken into account when we act, for circumstances themselves represent a definite crystallization of the doer's position.

In this connection we must not fail to distinguish between intentionality to the deed or object and intentionality itself as an act of the understanding. From the standpoint of this act as an act of the understanding of meanings, reality becomes a segment of circumstances. In my act of understanding I direct myself to a reality that is more extensive than the situation, even when I do not direct myself to reality in its totality. Within the vast expanse of reality I restrict the area of my intentionality to circumstances. From the standpoint of the relationship of the understanding we may say that the deed occurs within the perspective area, which is that of the situation already set aside and restricted by the intentionality of the understanding to reality. The deed itself, then, is a kind of intermediate sphere between the performed act, which contains an understanding, and reality, in which the deed takes place that produces changes within it.

It may be assumed that there is a connection between an act of the understanding of reality and the interpretation of this reality. In the very condensation of reality and its conversion to circumstances we interpret reality. This interpretation is not for the sake of knowledge but in order to restrict the area of reality to the limited segment set aside by our intentionality for our operations. The deed that takes place within the segment presupposes a reality that is more extensive than the segment. Reality is given prior to the deed, but the circumstances are created by the intentionality and the performance of the deed. The conversion of reality to circumstances, then, is not a matter of the deed itself *qua* intervention and change but the effect of the relation to reality prior to the deed, the relation of the understanding that meets the deed and accompanies it. We can thus discriminate between two types of changes caused by the deed: (*a*) the actual change that occurs in reality as a result of the deed happening and the residue of effects it leaves in its wake; (*b*) another prior change is that of the understanding of reality, which is not a change in the material order and arrangement of reality but a change in the faculty of the understanding. The essence of the understanding as such makes for changes on its level and not on the level of things to which it refers.

This perspective of the understanding which condenses reality to circumstances brings with it also the understanding of objects, the understanding for the sake of the deed or the understanding that is replete with the act of doing. In my practical attitude I feel myself to be something that is opposed to the object and I strive to change it.[1] I not only regard the object as an instrument of change, but I also understand it as circumstance, as an area of possible change through the introduction of the deed. Reality becomes for the understanding the arena for changes effected by the deed. This perspective of the object could be expressed, for example, by using the objects as goals that I posit for myself and making them serve these or similar goals. An object exists within reality as an object, but from the standpoint of knowledge prior to the deed or accompanying it the object is merely something to be acquired by me to serve some physical need.

C

We have distinguished between the act that gives rise to the deed and. the deed that is performed within reality. The act that engenders the deed is in no way severed from it, because the act prepares the area of circumstances in which the deed takes place. Thus the deed is not a mere occurrence like the movement of heavenly bodies or the fall of a stone, but an event — although not every event is a deed.

This distinction between the doer and the deed and the relation between·them takes us back to the traditional distinction between the two basic tendencies of the act. If the act is directed to the doer himself, it is essentially an act with an ethical tendency, that is, its purpose is to regulate the acts of the doer, to determine his aims, desires, and sentiments; if the act is basically directed to reality, it is a technical act calculated to effect a change, and this is a factor in reality and not in the intentionality to the doer himself. These distinctions are here set forth schematically and need to be defined more precisely. This need becomes apparent the moment we examine the two spheres of the act more closely, the ethical act and the technological act. What these two tendencies have in common is achievement or effect, whether it is an effect in the determination of the will and the curbing of desire or an effect in the position of objects and the defining of new arrangements in reality hitherto not present. In the one case the effect is ethical or educational, in the other it is technological. What these two tendencies of the act have in common is related to the purpose of the act. This also can be seen in Kant's ethical doctrine which is not directed to the achievement of results within reality but to the attainment of effects insofar as the determination of the will by means of the ethical law or the categorical imperative is concerned. By changing somewhat Kant's formulation in his discussion of the nature of the artistic activity, we can say that even according to Kant the ethical act is directed to the effect or result. This effect, however, is devoid of effects; with respect to the artistic activity Kant called it purposiveness without purpose. The ethical effect lies in the formation of the will, whereas the absence of the effect is the absence of intentionality toward the attainment of material ends, such as honor, happiness, benefits, and similar profitable effects that spring from the accomplished deed.

In any case we see that to the extent that the act contains an occurrence it involves a change in the things within reality in which the act is imbedded. This change springs from the occurrence within the act, but the act is not exhausted in the occurrence; it assumes a position, whether it is the position as the act that causes the deed or as the understanding of reality to which it is directed or which is condensed into circumstances by the act of the understanding prior to and concomitant with it. We now turn our attention to the problem of determining the nature of the relation between theory and practice.

NOTES

1   F. H. Bradley, "The Definition of Will" (II) in *Collected Essays* (Oxford: 1935), Vol. II, p. 517.

XIII. NON–PREFERENTIAL PRIMACY

A

The classical conceptions regarded theory as superior to practice because theory embodied the goal of man as a rational being. Kant took the ethical, practical sphere to be superior to the sphere of knowledge because in those contents with which it deals the latter is unable to decide whether or not beings denoted by these contents exist. The decision in favor of the existence of these contents come from ethical and not cognitive sources. Both the classical and the Kantian conceptions show a preference of one sphere as over against the other. Our purpose here shall be to indicate the primacy of the theoretical sphere with respect to the practical — a primacy that in no way entails a preference or superiority of theory over practice — and then show that there is no meaning to significant decisions in the practical sphere without first assuming such decisions in the theoretical.

B

We turn first to the view of Bradley, who holds that every theory or understanding has a real, practical aspect and that every practical activity as given in reality has a quality that is theoretical. Being active obliges me to do something, so that no matter what my theoretical activity may be, it must necessarily include a practical effect involving succession in time and change.[1] Bradley states in another passage that when an idea works ideally, the process is thought; and when an idea produces a fact in which the character of the idea and existence are no longer discrepant then this process is the will.[2] In this we cannot follow Bradley for he regards the theoretical and the practical as two aspects of the same thing. We distinguish between the nature of the theoretical relation to the world, which is one of understanding and does not change the face of things, and the practical relation that does

161

effect such a change involving a phenomenological difference between contemplation and intervention.

Despite our general disagreement with Bradley, his view seems to be justified in one particular: It is possible to look upon theory or the acts of theory as events or deeds. There is in theory an element of an act and from this point of view it is practical. The act of theory as an act involves intervention in the course of the world and its changes and as such must be taken as a practical sphere. The world in which an act of contemplation occurs is different from one in which such an act does not occur. We have already discussed the world as an aggregate of the acts of the understanding and as an aggregate of things and meanings. Since the world contains the acts, it undergoes a change when these are performed. Here we must emphasize the primacy of practice. Theory as a fact is practice, that is, the practical element is not the meaning of theory but its facticity. This assumption of the primacy of practice has nothing to do with any other assumption since it is within the limits of facticity and not within some scale of values or preferences.

This assumption of the factual primacy of theory as practice, however, does not necessarily imply the superiority of the content of practice over theory. Acts cannot be performed without the assumption of a theoretical attitude to the world and the principal contents of theory. Elements of theory are implied in acts, so that theory is the condition of acts and their spheres. Let us now analyze this problem.

C

From the viewpoint of its nature and content the theoretical position is implied in the facticity of the act because the relation of intentionality, as a relation of the consciousness of meanings, is an indispensable condition of the act. Theory, as a fact and as an act, does not cease to be theory, that is, the relation of the understanding to its objects. This activity is essentially a total one and as such may be viewed as an activity that serves as a step leading to a discrimination between theory, in its limited sense, and practice in its limited sense. Acts that are performed presuppose an activity of the consciousness as awareness and elucidation;[3] they are acts, therefore, only in the sense that they emanate from this total nature of the consciousness. Only against this background of total consciousness as awareness and elucidation can we distinguish between theory and practice as spheres having a special character containing both contemplation and inter-

ference. The difference between theory and practice, seen against the
background of their dependence on the nature of consciousness, is
that the essence of theory is in its attitude to meanings and that of
practice, in its creation of meanings expressed in the goals it sets for
our strivings and in converting the vast expanse of reality into situational segments.

This argument must now be carried a step further. We have stressed
the common connection of theory and practice to the character of the
intentional relation in general, the relation that presupposes the
awareness and elucidation of consciousness. In addition we must
remember that theory as an attitude to meanings is closer to the basic
nature of consciousness and of the intentional relation than it is to
practice. This may be stated as follows: Theory is closer to the nature
of consciousness, which is itself prior to the distinction between
theory and practice, because it is a relation to the world that has less
content than the relation of practice. Practice introduces into the
world a new content hitherto unknown and thus changes the established arrangement in reality as, for example, when I transfer something from one place to another. Theory, however, only discriminates
among the contents already within the world and thus has less intensity in terms of attitude to the world than practice. Theory is intensive
insofar as it is practice and as such changes the world. In its essential
content theory posits less with respect to the world than it does with
respect to practice. Theory reads the world, so to speak, but practice
dictates to it, the former being less intensive than the latter. But here
again no superiority of value is implied but only a primacy of elements
of which theory and practice are composed.

If we find in one of the components of practice a conversion of
reality into a segment of circumstances, then the relation that does
not contain such conversion presupposes a material priority to the
relation that does contain such conversion. Reality, as we have already
noted, is given *in extenso* but its restriction to circumstances has to be
brought about and presupposes a given reality in which it could be
effected. This is also true of the nature of decision as a disposition
toward a definite matter, object, or goal. Decision is an intentional act
and involves a relation of understanding to the world and to a definite
matter within it as well as an activity of the will or aspiration for the
sake of the object of decision. Decision involves an attitude toward its
object and this attitude is a more intensive relation than the intentionality of the understanding to a content. Decision, therefore, presupposes the relation of intentionality which includes understanding and
not, at least not yet or not necessarily, decision. Intentionality in

general, then, is prior to all decision. This primacy is based on the fact that intentionality contains within itself fewer elements and fewer components than decision. The rule we arrive at in our present discussion is, then, that the level with fewer elements has priority: Thus, when I come to create meanings within reality, I must first depend on my judgment of reality, on my orientation in the area in which I propose to create meanings by means of, or in conjunction with, an act. Since we find in the sphere of practice an element of intentional relation and thus an element of judgment, we can in no way sever the practical sphere from the doer; the basic relation of the doer to the world, however, is the relation of understanding. It follows that the relation of understanding is the condition for theory and for practice proper. Since theory proper, however, is a more extended realization of the relation of the understanding and since practice is based on the relation of the understanding, theory has a close affinity to this relation. Practice has primacy as a fact; theory has primacy from the standpoint of content.

D

The difference between the theoretical and the practical spheres becomes clear when we compare the relational abstraction of the former with the relational composition of the latter. In those fields that deal with meaning, such as the field of logic, the understanding of one meaning leads to another, for these are fields in which an inner determination of one content is made by another content. These relations between one content and another are found in the connections of implication, namely, that proposition a contains proposition b by implication in accordance with the formation "if a then b." The understanding of one meaning leads us to the understanding of another; we are thus guided by these meanings themselves. In the case of practice things are different, for here one act does not lead us by its inner meaning to another act. To the extent that practice concerns the creation of meanings in reality or in a segment of reality, meaning does not arise from out of itself but is produced from act to act. The creation of meaning in the practical sphere always requires an act of intervention in reality, so that meaning does not evolve of itself from one matter to another but must be coined, that is, the doer is indispensable in the creation of meaning. Hence, when we say to a person, "you should be consistent," referring not to the logical consistency of his thoughts but to his actions in the practical sphere – admonishing him, for example, "you must keep your promise" or "having acted once in this manner, you must also act now in the same manner" — our notion of consistency is not derived implicitly from the relation of one act to another but refers to the doer, explicitly or implicitly, with the expectation that he bear in mind the significance of consistency and incorporate it concretely in his actions. Since the act is opaque to a certain extent, it can be penetrated and illumined through the intervention of the doer and by his attribution of the formal or material meaning of consistency.

Another distinction must be considered in dealing with these acts of the understanding of meanings in the sphere of theory. In some of these acts the understanding is not dependent on the decision of the one who performs these acts. Where it does depend upon it, we say that he who executed the act did not behave rationally. He behaved without considering the inner criterion of the theoretical sphere, as when a rational man, for example, violates the law of contradiction or when he fails to discern the implication of a judgment he has made. Since there are determinations of one content with respect to another, there are also in the sphere of theory determinations of a content with respect to acts of the understanding that refer to this content. The content limits the direction of the act related to it. This determination by means of a content imposed on the act facilitates to a certain extent depersonalization in the theoretical sphere. This is clearly seen, for example, in the fact that from the standpoint of the total sum of knowledge of the world it does not matter who thought a particular thought or discerned some natural phenomenon and created a physical theory. From the standpoint of human history it is important to know who created a theory, since human history is concerned, among other things, with acts that bear the imprint of great personalities. But this is of no importance over against the contents themselves. In the practical sphere, however, the doer or agent is posited not only as a real condition for himself but also in regard to his content. Involved in practice is an act of decision or a conversion of reality into a situation. Hence, if there were no act by a doer, we would be in the sphere of occurrences and not of deeds: Remove the agent and you have removed the deed. The depersonalization of a kind found in the theoretical sphere is impossible in the practical sphere without changing the essence of this sphere. The doer belongs to the deed and he is also separated from it; more than the act itself belongs to the practical sphere, since the act contains an inner connection with the doer. In the practical sphere we inquire after the doer and it is important to know who performed a given act and under what circumstances and

for what reasons. There is a content to an act such as the waging of a
war, but it is also important to determine who struck the first blow
and for what reason. Here as well the practical sphere seems to contain
more components than the theoretical sphere. To understand this
nature of the practical sphere we must reduce the theoretical discernment implied in the meaningful aspects of the practical sphere. This
explains the fact that the connecting link between the practical sphere
and the theoretical sphere, as already intimated, is the content 'man'.
But it is not only this content 'man' that is presupposed by the practical sphere but also the content of the area of reality in which the act
is performed and which has been condensed by the act into a segment
of reality. We may say, in other words, that the act presupposes also
the content 'world' in addition to the content 'man', both being
contents of theory. The world is the scene of the act and is converted
by man into a situation. A deed performed by man has two aspects,
the perspective aspect as the conversion of reality into a situation, and
the material aspect of the content as procedure, acquisition, formation, and other similar possibilities open to the act. The act of intervention presupposes, as it were, a defect in reality and this is related to
man who sets himself to remedy it.

Here we see that theory, from the standpoint of the objects to
which it refers, is more extensive than practice. The extension of
theory is the condition for practice precisely because practice is
restricted and restricting. Restriction is secondary to extension and is
dependent on the meaningful act of restriction, an act that takes place
in extension by focusing the act on decision or on dividing reality into
segments.

In this matter practice is conditioned by theory in two respects: As
a meaningful relation as understanding and as an aggregate of revealed
contents, which we have termed above spherical objects of the understanding, to which theory refers. We see that an analysis of the nature
of practice reveals the dependence of the act on the spherical contents
'world' and 'man' — world as the expanse in which condensation
occurs and man as the doer in distinction to the deed. World and man
are the objective, ontological conditions of practice; but these contents, which are the conditions with respect to practice, are the
contents of theory with respect to themselves. The sphere of practice
thus presupposes that of theory. The theoretical relation as discernment of the contents is the condition for the practical relation from
the standpoint of its condensation into a segment, on the one hand,
and the doer's concentration on this segment on the other. Practice
does not change the aggregate of the world's contents by directing

itself to a change of the totality but at most to a segment of the contents. The change that occurs in the world is a change that takes place in the means of change within the segment.

This segmentation raises for the doer the question of the integration of his act in two senses: (a) integration in the doer's private sphere, that is, the relation between him as a total doer and the definite deed he performs or the meaning of that deed with respect to the total doer; (b) the doer is also faced with the problem of integration on the plane of the deed, that is, the aspects of reality outside of him wherein he lives and to which his acts are directed. Reality is changed as a result of the acts he performs: How, then, will he continue to live and work in this reality which he was instrumental in changing? Integration is not accomplished automatically, for in the practical sphere there is no independent determination of contents. Integration is possible by means of additional acts that are performed and by means of additional relations of the doer to the acts and to the circumstances. Since this dependence on integration is effected by acts, integration is partial and fragmentized in accordance with the nature of the acts which are themselves partial and fragmentized. A system of acts does not exist, but a system of theory is an inner norm of theory because of the nature of the theoretical contents as contents that have inner relations. The discernment of these inner relations is an inner norm imbedded within the very nature of theory. The systematization of theory is the integration in the theoretical sphere, and the progression from act to act which continues unceasingly is the rhythm of integration in the practical sphere. This integration is without end because every integrative act changes reality. This is true even when I carry out an act directed toward integration, as when I correct in one act a mistake I made in a previous act. The means of integration are themselves acts that change reality and thus disrupt integration automatically. The relative simplicity of the theoretical sphere over against the denser composition of the practical sphere becomes apparent when we consider the peculiar circumstances that the system is possible in the theoretical sphere because of the relative simplicity of that sphere, and it is not possible in the practical sphere because of the complexity of that sphere. Now, as a result of the preceding distinctions, we understand simplicity as an immanent determination, and complexity as the pursuit of an unattainable total integration. It has already been made clear that this complexity has an additional aspect, namely, the dependence of the practical sphere on the contents of the theoretical sphere, a dependence that is irreversible since the theoretical sphere does not depend on the practical. This latter non-dependence has another aspect, namely, that practice has no contents *par excellence* or spherical objects, whereas theory has. An act that is performed by man in the world is bound up with these two contents which are the contents of theory, from the standpoint of theory, and are the conditions of practice, from the standpoint of the dependence of practice on theory. This complex nature of practice is clearly evident in this instance for, whereas every act depends on the contents of theory and is meaningless without them, the contents of theory are not the essential, inner contents of practice. Every act has its own content and its own meaning within the world which serves as a framework and not as the content of the act. The dependence of the act on theory is a dependence on the framework; the problem of the act is decision in favor of a definite partial content within the total framework.

A common adage drawn from daily experience has it that it is easy to know but difficult to act. We deplore the fact that man's ethical life has not kept pace with his intellectual accomplishments. In the practical sphere there is the problem of integration; the systematic integration in the theoretical sphere does not involve material incorporation in practice. Furthermore, in the practical sphere there is a need of integrating not only acts that are openly carried out, such as acts of war or of economic development, but also a need of integration on the level of theory within practice. It is well known that this integration of the spheres is a much graver problem than integration within the practical sphere alone. Since man lives on different levels at the same time, the different levels of the understanding and of conduct, he often fails to achieve integration at all or must remain content with partial integration. Integration is always an open problem; it cannot be avoided because acts are related to man as a whole and to the world as a whole. This relationship, however, is not of the nature of an integrative content of definite, individual acts whose complete fusion in the world and in man is not a material fusion that is actively carried out. The fact that everything is done in one world does not make acts one cohesive sphere.

Man's actual adaptability to reality is not assured by the systematization of theory and knowledge; it is acquired piecemeal and it is not possible for thought to achieve integration with reality. The dependence of acts on the relation of the understanding as the nucleus of theory does not mean that theory can serve as a model or pattern for acts or *a fortiori* as a guarantee for their success. The dependence of acts on theory does not abolish the gap between them.

This subject of the difference between the directions of integration of the theoretical position compared to those of the practical position brings us to another distinction. The theoretical relation is at bottom a relation of an attitude to meanings. This is true of all knowledge and, more particularly, the knowledge of spherical objects — world, man, and time. When we discern meanings we adopt an analytical attitude. We distinguish one meaning from another and on the basis of evidence derived from definite meanings proceed to make connections between one meaning and another. Furthermore, the theoretical position is primarily a discriminating position, for it is based on the distinction between the understanding and its object. Only on the basis of this prior distinction can a relationship arise to unite these two elements; the inner problem of the theoretical sphere is thus the problem of the connection between objects that have been discriminated — a problem that since the earliest days, has engaged philosophers, whether they have considered such objects as ideas as did Plato, or as categories, as did Aristotle, Kant, Hegel, and others. The analytical *terminus a quo* is the point at which the inner problem of the theoretical sphere becomes a problem of system, as explained above.

The nature of the practical sphere and its inner logic are different. Here the deed is synthetic from the very outset since it combines the act with meaning, confers meaning on a definite segment of reality, or else directs it to definite ends and effects. Insofar as the deed changes given reality it imparts to it content. The distinction between the doer and the reality in which he works is the condition for the proposed deed, for without such a distinction there could be no intervention on the part of the doer. That which is distinct from reality intervenes in it; the distinction is a position embodied in the theoretical position which has its place over against, but not within, reality, so that the separation of the doer from reality is rooted in the understanding as a separate position. The basic analysis of the understanding as a theoretical position is then a starting point and presupposition of the practical position as a synthetic position. Integration is imbedded in the deed *qua* deed. Therefore, the sphere of the deeds as a sphere that combines and unites is concerned with the integration of integrating, while the sphere of theory which is basically that of analysis is concerned with the integration of the analytical findings resulting from analysis.

In short, we can say that since the deeds are separate and distinct from one another, the integration of the practical sphere is either an extension of the problem of integration as an inner problem of the theoretical sphere or a problem of man with respect to himself as a doer. The doer may expect the deeds to serve as his expression and as a reflection of his inner self. The problem of the systematization of deeds is a kind of an attempt to embody in the practical sphere a systematization analogous to the inner problem of the theoretical sphere; it is basically an attempt to transfer the meaning of the spherical entity 'man' from man's personal sphere to the public sphere of deeds as a reflection of his inner unity. Whether from the standpoint of systematization or from the standpoint of man, there is a connection between the demand for systematization in the practical sphere and the position of systematization in the theoretical sphere. We are here presented with a connection between the practical sphere and a criterion ultimately exterior to it.

E

We have attempted to clarify the relation between man as a totality and his isolated deeds. There is another aspect to this relationship to the content 'man' in the practical sphere. This aspect is derived not from the standpoint of the spherical entity 'man' but from the fact that in deeds, at least in certain deeds, we take into consideration a concrete, material component, that is, other people who become implicated in our deeds and to whom our deeds are directed for good or ill. Since the deed converts reality into a situational segment, we find this segment to be inhabited with real people outside ourselves who in our daily conduct we assume to be human creatures like ourselves.[4] The view that regards others as partners to our deed or as constituting its system of relationships is in itself no concern of the deed but of the cognitive determination implied in the deed we perform. The reality of people as human beings and not as objects becomes then a material component of a definite class of deeds we perform. In short, we can say that the sphere of deeds presupposes the factual determination or the determination on the qualitative level of the reality of many people united to one another or who have become so by reason of the deed performed.

F

From the foregoing discussion we may conclude that the sphere of practice and the happenings within it presuppose the position of the theoretical sphere in three fundamental matters: (a) we presuppose the position of understanding; (*b*) we presuppose the spherical entities 'world' and 'man'; (*c*) we presuppose a definite material component, a cognitive determination, namely, the reality of other people.

However, with respect to the character of the reality in which we act or in which we intend to act by intervention an additional supposition must be made. We assume that in order to make intervention in reality possible, intervention being the essential characteristic of deeds, reality must not be closed or impervious to the thrust of the intervening component. If all things were impeccable and flawless and constituted a well-rounded whole, intervention would be impossible and even unimaginable. Even if one should come along and insist that all intervention in reality can be explained by causal factors, there are still various factors in reality that remain. Intervention is possible in some area of reality where it is not part of the inner process of reality itself. When a tree grows as a result of organic forces, intervention by irrigation or fertilization still contributes to its growth. This minimal contributory intervention is the presupposition of every deed, whether it is explicit to the doer or not; it is the presupposition of the doer with respect to reality toward which his deed is directed. Just as the deed posits the supposition of a doer, so also does it posit the supposition that the doer posits with respect to the reality that he converts into a situation and in which his intervention takes place. This supposition does not pertain to the deed but explicitly to the doer; it is theoretical or cognitive *par excellence*, first, because it pertains to the order and nature of reality, being interpreted for the deed but not decisive for its needs, and second, because it is not found on the level of deeds. This supposition is pre-practical and is thus cognitive or theoretical with regard to the nature of reality in its totality beyond the deed or in the area in which the deed takes place. We will have a clearer conception of this complex matter after we explain the connection between the supposition of the open character of reality and the supposition of the connection between deeds and time.

The deed is in need of a supposition or hypothesis which teaches that time does not terminate, that is, the duration of the deed adds a segment to the process in time that brings it up to the present. The deed needs a supposition that time has already elapsed up to the moment of the deed and that now the segment of the deed has joined the flow of time up to now. Furthermore, as stated before, the deed cuts the total reality into segments and converts it into a situation. The essence of intervention in reality effected by the deed lies in creating a situation. To the same extent that the deed segmentizes reality it also segmentizes time: It draws a line that divides time until the present from time henceforth, or it segmentizes total time and concentrates it on that interval of time to which the doer directs the deed, even though it be the most elementary deed such as walking from one room to another. Temporal duration is a correlate of the deed. But a deed, this definite deed, is directed to this definite segment within an interval of time. Here time appears as an objective correlate of the deed, the correlate to which the condensation characteristic of time pertains with respect to the deed.

In addition to the relation of the deed to time as a correlate, time appears as the background for the deed since the deed is an event from the standpoint of its facticity. The event occurs in time, following another event (the aspect of succession in time) and occupying a segment of time (the aspect of duration in time). Time here appears not as a correlate of the understanding with respect to the deed but as the background of the deed. As the former it is a member of a relationship — the whole of time limited by circumstances; as the latter it is the medium of comprehensiveness since the deed occurs within the comprehensive sphere of time. From these two points of view time may be regarded as a material component of the deed. Time is, as has been stated, a spherical content of theory, and this connection of the deed to time then gives rise to the connection of the deed to theory. Time as content is the condition of the deed and is also an inner element embedded in the deed itself from the standpoint of its event and of its duration.

Moreover, to the extent that I presuppose that reality is open to the deed and as such is the condition of the intervention of the deed, I am obliged to assume that time has not yet reached its end and does go on. Time as continuing is not a datum of knowledge. The act of the understanding before us considers time as a transition beyond given time, as a "not-yet" with respect to the deed. We have here a combination of views of time that is required for the deed. Time in its extension is implied in the deed by means of its segmentation corresponding to a segment of the world. Time that is not yet is a supposition for the deed, and this supposition corresponds to the one that reality is open. In all this we understand the significance of time with respect to the sphere of deeds and also the connection of the deed to time as a spherical content and to understanding as an understanding of spherical contents. Time is a phenomenological component of every event and of every deed as an event, and it is the condition of every event and of every deed as an event

A deed is not an event simply because of its connection to the doer. The doer assumes as a matter of course that time has not yet terminated and that reality is open, and with this assumption he performs his deed whereby he intervenes in reality and adds to the duration of time up to now. The assumption of the open nature of the deed and of reality is an attitude of anticipation of that which is not yet from the standpoint of its spherical extension, that is, it takes into consideration and anticipates future time. The deed itself has duration the instant it is performed; the doer assumes or takes into consideration the residue of the deed together with its duration in the effect that the deed will have in the future. The effect takes place later than the time of the performance of the deed. It is thus relegated by the doer to the future. The anticipation of the future proceeds from the doer and not from the deed, yet anticipation in itself is not a practical attitude for it is not by itself intervention but a cognitive, and hence a theoretical, attitude. We here have a knowledge of the nature of time as a sphere or a spherical content prior to the knowledge of the definite effects of events or deeds. A distinction must be made between the material knowledge concerning something that happens in reality (whether or not some object is acquired, whether an eclipse has taken place or whether an economic crisis has occurred) and the spherical knowledge of the nature of time that continues from the past to the present. Since the anticipation of time that has not yet come assumes the form of content, it is possible to speak of foresight in anticipating effects, of intentionality to effects and similar relationships of content. But such relations presuppose a relation to continuous time. Every effect, every achievement or goal that we seek to attain by means of deeds, is itself in the future with respect to the deed. From this point of view the future appears as a term of the understanding that is presupposed with reference to every content in the future.

In this matter, too, we cannot agree with one of the basic principles of the philosophy of existence, namely, that the understanding itself is 'thrown' and that this 'thrownness' or *Geworfenheit* is a mode of man's reality or existence.[5] A distinction must be made between anticipation as a total relation of the understanding to time and the future as time beyond the instantaneous moment or projection which is the possibility realized in the future. The presupposition of all *Geworfenheit* with respect to the future is essentially the relation of the understanding to the future. The two relations are not identical. The relation of *Geworfenheit* assumes the nature of time and of non-existent time, that is, it presupposes a future. Anticipation is a more comprehensive and a more minimal relation than *Geworfenheit*. Totality precedes particularity, and the minimal precedes the composite — in accordance with the principle we explained with respect to

the relations between theory and practice, a principle that applies
more specifically to the relations between anticipation and *Geworfenheit*. Anticipation is an attitude of intentionality and as such
precedes this or that content of the attitude of intentionality. Intentionality is a more extensive relation than anticipation, and anticipation is more extensive than *Geworfenheit*, so that *Geworfenheit* is
rooted in anticipation just as anticipation is rooted in intentionality.[6]

                                        G

We see that the total relation to the future is a condition for regarding
the future as the field for the realization of the intention we wish to
carry out. This obliges us to distinguish between the aspect of ends
and the aspect of effects within deeds. This comment throws light on
an additional factor in the relations between the spheres of theory and
practice.
    We speak of attaining an end when that which is achieved by the
deed corresponds with the intention of the deed — for example, when
the purpose of the deed is to reach a definite place and our intention
to reach that same place is realized. The intention of the deed
amounts to the anticipation of the end involved in the instance before
us. When anticipation and the state arrived at are in agreement, we
speak of having attained the end. Anticipation in this case is expectation. But the end is not always attained since the intention is not
always realized nor is the condition brought about by the deed always
commensurate with the expectation. But something does arise as a
result of a deed that is performed: I go forth to meet a man and I do
not meet him, but I arrive at the place of the appointment. What has
been achieved does not correspond to the intention and hence the end
has not been attained, but an effect has resulted. It follows that if we
look at the deed only from the standpoint of the event, we cannot
distinguish between effect and end, for the effect is always beyond the
present time in which the deed is performed. The distinction between
effect and end is bound up with the nature of the relation between the
condition created or brought about by the deed and helps us to
determine the significance of the doer for the deed. From the standpoint of the doer there is a distinction between end and effect. The
intention is not that of the deed but of the doer; the distinction
between the effect and the end, then, is bound up with the determination of the relation of the situation to the anticipation and the
planning of the doer. The effect or the result is the minimal residue of

the deed, whereas the end is the residue of the deed when among the components of the residue we also find the accordance with the doer's intention. The intention, then, is an expression of intentionality, of anticipation. Intention presupposes intentionality; it is a definite concentration of intentionality not simply in the direction of the future but toward a definite state of things that is to arise in the future. The effect presupposes anticipation; the end presupposes anticipation as well as intention. A cognitive, pre-practical attitude is therefore established with respect to the effect and *a fortiori* with respect to the end.

When this attitude of anticipation refers to the deed that we are performing, it is called planning. In planning I determine that which I wish to achieve with a deed I perform and which will be achieved beyond the deed at a future time. By anticipation I take the future into account and address myself to the future. In planning I take into account that which will happen in the future or, so to speak, that which will fill the empty space of the future simply as a dimension of time. There is thus more content in planning than in anticipation. We are again presented in this connection with the aspect of knowledge that accompanies the deed and thus with that aspect of theory which is the condition of practice: Anticipation is a relation to a segment of time. Since time is a spherical content of theory, anticipation pertains to the content of theory. Time is a spherical content whereas whatever fills time, including the effect of a deed or the end which the deed seeks to attain by way of intention, are fragmentary objects of the cognitive relationship. Achievement in the future, insofar as we direct ourselves to it, is not only something that is bound up with the deed; it also has a position in terms of knowledge. As such it is not an achievement either as end or effect but is also an object of knowledge among other objects of knowledge which happen not to be objects pertaining to the sphere of deeds. The practical attitude interprets the status of the object as an end or as an effect and does so also according to the motives in the deed; with respect to the deed the attainment in the future is an end or an effect which we take into account in planning. This planning contains a cognitive component, the component of anticipation. With respect to this component the end or the effect is an object. From the standpoint of the practical sphere we add to the object an element of purpose or effect, although these elements do not nullify the status of the object that accrues to the end or to the achievement. The practical relationship does not nullify the status of the object although it obscures it, for the motive of the relationship in this case is practical and not cognitive and has absorbed within itself the status of the object that has been posited from the standpoint of knowledge.

As soon as we speak of the knowledge in anticipation and the knowledge that refers to the object in the effect or in the end to which anticipation is directed, we are unable to omit the additional steps in the sphere of the relationship of knowledge and not in that of practice, either as intention or as planning. The moment we know that we are related to the future, we know that the future is beyond us. A gap intervenes between the present as a level of relationship and the future as the level of that to which we are related, whether from the standpoint of practice or ends or effects. When I am aware of the gap between the present and the future, I am also aware of the duration, not exactly as measured in hours or in years, but I am aware of the fact that there is duration. Duration is the other aspect of distance, the distance between the present as a level of our relationship, and the future as a level of achievement. I also know that there is a way, or that a way will be found, that leads from the present to the future. In all this we see that reflection, that is, the understanding of my position in the present and my relation to the future, accompanies the deed and is absorbed in it. Reflection is also involved when I consider its extent, a reflection that expresses itself in the fact that I take an attitude to the future as, for example, when I foresee or look forward to an effect or an end. The assumption of this attitude of expectation places me in the practical sphere. However, I do nothing; I merely look forward to the future, which is an attitude of anticipation. To look into the future with anticipation or expectancy is an activity, an activity that concerns the practical sphere but which is itself not of its character.

The assumption of an attitude in this matter serves as a kind of a general background of our intentionality. In looking forward with anticipation and expectancy to a given effect I form the decision to act in that direction. The decision is a kind of deed although it is not yet entirely within the practical sphere. Decision involves a concentrated attitude directed to a deed, but it is not yet a deed that occurs in the public realm or in public time. It is an act, directed by planning, that takes place in the present and produces the deed that I anticipate and whose effects I expect. In making decisions I adopt preferences; I prefer one procedure to another. In planning I endeavor to envisage the sequence of events from the deed I perform here and now until the effect or the end that is external to the here and now and hence lies in the future. In adopting preferences I condense and restrict the future to the very object I desire to attain; I take into account the future and its manifold possibilities and direct the course of things in such a manner that one possibility and not another is to be realized in reality. All these aspects of decision and preference contain an element of judgment, an element that discerns the state of things as they are and as they might be in the light of my preferences. These aspects of judgment are the various aspects of knowledge implied in the deed; knowledge accompanies the deed in that the doer is related to his own deed. The relationship of the doer to his own deed is one of the manifestations of the reflective attitude. The knowledge that accompanies the deed is a knowledge of the circumstances here and now and in the future, but the circumstances here and now and in the future are segments of time. The knowledge that accompanies the deed condenses time into segments; this condensation presupposes the knowledge of the extension of time in its totality and this knowledge is in turn theoretical. The knowledge that accompanies the deed presupposes the extensive knowledge of time in its totality. Theory, then, is required for practice just as extension is required for condensation to take place.

It is plain from all this that theory is a condition for the deed, for theory is an attitude that is more extensive than that of practice. We do not interpret this to mean that theory is superior to practice but only that it is a condition of practice. The principle of dependency, from the standpoint of the relation of practice to theory, is the general principle of this dependency, namely, the dependency of condensation on extension. Theory, which refers to time in its totality, is more extensive than practice. We see this extensive aspect of theory over against the intensive aspect of practice in the fact that in theory as such there is understanding but not planning. Planning is a cognitive attitude for the sake of the deed or its motivation; theory is neutral with respect to the contents to be preferred, whereas planning presupposes preferences which serve as a cognitive attitude for the deed. The preference is not a deed and not merely knowledge; it is knowledge for the sake of the deed or it is knowledge that the doer knows because he is both a knower and a producer of deeds.

The expanse of theory is another aspect of its extension, another aspect of its neutrality that can be directed to any content whatever and not to any particular content; preference, however, and the judgment that accompanies it and planning, fall within the sphere of intensive knowledge and thus have choice or selectivity. Preference is essentially selective and as such differs from neutral knowledge which is devoid of selection.

It seems that this distinction between the neutrality of theory and the selectivity of practice can shed light on some of the vexing philosophical questions of our century. The question we ask concerning the meaning of the world is derived from the standpoint of practice and not theory. From the standpoint of theory there is always meaning, and this meaning adheres to the world by virtue of the fact that it is open to interpretation or that it could be interpreted step by step. Interpretation is subject to the highest principle of all knowledge, namely, the principle of truth. According to the principle of truth, meaning is restricted to having statements correspond to the state of things as they are and from this standpoint constitutes no addition to the layer of meanings. Questions that are called existential are those that are concerned with the meaning of the world as to whether it corresponds or not to what we expect from it and is likely to promote these expectations. Existential questions are thus more intensive than the question concerning the meanings of our determinations from the standpoint of their submission to the principle of truth. The principle of truth, as the principle of theory, applies to all judgments, whereas the principle of the meanings of the response or non-response of our expectations is a more selective — and thus limited — principle than that of truth. The significance given to existential questions is one preceded by the preference of meaning of the practical sphere over against the neutral meaning of the theoretical sphere. In other words, it is not the world that poses these existential questions but man who prefers the existential to the theoretical attitude, or man who regards the theoretical attitude as secondary and places the decisive value on existential questions. This analysis of the relation between theory and practice leads us to conclude that the attribution of greater value to existential questions does not correspond to the relation of the dependence of practice on theory. We find that this preference granted to existential questions extends to the relations of the understanding between theory and practice. This granting of preference does not conform to the structure of the fundamental relations between the two spheres — of theory and of practice. The practical attitude as one of preference gives rise to the preference of existential meaning over against the material structure of the relations between the theoretical sphere and the practical sphere. The preference accorded to existential questions is based on the argument that the practical sphere is absorbed by the theoretical sphere and superseded by it, an argument frequently heard since the days of Kierkegaard. Our present analysis is designed to refute this argument by demonstrating that no such absorption takes place, for the practical sphere is dependent upon the theoretical sphere from the standpoint of the understanding and its objects. The existential argument is from this point of view a protest and not a conclusion derived from an adequate interpretation of the material structure of the spheres.

The relation between deed and preference — and the problem of the principle of preference as a problem that resides in the very nature of the practical sphere — will appear clearer when we come to discuss the sphere of ethical deeds.

NOTES

1 F. H. Bradley, "On Theoretical and Practical Activity," in *The Principles of Logic* (Oxford: 1950), Vol. II, pp. 714 ff.
2 F.H. Bradley, "On Pleasure, Pain, Desire, and Volition," in *Collected Essays* (Oxford: 1935), Vol. I, p. 272.
3 See Nathan Rotenstreich, *Spirit and Man, An Essay on Being and Value* (The Hague: 1963), pp. 3 ff.
4 See A. Schutzs, "Common-Sense and Scientific Interpretation of Human Action," in *Philosophy of the Social Sciences, A Reader*, edited by M. Natanson (New York: 1963), p. 310.
5 M. Heidegger, *Sein und Zeit* (Halle a.d. S: 1927), Part I, p. 144.
6 See Nathan Rotenstreich, "The Ontological Status of History," *American Philosophical Quarterly*, Vol. 9, No. 1 (January 1972), pp. 49 ff.

XIV. THE ETHICAL DEED

A

Having elucidated the main features of the nature of the practical sphere, we are now prepared to examine the specific nature of the ethical deed. The first question that arises is whether it is possible to consider the nature of the ethical deed without first considering the nature of the ethical norm — that is, the nature of the good to which the deed as an ethical deed is related. This problem is beset with grave difficulties; indeed, there is room for doubt as to the phenomenological isolation that separates the deed in its dynamic character from the good as representing the aspect of content. This difficult question can be answered only at the end of our inquiry, though even then some doubts will remain concerning this methodological and material isolation.

Nevertheless, if we are at times able to discern some features of the ethical deed as described in different ethical systems, we will have some standard for judging the plausibility of the method suggested here. It seems that there are aspects of the ethical deed that receive their peculiar nuance from the ethical system to which they are attached, yet these aspects also reveal qualities that are independent of these systems. Furthermore, the dynamic aspect of the ethical deed gives rise to the question concerning the source of the connection between the deed and the good, or rather, concerning the qualities of the deed that can reveal the connection between it and the good and not some other content, such as beauty. Here the isolation of the nature of the deed from that of the good in the last analysis contributes somewhat also to the clarification of the nature of the good. The isolation we are confronted with is a methodological one and it is introduced with the view to the normative pole of the deed *qua* ethical deed, a good deed, one that is related to the good or activated by it. These methodological observations are by way of an introduction to the discussion before us.

B

The ethical deed does not cease being a deed although it is characterized by a special quality. The above-mentioned qualities of the deed
and of the practical sphere are also found in the ethical deed, which
has an additional characteristic or an additional condensation of the
deed in general. We shall point out some of these qualities in the
nature of deeds in general that lend themselves to the condensation
leading the deed precisely along the path of the ethical deed.

Every deed points to an anticipation of the future. This anticipation
is a pre-practical relationship that accompanies the deed and imparts
to it the structure of a deed insofar as it is a pre-practical attitude. An
ethical deed is one that has a definite direction, from the standpoint
of the content, as to the general position of anticipation. In this, the
ethical deed is bound up with a definite, limited characteristic of the
end to which every deed is directed. In discussing the difference
between effect and end we pointed out above that the end is an
attainment that corresponds with the intention; the effect is an attainment that is not measured by the criterion of correspondence or
non-correspondence with the intention. From the standpoint of
the ethical deed we can here indicate two possibilities of understanding the relation between deed and intention. According to the
type of ethical doctrine represented by Aristotle, the ethical deed,
which is a materialization of the faculty hidden in man the doer, is
concerned with the deliberate realization of this faculty, namely,
man's intellectual faculty. The type of ethical doctrine represented by
Kant regards the ethical deed as one that incorporates an intention to
act in accordance with a principle. The principle is not rooted in a
faculty of man the doer nor is it a development of such a faculty. In
both of these types, however, intention is activated for the sake of an
end, whether the end be self-realization or the performance of deeds
motivated by a principle. In either case we see that the ethical deed is
one that is guided by a principle, whether this principle is the realization of a faculty of man the doer or the universal imperative of
reason that determines the the will of the doer.

The ethical deed is different from the deed as such in that it is
guided by a principle; this guidance, however, does not proceed
automatically. It is not in the nature of a deed to present itself as such
before us; what is presented to us is a decision in favor of a principle,
and the carrying out of this decision directs the deed. In the ethical
deed we have the intention through the principle and the intention
through the decision for the sake of the principle. The principle

awakens decision, and decision causes the doer to direct himself to the principle. If in every deed we can compare the achievement of the deed to the intention, in the ethical deed it is determined at the outset that we must compare the effect of the deed to the decision that led us to perform it. Here again we meet with two types of ethical doctrine. The first type is concerned with the effect of the deed as, for example, when it deals with the question whether a deed promotes the greatest happiness for the greatest number of human beings. The second type, however, revolves around the intention or motive of the deed, the manner in which we conceive its purpose, whether the purpose is to magnify the importance and prestige of the doer or to benefit one's fellowman. In both cases we value the deed because in the very nature of the deed there is an evaluation of a definite active direction or an end to which the intention of the doer is directed. A decision in favor of an active principle is an evaluation or a preference of this principle as a motive for deeds. Since we are in the sphere of value we can evaluate the deed according to a logic of value, including the value whether the deed is done according to the principle that is a principle of value or not.

In other words, in the sphere of the ethical deed we find ourselves confronting the problem of the justification for the deed. We apply to the deed the test of whether it was done in accordance with a principle, no matter what that principle may be. Thus, the principle itself is the justification of the deed. We evaluate the deed as to whether the principle applies to it or not — for example, the principle justifying a deed may be greater happiness for a greater number of people. But actually in practice we see that disappointment and distress follow in the wake of the deed; we then compare the results of the deed with the principle of its justification and thus evaluate the deed as ethical deed. We adopt this criterion of comparison in discussing many social problems, whether the principle of the deed's justification is human freedom or other social or political ends. Here the interpretation of the question concerning evaluation is one of the justification or non-justification of the deed performed. According to this principle of justification we compare the intention to the end to which it refers, and we measure the end in accordance with the intention that caused it or is related to it. In the very separation between effect that is only effect and effect that is achievement we have already instituted a comparison between achievement and intention. The aggregate of deeds presents us with qualities that are peculiar to the sphere of ethical deeds: (a) decision, which is a quality of the deed — and this is the difference between deed and simple occurrence — confronts us in the ethical sphere as decision for a definite direction of an occurrence when this direction is guided by a principle; (b) evaluation is the attribution of preference to a principle or to a direction of conduct that is guided by a principle; (c) justification is the principle according to which it is proper to grant preference to a particular direction of conduct over against another; evaluation as the granting of preference is bound up with justification and justification is realized in evaluation.

A reservation must be made at this point. The sphere of ethical deeds needs the doer, and from this point of view there is no difference whether we speak of a type of ethical doctrine where the principle resides in the effect or one where it resides in intention. Clearly, in the latter we must always assume a doer, for intention can pertain only to a doer. This can be seen in the formulation of Kant's categorical imperative which begins "Act so . . . " — the one who acts is the doer. But even the type of ethical doctrine concerned with the effects of deeds cannot escape from the doer: This type also assumes that the greatest happiness is not an automatic effect but that it involves intention on the part of the doer toward effects; the doer is guided by the results he wishes to attain. This guidance is an inner function that can be described as intention or the intention of the doer. Every principle of justification turns to the doer and is concerned with having him see the connection between the deed he performs and the reason for doing it or for what purpose it was initiated.

C

We do not wish to suggest that harmony reigns in the ethical sphere between the doer and the deed. On the contrary, in our view this sphere contains two indispensable components, doer and deed, thus permitting us to inquire into the relation of the doer to the deed and vice versa. Every ethical deed, containing as it does a preference for a given direction or a preference in accordance with a definite principle of justification, presupposes a doer as a factual or real cause of the preference. Even when the principle of preference is a universal principle, such as Kant's imperative to act in such a way that the rule that guides your deeds might become a universal principle, it assumes a particular individual who gives preference to the universality of the content of reason over against his particularistic urge. Even Kant's universal principle presupposes empirical man not yet absorbed in the universal plane, for without the positing of an empirical man there would be no room for a preference in a definite direction. Without the assumption of a man who is able not to prefer the universal and in spite of this chooses the universal there would be no point to this ethical doctrine propounded by Kant and, *a fortiori*, to that of Aristotle; for Aristotle was concerned with the fulfillment of the faculty which is always a faculty of a real being — that is, of a man who possesses the faculty of being rational but does not develop it without intention, unlike his organism, which grows without any special guidance. This quality that adheres to every deed that has a doer is most evident in the ethical deed, which involves deliberate preference on the part of the doer. The deed itself is a manifestation of such preference. Within the province of preferences itself we find various fundamental directions that these can take: The preference in the direction of effect to be attained or a preference in the direction of shaping the personality of the doer himself, as when we speak of an educational or ethical direction of character formation or the development of personality. Since the ethical sphere contains these two components, the deed and the doer, we have different possibilities of interpreting ethical doctrines. We can thus see in the sphere of ethical deeds either a direction toward a preference of goals, affairs, values, and similar formulations of the objectivistic direction — giving one's life for one's country, permitting one's self to be killed for the truth, and so forth — or we see a direction that stresses the value of the doer, such as a Stoic philosopher, a universal man of the Renaissance, or a genius of the Romantic period. We are not, of course, deciding here in favor of any of these directions but merely wish to point out that different conceptions of ethics or of the nature of the good depend on the poles in the sphere of the ethical deed. These conceptions attribute preferences to one of these two poles, an attribution that adheres particularly to the sphere of ethical deeds and is possible because of the structure of this sphere but is not necessarily indispensable to it.

D

The status of the doer with respect to the deed is expressed from the standpoint of the ethical deed in the concept of responsibility, a concept fraught with ethical meaning *par excellence* in that it is bound up with the character of the deed *qua* deed. In responsibility we find, first, an expression of the causal aspect of the doer with respect to the deed, this being simply its factual aspect. Only the doer who is the cause of the factual deed can assume the burden of the relation of the deed to himself as one involving guilt or innocence — both being kinds of responsibility. It is not the deed but the doer who is responsible, for it is the doer who occupies a total or extensive status over against his deeds or over against a particular deed. In responsibility the doer is judged in terms of the deed: The doer is the one who is judged and the deed determines the direction of the judgment, whether of guilt or of innocence. This does not mean to imply that there is a connection between the determination of responsibility as a relation of effect of the deed to the doer and the question concerning the freedom of the will and similar questions that pertain to this sphere. The important thing is to determine that the actual contact between the deed and the doer constitutes an ethical problem. The question of responsibility is an expression of this ethical problem within the area between the deed and the doer. This question, furthermore, presupposes a status of the doer that is not exhausted in a definite deed — which is the particular case — nor in a number of isolated deeds; the doer has a total status with respect to responsibility. Here we come upon the status of the content 'man' which is a content of theory, as explained above. The connection between the doer and the principle of justification has been noted; we can now say that the doer's reliance on responsibility with respect to the deed is based upon the principle of justification — that is, the doer is obliged to justify his deed or he will be judged guilty. It is understood, of course, that such a judgment of guilt, objectively expressed by punishment or fine, is a judgment within the context of justification. The general determination of responsibility is not bound up with any particular tendency of any ethical doctrine. Man becomes responsible both from the point of view of the pursuit of an end and from that of his obedience to an imperative. Or, *vice versa*, when we argue from the empirical point of view that man is not responsible for his deeds, we do not mean that there is no total doer who causes or performs the deed but that he is immersed in his atomic deeds. Obliteration of the category of the total doer, or in other words the category of man not identified with his deed, serves as a reason for liberating man from his responsibility. The connection thus arises between the question of man's totality and the question as to whether he has a faculty for distinguishing between good and evil, the faculty that is considered as the condition for attributing to man any responsibility whatever. It is clear that the distinction between good and evil is not to be identified with a particular deed but is a faculty that hovers, so to speak, above the deed. It is a faculty that finds expression in a definite deed accomplished by man. The obliteration of the

distinction between good and evil does away with evaluation, preferences, and principles of justification. These involve the status of the
doer over against the deed. The connection between the sphere of
ethical deeds and that of theory emerges in this context since the
problem of responsibility as an attitude with ethical meaning presupposes as a condition the integral character of man who from the
practical standpoint is a doer and from the standpoint of the ethical
deed is one that may be held responsible. The ethical category of
responsibility does not create the integral man but merely assumes
such a man as a presupposition. We cannot, therefore, say that man is
a postulate of ethics — that is, for ethics to be realized it is necessary
to assume or postulate the existence of man. Man is a prerequisite for
ethics but one that has no basis in the ethical sphere itself or in the
sphere of deeds as such; he is in reality a spherical content of theory.
Man the doer is an expression of man in his total status; responsible
man is an aspect of total man conceived from the standpoint of the
deed or of deeds.

This discussion may be summed up by distinguishing the elements
of the deed whereby the deed becomes an ethical deed. The first
component is the doer with respect to the deed. This is not yet a
determination with respect to the status of the doer himself over
against the deed, but since we have the theoretical content 'man', we
identify by way of interpretation this theoretical content with the
aspect of the practical sphere. We determine that the doer is man in
his totality or, at least, that he is more extensive than his deed.
Finally, the special ethical significance of man with respect to the
deed or of man as doer with respect to the deed is the meaning of
responsibility; this emerges from the ethical status of man as an active
cause of the deed in the direction of the doer to the deed, and the
meaning of material appropriation of his responsibility in the direction
of the deed to the doer. In responsibility the preference of the doer
with regard to the deed is evident, or the voice of responsibility
summons man to recognize this preference.

In the problem of responsibility we note the fusion between the
theoretical-factual approach, which determines that a certain person is
the performer of the deed *qua* its cause, and the approach that may be
called appropriation — that is, we attribute to a certain person or a
certain person attributes to himself a special relationship with respect
to the deed. In accordance with this relationship he calls himself
responsible as one to be judged for his deed, or he is called upon by
another to be judged for his deed either as innocent or guilty. In the
appropriation of the deed by the doer we have an act of integration on

the part of the doer over against himself. The act of appropriation is an integrative act and it presupposes man in a status of integration; or it may be said that when another calls me responsible he presupposes my integrality or he imposes his integrality upon me and as a result I am required to appropriate the deed to myself with all the consequences it entails. The theoretical assumption of total man, then, is the *terminus a quo* for the transition to the attribution of appropriation in the sphere of the ethical deed. From this point of view it is evident that the quality of the ethical deed from the aspect of its appropriation by the doer and from the aspect of his responsibility is not a quality derived from the practical sphere. It is one that is bound up with the ethical significance of the theoretical presupposition of the position of man.

E

The connection between the ethical sphere and the theoretical content 'man' is conspicuous because the intermediate link between the sphere of ethics and the sphere of theory is that of responsibility. The connection between the spheres, however, is also apparent in the other spherical contents of theory, 'world' and 'time', even though it is not as significant with respect to the direction of ethical deeds as is the content 'man'. We shall continue with a clarification of the content 'time' and then return to the topic of responsibility.

The content 'time' is implied in every analysis of responsibility and in every relation between deeds and doer. In speaking of responsibility we assume an event that preceded in time, that is, that a deed done cannot be undone. A deed once performed, then, will have effects in subsequent time. The deed itself, insofar as it has its source in the doer, takes place in time. It thus has some of the formal qualities of time, namely, that it comes after the deed or the event that preceded it and is in turn followed by deeds and events. The assumption of responsibility means that there is succession in time and that it proceeds in one direction only and that doer and deed are reciprocally related. The sphere of ethical conduct, whose axis is in the concept of responsibility, does not invalidate the status of time; but the ethical meaning of responsibility makes a breach into time, as it were, and thus adds to it an extratemporal dimension. It is clear that we here have a relation to time since we speak of responsibility in connection with deeds within time. It is precisely because deeds are isolated and dispersed and scattered through time that we have the problem of their integration. This problem does not exist on the level of deeds themselves but only on the level of their appropriation by the doer. The concept of responsibility and the problem connected with it, then, presuppose time but they are characterized by a kind of an ideal estrangement with respect to it. The deed that is done cannot be undone, but it can be attributed to the whole man who is within time and who has also a status over against it. As far as the theoretical content of time is concerned, we cannot argue that this content itself has ethical meaning as does the content 'man'. But the content 'time' has a secondary ethical meaning since it is a correlative member of the ethical content of responsibility rooted in the theoretical content 'man'.

This also applies to the theoretical content 'world'. We have already observed that this content denotes totality and, among others, the totality of eventualities. In ethical discourse the world appears as the correlative term to doing, that is, the world is the sphere in which the deed takes place and which also contains its active cause, the doer. The doer is not exhausted in the world because of his integrative meaning, a meaning that pertains to him and not to the visible world. But the doer, insofar as he is the cause of a deed performed in time, introduces the deed into the world either because of an end he desires to attain through it or because of some effect he anticipates from it. Deeds are always fragmentary, and the world as a totality permits these fragmentary deeds and accepts them.

The world is the total sphere of realization, and thus appears as a neutral and not as an ethical content. The ethical content of deeds is concerned with the attribution of uniqueness or particularity to events which, in the final analysis, are included in the common sphere of the world. The world appears as an expanse over against which and in which condensation takes place. The course of things within the world is that of organic decay, to select one example, and the ethical deed which is designed to bring health to the organism intervenes in this process of the world with a remedy for the organism. It thus gives definite direction to the course of events in the world by choosing one of many possibilities to effect this end as, in the example cited above, by choosing a remedy instead of decay. We might say, in other words, that the world offers a number of possibilities; the ethical deed selects one of these possibilities by preference and realizes it in one direction and not another. The world has also the possibility of destruction as well as recovery; the ethical deed chooses the latter and directs events to that end.

This connection with the world is expressed in another phase of the ethical deed. When the ethical deed envisages some future act, such as an increase of happiness for posterity, it assumes that there will be people in the future whom the present deed will benefit. The existence of people in the future is not an effect of the ethical deed itself but an assumption or anticipation preceding the deed. Anticipation refers not only to a future end but also to the human subjects to whom this end is related. The ethical deed assumes as an extra-ethical datum the existence of men in the future. As a result of this assumption it is able to direct itself to the level of a content and conduct beyond the basic level of the existence of men. This relationship to the existence of men is a relationship to time and the world at once; it has no direct ethical meaning but an indirect, secondary ethical meaning because of the additional aspects of ethical conduct that are not possible without the assumption of time and the world. The ethical deed erects an additional story above this basic, implied assumption.

This difference, from the standpoint of the ethical deed, between the status of the content 'man' and the status of the contents 'time' and 'world' indicate that the ethical deed is the work of man and not of time and the world, being a deed that requires man as the doer. The content 'man' thus is an active factor in the very nature of the ethical deed; the contents 'time' and 'world' are only correlatives to which the ethical deed is related but which are not part of its content in the restricted sense of this concept. Even when the ethical deed refers to inanimate nature, the organic world of material data, and even when it is directed by the imperative "Thou shalt not destroy" in its all-inclusive sense, it does not cease to be a deed performed by man. Man is the subject of the ethical deed since he is its cause, and this gives him a superior ethical status compared to the other spherical entities of theory. We find ourselves within a broad system of spherical contents of theory, but from the standpoint of the ethical deed these contents have a specific value: One content is central and the others are correlatives — the spherical content 'man' is central and the contents 'time' and 'world' are correlative.

F

This special connection of the ethical deed to the content 'man' again obliges us to posit the central status of the category of responsibility in the sphere of the ethical deed, a category that is nothing but the ethical interpretation of man's total status within the sphere of the

ethical deed. The connection between man as a whole and the ethical
deed, which is mediated through the category of responsibility, is
concerned with the determination that man as a totality can be
responsible, that he can appropriate the deed and as its cause and
originator justify it, that is, he can be evaluated on the basis of his
deed. This ability of man to be responsible makes it possible for us to
formulate some imperatives in connection with the category of
responsibility.

A. "Act in such a manner that you will consent to be responsible
for the deed you perform" — that is, be prepared to appropriate to
yourself the deed you have done. This imperative refers to the formal
relation between the deed and the doer. In terms of this relation man
will not disappear; he acknowledges his causal relation to the deed as a
factual relation. But to the determination of this fact the imperative
adds the acknowledgment on man's part of the existence of this causal
relation.

B. "Act in such a manner that you would wish to be responsible for
the deed you perform because of its content." This imperative no
longer refers to the causal relationship between the doer and the deed
from the factual point of view, but urges man to perform a deed
whose content, to put it negatively, will not discourage him from
wishing to be responsible for the deed or, in positive terms, whose
content is such that man would wish to identify himself with the deed
since it is a deed that should be done. This can be illustrated by a
simple example: A man causes an accident and, according to the first
imperative, he should regard himself as being the cause and acknowledge it. According to the second imperative, man is required to do a
deed that is helpful and not harmful; he should wish to assume responsibility for the deed not because he caused it, but because the deed is
such that it is proper that man should perform it and be responsible
for it. The element of an evaluative justification is here introduced in
the second imperative; because of justification man has reasons why
he is pleased with a deed that he performs and does not reject it. Not
only does he relate himself to his deed, according to the first imperative, but he does so because of the identification in the content
between his intention to carry out the deed and the deed he performs.
The justification in this case is expressed in the fact that man could
say that the deed corresponds to his intention. Man is able, according
to the first formulation, to take upon himself a formal responsibility
but he can argue that the deed he has performed does not correspond
to his intention; according to the second formulation of the imperative of responsibility, man should be prepared to assume responsi-

bility by acknowledging that the accomplished deed corresponds to his intention and is not merely the effect of his action but the objective of it. It is evident that the second imperative presupposes the first, that is, the meaningful relation between the deed and the doer presupposes a causal relation between them. But this reciprocal dependency does not blur the distinction between these aspects in the attribution of the deed to the doer. In the first imperative we find support for the view that the deed must not be arbitrary; in the second imperative the opposition to arbitrariness is explicit, for it is in the nature of the deed that I assume responsibility in accordance with a justification that is not arbitrary, arbitrariness and justification being contradictory and mutually exclusive.

This phenomenological explanation of the ethical deed leads us to the content or rather to the threshold of the content of this deed. We have thus far discussed the direction and the demand for preference without implying, however, that the latter was a result of the former. There is a gap between actual conduct and demand, so that the one cannot be derived from the other; but the attribution of the deed to the doer makes it possible, but not more, to demand such attribution. The demand for preference is ultimately a demand for responsibility in accordance with the second imperative, namely, to act so that we can be judged in the light of the deed we preferred to do in conformity with the principle of the justification of deeds. We can be thus judged because we have a total functional status with respect to deeds and we are not opaque or dispersed as are deeds.

If we understand the spherical entity 'man' as theoretical and not practical, we cannot support Kant's trenchant formulation "You can because you ought."[1] We would rather say: Since you can, that is, since you have a causal status with respect to deeds from the theoretical standpoint of the attribution of deeds to the doer, then you ought — that is, then you are obliged to take responsibility upon yourself and to acknowledge attribution on the factual level and the principle of justification on the level of meaning. Justification is an addition to the character of deeds in their connection with the doer, but it is not the product of invention or whim. The imperative in its second formulation is an extended interpretation of the first imperative in accordance with the inner logic of the ethical system.[2]

Within the relationship of responsibility we find the relationship of the doer to himself. The doer attributes to himself the deeds he performs or someone else attributes them to him. The moment I perform a definite deed there arises the question of responsibility according to the two formulations set forth above: That I consent to assume responsibility and desire to endure it from the standpoint of the direction of deeds. In this relation of the doer to himself incorporated in responsibility there is a definite paradox of ethical conduct and deeds. These ethical deeds are a material realization outside the doer, on the one hand, and have an egocentric element of relations to the doer on the other hand. This duality of the direction to the deeds and the relationship of the doer to himself is another expression of the duality of the sphere of ethical deeds which is based on the relation between the two poles of deed and doer. Another expression of this duality is in the sphere of religion when in a given custom or rite one expresses obedience to the will of God and at the same time, however, is concerned with his personal salvation. Because of this duality and because the concept of responsibility always refers to the doer himself, we see once more that complete de-personalization is not possible in the sphere of deeds and *a fortiori* in the sphere of ethical deeds.[3]

This relation of the doer to himself constitutes a situation in which the doer takes into account the next stage in the future. The connection to time is clear and need not be stressed here. In the doer's relation to himself he envisages the next stage, that is, whether he will consent to assume responsibility and wish to see it through or, in short, whether he will be able to take upon himself the consequences of the principle of justification. This stage, in which the doer envisages a subsequent stage, may be formulated as follows: The doer selects one particular course in preference to others for he takes into consideration the responsibility imposed upon him or which he has imposed upon himself. I prefer not to harm another person because I take him into consideration, this being the material side of the deed. I prefer a certain course because I weigh the value of my deed with respect to my responsibility and to myself as a responsible agent, this being the egocentric side of the deed. In preferring one course to another I also take my stand as a doer in the subsequent stage of my conduct and as the responsible agent of my acts. Preference in this case is the manifestation of consideration, or consideration is the reason for those deeds that are preferred. When I prefer a definite deed, I consent to a certain course of events of which I am the cause and which are directed by my preference. This consent, however, is for the sake of the preference, that is, it is a consenting in the direction of deeds that I consider proper to prefer and in my status as a doer in the next stage of my conduct. In this consideration of the effects of deeds with respect to the direction of the deed and with respect to the responsibility of the doer we find a fusion between a cognitive and an active element.

Concerning the status of preference and consideration it should be observed that these engender deeds and give them expression in the sphere of social intercourse among men. Preference induces me not to harm my fellowman or to benefit him, this being the manifest aspect as it appears in public acts. This external aspect of preference places it in the sphere of public conduct. But preference also has an inner aspect, for although the deed itself is visible the motives that prompted it remain hidden. The reason for a deed is the consideration of one's fellowman or the consideration of the doer. These aspects of the deed are not manifest; they exist between the doer and the deed. We thus find in the sphere of ethical deeds an element that is considered the condition of deeds, the element of preference, which is not a visible, public deed.

G

This explains the connection between the element of preference in ethical deeds and the element of restraint. Faced with several possibilities of action, of these we prefer one because of one of the considerations presented before. In the very act of preferring I restrain my activity in a definite direction and prepare myself for a subsequent assumption of responsibility because of the definite direction I have chosen or preferred. The empirical hypothesis of ethical conduct is that there are various paths of conduct in life and that there are various forces at work that impel us in different directions. In the act of preference I limit the world and constrain it into a definite path and thereby also constrain myself to follow in this path. The element of preference is a positive element that gives direction to deeds; the element of restraint is a negative element that is a concomitant of the positive element and serves as a kind of a check in the adoption of various possible courses by rejecting those that are not conducive to the desired end. In preference, guidance is implied, and in restraint, a curbing or bridling.

This notion of restraint is to be found in the various types of ethical systems. In the Aristotelian doctrine it appears as the golden mean between extremes, in Stoicism as the subjection of conduct to contemplation, in Kant as the rejection of considerations of happiness in ethical conduct, and for the Utilitarians as the sacrifice of immediate pleasures for future rewards. The element of restraint, even more than that of preference, refers to empirical faculties of man that are designed for the purpose of finding a channel for themselves in various

activities. Restraint, however, curbs these empirical urges and inclinations. We can say that the principle of ethical deeds is manifest to us
in the principle of justification of deeds. It therefore reveals itself to
us as a principle that conducts us in a definite direction of preference,
a preference of deeds or of the doer who assumes responsibility. With
regard to the concept of responsibility it may be said that the doer
exercises restraint because he takes into consideration the possibility
or the impossibility of undertaking responsibility at the next stage. We
notice once more how these various elements in the nature of the
ethical deed converge in the notion of the formation or the molding
of the doer, a notion that is complementary to the direction of the
deed or parallel to it. The sphere of ethics is concerned not only with
isolated deeds but also with the nature of the doer or, in other words,
the principle of justification applies both to deeds and doer. The
double expression of the principle of justification as a single principle
should be stressed. To put it another way, the sphere of ethical deeds
has onè pole in accordance with its material direction and another
pole in accordance with the doer's status with respect to deeds.

C. The ethical imperative of conduct may thus also be formulated:
"Act so as to establish a connection between the direction of deeds
and the status of the doer," or "Act so that the multitude of deeds
will not conceal or efface the doer and, conversely, as a result of the
multitude of his concerns the doer will not fall into a state where he
will refrain from performing deeds." This formulation requires an
explanation. The first part states that the man who performs many
deeds that have a definite form or *Gestalt* performs them in accordance with imperatives or commandments. With respect to the many
deeds he performs, man is the bearer of intentions and decisions to
perform deeds in a definite direction. The ethical imperative in this
formulation obliges us to heed the two poles of the ethical sphere:
Deeds with a definite direction and man, who decides the direction in
the light of imperatives and commandments. According to the second
part of the formulation man is apprehensive lest his deed should make
him responsible for its consequences and effects in reality. The fear of
responsibility may cause man to refrain from performing his deeds and
render him inactive. But since the status of the doer is one of the
expressions of man as a totality, man is required to find a way
between the preservation of his position among deeds and at the same
time outside of deeds. It is always possible to argue that to refrain
from doing a thing is also a deed and involves the same responsibility
as its performance: There is no way of escaping responsibility.

Another thought requires stressing at this point, namely, that the expression of the doer with respect to the direction of the deeds he performs is an expression of preference. Preference has, as already stated, a public aspect which consists in the doing of one definite thing and not another, and it has in addition an inner or private aspect.

  D. Finally, the ethical imperative also may be formulated as follows: "Act so that there will always be a possibility of preference, a preference for you and for your fellowman." The operative meaning of this formulation of the ethical imperative requires us to act so as never to preclude a decision of preference that would remove us from the next stage of our conduct. More exactly, it requires that we do not cause our fellowman to fear that he will be deprived of the possibility of preference within the sphere of his activities or that his deeds will be circumscribed by submission to us or interfered with chemically or mechanically, so that in the end he would think of himself as a puppet rather than as a creator of preferences. This matter finds concrete meaning in the social intercourse between men and within organized society. The preservation of the possibiility of preference means the creation of social relations that involve matters for decision and permit men to exercise their preferences. In such a social reality which preserves and acknowledges the element of preference, all things are not made to depend on traditional patterns and arrangements embodied in institutions created by a small minority and imposed upon the majority. Our fellowman is not the object but the subject of preferences. In formulating the imperative concerning the preservation of preferences and possibilities resulting from them, we have in mind all people and not any particular individual.

  From the importance attached to the imperative of preference we see again that in the sphere of ethics we are dealing not only with the direction of deeds but also with the status of the doer, a circumstance that is evident from the value of the doer within this sphere as well as from the ontological and ethical value attached to the category of responsibility. The ethical sphere is a sphere that embraces both deed and a doer who exercises preferences. Here again we come upon the status of man as a total being in the ethical sphere since the imperative now refers to the possibilities of preferences open to man as a doer. A parallelism thus emerges between man's status from the standpoint of responsibility and his status from the standpoint of preference. In these two aspects of the sphere of ethical deeds we see that man finds expression in his deeds and that he is at the same time separated from them. This is the status of man judging himself and consequently the status of a reflective man. We thus find that the sphere of ethics

presupposes man as a reflective being, and the ethical expression of
this reflection is to be found in responsibility and in preference.

H

Discussion of the ethical deed rests on the discernment of structural or
formal qualities of the deed as such; it also leads us to a consideration
of the qualities of the good, for these qualities constitute one aspect
of the qualities of deeds. In this context 'the good' means the principle that underlies the formulation of previous imperatives. We may
thus say: It is good to act so that the doer will be responsible with
respect to the deed or deeds of which he is the cause; it is good to
arrange patterns of reality in which man is responsible; it is good to
act so that the doer will be presented with preferences, for these are
the factual and material background of his existence as well as that of
his fellowman; it is good to act so that there will be social arrangements containing areas that are not determined or organized any more
than is necessary; it is good to act in a definite direction of preferences
— that is, good is a preference, but better is a preference in the
direction of good. It is good to maintain a preference in the direction
of the preservation of life, and this is better than a preference in the
direction of the destruction of life; the preference in the direction of
giving all men opportunities is better than restricting them to the few,
and so forth.

We understand the material aspect of the ethical deed as a deed that
is directed to the good; the directions of the good or of preference
toward the good are not necessarily those that make for harmony. We
say, for example, that it is good that there are preferences and it is
good that there are preferences in the direction of the good. This
matter has ethical significance and sometimes concrete political significance. The fact that it is good that there are preferences is a statement that can be translated to the concrete sphere: It is good for men
to live in a society and take part in its political and social institutions
which they shall be able to change in the light of their preferences,
and so forth. This is one aspect of the sphere of deeds: The core of
the deed resides in the fact that its source is in preference and
conditions that make it possible. Thus, it is good if the way is open for
preferences, that is, always to decide in favor of preferences and to
prefer preferences. But to stress this aspect of the practical sphere is
no assurance of the direction these preferences will take, for we are
certain only of the nature of the attitude of the preference and not of

its quality. The question still remains: Formal preference can decide in favor of the death penalty or waging a war or pursuing a policy of appeasement and similar matters whose ethical and political content is, to say the least, controversial. It may therefore be concluded that it is better to have preferences than not to have them, it is better to preserve life than to wage war; but it may sometimes be better to wage war, against the Nazis for example, for this may be preferable to appeasing them or being subjugated by them. It is proper, to cite another example, for a man to insist on his rights and have them defended in the courts of law; he may not always be justified in his demands but he is entitled to a hearing and his very complaint is in itself a part of justice. We thus see that the directions of preference have different and sometimes contradictory aspects as, for example, a war of national liberation over against the destruction it brings in its wake or the conflict of loyalty between family and country. Conflicting loyalties are also apparent in ethical decisions, such as refusing to tell a lie to save a friend or preserve life. There are conflicting preferences in choosing among the different kinds of good itself, such as telling the truth and preserving life. Preference does not constitute a unified whole; neither are acts performed in the practical sphere a total unity. Acts are isolated and dispersed, and their relations to the principle of justification or to the principle of the good are not given at the outset. The conflict between telling the truth and the preservation of life can be seen as a conflict between a material good and a good in its relation to the doer. When I refrain from telling a lie even at the risk of jeopardizing human life, I take the strict position that the direction of preference is that of truth; and when I forego speaking the truth in order to preserve life, I regard the preservation of life to be the prime duty of the responsible doer. A decision or preference with respect to the direction of responsibility is not given in this instance at the outset, and no one preference may be considered arbitrary. Preferences are rooted in the inner logic of the sphere of ethical deeds and in their various relations to the good, the good in the preservation of the doer and the good in the preference of the material direction of conduct, as in the example of speaking the truth; the practical character of deeds that are directed to the good entail other determinations of its content, for the good is not one unified whole. The fragmentation of the good has two manifestations: Even when the good means the preservation of life, there is no one total act that can establish this principle for all time. I may on one occasion have performed a deed that saved a human life; a moment later I am faced with the same problem and have to apply this principle with respect to another life. Not only is there no deed that can totally realize a principle, but there is no deed that can totally realize all principles, that is, the principles of the various directions of preferences. It is possible that each one of these directions may be justified in itself and thus bring the doer into conflict with some other preference, as the conflict between the preservation of life and speaking the truth.

This matter becomes clearer when we recall that the deed, including the ethical deed, occurs in a definite empirical reality and that at the time when the ethical act occurs, the whole of reality is not totally imbued with ethical principles. Reality is given and it is for us to perform the ethical deed that we have preferred within this reality as it is. It may be that the strict principle of justice cannot be applied to it, for justice, in the limited sense of this term, may be contested: For example, when a pupil in school interprets his punishment as a total misfortune and not commensurate with his misdeed, and as a result leaves school. There are cases where we would argue that the abstract principle of justice calls for a prison sentence — for example, when a mother steals bread for her children. But a sentence may not be imposed in a concrete case. Here we necessarily come upon a definite interpretation of the principle of justice because of material consider-ations relative to the application of this principle in reality where the empirical background of the deed and the doer have to be taken into consideration. We must consider our responsibility to the doer and this may conflict with our responsibility toward the material principle of our deeds, such as the principle of not depriving another of his property. This does not mean that conduct in accordance with the observance of empirical facts obliges us not to conduct ourselves in a definite normative manner, but our consideration for the human agent of the deed must also consider his empirical situation. We are thus faced with the possibility of a real conflict in terms of acting in accordance with a material principle on the one hand, or in accord-ance with our responsibility to the doer, a human being acting under definite empirical conditions on the other.

To take empirical conditions into consideration involves knowledge; we must be able to describe the empirical conditions in which the doer found himself and the conclusions we arrived at as a result of our observations. Consideration is normative behavior, but knowledge is cognitive or material behavior, in the broad sense of this term. Consider-ation leads us to a knowledge of the empirical conditions of the doer; knowledge or the discovery of knowledge leads us to adopt a certain mode of behavior over against the doer placed amid conditions that have been clarified to us through our cognitive relationship to them. The reasons that impel us to obtain knowledge are in this case normative, that is, they are rooted in the principle of consideration; knowledge itself is from the normative point of view neutral. But since we began with knowledge for the sake of normative behavior, we arrive at the normative by translating the findings of knowledge into normative conclusions, just as we do in the case of the doer placed amid definite social conditions. The element of knowledge, however, is not limited to the empirical aspects of any particular condition, but applies to the status of the doer as a responsible being. The doer is responsible even when he does not follow the strict principle of doing justice and, as in the case of the mother who steals bread for her hungry children, we decide that this responsibility is prior or superior to that of safeguarding the property of others or considering it to be inviolate. We do not pass beyond the limits of the category of responsibility; we interpret this category in the light of the circumstances involved. Our cognitive insight into man as a responsible being remains unshaken: From the standpoint of ethical deeds we hold every man responsible. This cognitive insight is the substratum of ethical determination.

I

From all this there emerges the place occupied by the will in the sphere of ethical deeds. The will bears a definite relation to what is called choice, that is, the will is the human faculty to act from motives that stem from attitudes, the ability to make decisions and to act upon them. In connection with this ability we should bear in mind the distinction between the will, strictly speaking, and a stimulus, impulse, or desire. The nature of the will reveals the connection between it and preference: The will is the motive of preference and contains within it the direction indicated by preference. The desire to attain some definite end is present in urges and impulses, on the one hand, and in the will on the other. The difference between the two lies in that the former is attracted toward a definite direction whereas the latter is guided by the goal it wishes to reach; the one seeks an outlet and the other pursues an end. The will is a correlate of an end, being the motive to that end. A stimulus leads to an effect but not to an end, for it does not contain the element of intention. Preference is both motive and direction; the will is the active element or the operational aspect of preference.

Different ethical doctrines speak of the guiding or formative func-

tion of the will derived from the principle of preference on the part of
the will seeking to attain that which has been determined to be the
proper object of its striving. The formative function of the will implies
the existence of motives for proper actions even though there may be
no opportunity for exercising them here and now; it involves the
summoning up of hidden forces to perform acts indicated by preference, so that it may be said to constitute a kind of educational discipline for ethical deeds, although in speaking of direction of the
formative power of the will we refer to the direction toward the doer
and not toward the deed. The will is the motive for deeds, giving rise
to them and directing them. The formed will is the peculiar attribute
of the doer revealed in his deeds. The formation of the will is also the
formation of the doer or the definite manifestation of the doer to
whom the ethical direction or the ethical imperative refers. When we
formulate the ethical imperative in the general statement "act so,"
we have in mind the outer manifestation of the deed as well as the will
of the doer revealed in the deed. This imperative thus refers to both
the deed and the will. The will appears as an operational factor in the
service of the deed, of the preference and of the responsibility. When
the will functions in a certain direction, responsibility becomes possible; but responsibility is possible because the will has already been
posited as the motive of the deed. We must again point out the union
of the factitive element and the ethical component, in the limited
sense of the term, within the will. The will as motive is a factitive
element, although not an evident one as the external act itself. As such
it is also the element that makes possible the attribution of the deed
to the doer within the will. It makes possible the transfer of the deed
in its facticity to the level of attribution that is the bearer of ethical
meaning, this being the double meaning of the determination of
responsibility.

The will, then, is a motive force, an operational and dynamic element. The distinction between the will as motive and impulse or desire
as motives is that the will implies an element of knowledge, an element of consent to act in a certain direction. This consent consists in a
cognitive acknowledgment of this direction and its content and of the
authority of this direction to use a preferred content to stimulate the
will. These aspects of the will lie in its dynamic nature but they are
themselves bound up with a content and are hence objects of knowledge. The formation of the will is a formation of the motives of
action in the direction of consent or in a direction that merits consent,
and we cannot speak of the will apart from these cognitive aspects.
Furthermore, the will as a stimulus of motive is a concomitant of

consent, and it is accompanied by an anticipation of the conceived end and of the direction of preference. To the extent that the will is motive and preference it is an act. We make a distinction between the operational factor, the will, and the direction of activity, preference. Because of this distinction we must include in the will a definite anticipation of the direction of activity found in preference, so that it appears again that an element of cognition is implied or absorbed in the will. This element of consent is to be found in the various types of ethical doctrine: In Aristotle it appears as the consent to realize man's end in knowledge, a consent which precedes realization for it is the motive force that impels us to realization; in Kant it appears as the consent to make the general principle of conduct the regulative maxim of conduct and the consent to the meaning of equality in the general principle and in the status of man as an end in himself and not merely a means. The formation of the will, then, is at the same time an incentive of consent and a preparation for consent. Corresponding to what has been said before concerning the variations of the ethical imperative, we can now formulate it as follows: "Act so, that there will always be a will for preference and a will for preference in the direction of the ought," and "Act so, that the act will always be made with the consent to act and to act in the direction of the ought." This formulation shows that the interest of the will in the deed and the reliance on the will require an element of a knowledge of content, a knowledge that consists of the dynamic factors included under the broad concept of the 'will'. The motives of the act are thus dynamic-volitional, on the one hand, and material-cognitive on the other. Knowledge is not introduced here for the sake of knowledge but in order to direct the dynamic motive, the will; but the instrumental status of knowledge for the sake of the dynamic motive cannot remove the cognitive factor from the sphere of the ethical act. The ethical act is bound up with man the doer, that is, to one who in this matter knows how to channel his knowledge in the direction of the act; but this does not affect the deed and its motives from the standpoint of the will; the subjection of knowledge in the service of the act is the concern of consent, that is, it cannot be without an understanding of the relations between the cognitive and the practical sphere or the relations between a definite area of knowledge and a definite area of acts. For not everything that is known in the act is a content of preference; it is not the entire world of knowledge, including its physical and biological aspects, that is of value for acts; from this world of knowledge we select those elements that are significant for our acts and this selection involves knowledge and an understanding of what is significant and what is not significant for our acts. We have here the tendency not to use knowledge merely for its own sake but as a starting point for deeds.

J

The foregoing discussion has shown that the directions of preference of the ethical deed are two in number, a direction toward the preferred object and a direction toward the preferring subject. The significance of the latter is evident in all the imperatives in the ethical sphere that refer to man's body as, for example, the ethical imperative not to inflict bodily harm both as a daily precept and as a maxim of the medical practice with reference to patients, and similar imperatives with respect to the body in a positive sense, such as extending physical help, promoting health, and other corollaries of the ethical imperative. Preference applies not only to the ends toward which we strive and which we create by our intentionality as, for example, the creation of equality which is an end in the ethical sphere and which is realized by deeds within that sphere. In contradistinction to this the end of preserving the body falls within the ethical sphere, but it is connected with man's body which has a status in the factual sphere and as such is an ethical subject in accordance with its first definition. The pre-ethical, factual status of the body becomes an ethical status because of the logic of the ethical sphere, a logic that operates in a direction toward things outside the doer and also toward things involved in the doer. The body is granted an ethical status, or rather, it is raised from the factual level to the level of ethical meaning because of the relationship between the body and its owner, man the doer, who has an ethical status in accordance with the interpretation given to the content 'man' from the standpoint of the sphere of ethical deeds. We can express this thought in other words by saying that since the matter for the sake of which we act demands acknowledgment or is on a plane that is already acknowledged, man the doer, including his body, also demands acknowledgment. The man who acts is an extensive entity, an entity that is particularized in various subsidiary spheres. These are man's body, his private domain that demands acknowledgment for itself and hence protection from infringement and violation by the public domain without; the cultivation of his capacities through education; and similar definte expressions of the whole man in his various particularized functions and activities. Because of the relationship to the total content 'man', there is a continuous transformation of definite contents that express this total content, a transformation from the level of facticity to the level of ethical demand, including the demand for the preference of these empirical expressions of man.

We see then a definite relation of man the doer to the ends he has preferred, and the relation of man to himself as a doer and as immersed in definite expressions of his bodily, educational, social existence, and so forth. These two directions of relations presuppose the existence of man the doer, a spontaneous being capable of assuming a position of relation to himself. As a spontaneous being, man is the ontological condition for the existence of ethical deeds and his preservation as such a being is one of the contents of the ethical deeds. The ontological condition of ethics also becomes one of the norms of ethics. The interpretation of the ontological status of man as having normative meaning thus falls within the limits of ethics. This interpretation is an act of man himself and an expression of spontaneity, which in this case is the spontaneity of man's self-understanding or the spontaneity whereby man interprets himself from the standpoint of his factual qualities and from the standpoint of their normative meaning. In the interpretation of factual qualities we are confronted with an act of contemplation, of understanding or reflection. No logical conclusion is drawn here; things are here interpreted and apprehended from the factual point of view and a leap is made to the normative point of view. We cannot derive the normative meaning of man's existence as a spontaneous or reflective being from the fact that he is a spontaneous or reflective being. Our involvement in the sphere of ethics is an act of contemplation or of reflection. It is an act in which man abstracts himself from a description of factual qualities and imparts ethical-normative meaning to the qualities revealed by his self-understanding which interprets these qualities in an ethical sense. In this we do not forfeit the connection to man's factual qualities; yet we no longer adhere only to the description of these qualities the moment we discuss the nature of ethical deeds and the understanding of these deeds in accordance with the directions of the preference that distinguishes them. The sphere of ethical deeds involves a constant decision in favor of the leap from the factitious to the normative, a leap whereby the level of preference is created. This level becomes manifest also when the preference refers to man himself as he interprets himself on the factual level by means of a cognitive process that deals with facts. Decision takes place not only with respect to definite contents in the sphere of the ethical deed, but also with respect to our connection with the sphere of ethical deeds. It is thus possible to argue that the ethical sphere is based on a kind of *petitio principi*, that is, it takes for granted a premise which is equivalent to the conclusion. This argument loses some of its force when it is pointed out that this constant decision in favor of the content of ethics is possible because man, being a creature of understanding, is able to understand himself and be in a position to make decisions. This position is different from that of the understanding, but it presupposes the position of the understanding as one of its necessary conditions. The fact that there is a connection between the understanding and decision, the understanding being a condition for decision, leads us to conclude that the sphere of ethical deeds is a sphere that constructs itself, that is, there is no first step in the direction of the transition from the sphere of facts to the sphere of ethics. Every first step presupposes a previous step and hence it is always a second step. The understanding is an element of ethics, but it does not constitute a sufficient condition for it; without understanding there is no ethics, but understanding alone is not ethics. Decision itself is interpretation; interpretation is an act of understanding, but decision contains more than understanding and this something more cannot be derived from understanding.

K

From all this we can draw a conclusion concerning the nature of the relations between the theoretical sphere and the sphere of ethical deeds. The sphere of ethical deeds differs from the sphere of theory just as the sphere of acts in general differs from the sphere of theory; whatever is found in deeds is to be found in the sphere of ethical deeds, only that the latter is characterized by some peculiar features of its own which clearly relate it to the basic act of theory, which is an act of the understanding, and to one of the spherical contents of theory, namely, man. The sphere of ethical deeds assumes as its conceptual presupposition the content 'man' and bestows an ethical status on this content. Without the theoretical content 'man' we have no ethics; for the sake of ethics this content confers upon itself not only a status of the understanding that is neutral but also a normative status. The conceptual tool of interpretation is within the domain of ethics but the content of interpretation, the content from the standpoint of preference, is an addition in accordance with the logical faculty of the sphere of ethical deeds. We have here a material dependence of the sphere of ethical deeds, but we also have an addition that belongs to the essence of this sphere, an addition that refers to the sphere of theory which is the condition for the sphere of ethical deeds. The content of theory, which is the content 'man', has an independent status with respect to the sphere of ethical deeds. From the standpoint of this sphere the independent status of man is deepened, so to speak, because it acquires for itself a content and a value beyond the qualities put forward from a theoretical point of view. Ethics has a status conditioned by theory in its ontological aspect, but it also has an independent status in its aspect as meaning. We no longer speak of a preference for theory over against practice or deeds but of a dependence of deeds on theory. In the matter of ethical deeds, however, we return to the content of theory after discussing the qualities of deeds.

1 Kant's formulation is as follows: "He [man] judges, therefore, that he can do something because he knows that he ought" (*Critique of Practical Reason*, § 6, quoted from Lewis White Beck's translation, p. 30).

2 This has been dealt with exhaustively in my book, *On the Human Subject, Studies in the Phenomenology of Ethics and Politics* (Springfield, Illinois: 1966).

3 There is a difference here between the sphere of knowledge and the sphere of ethics: In knowledge the direction is toward objectivity, that is, to give an account of the state of things as it is. The principle of giving such an account is the principle of truth, because this principle guides the direction from the knower to the known. In the sphere of ethics the direction has two arrows at once; toward the meaning of the deed and the status of the doer. See my article, "Person and Responsibility," in *Der Mensch – Subjekt und Objekt, Fesbilinft für Adam Schaff* (Vienna: 1973) pp. 263 ff.

XV. THE TECHNICAL ACT AND TECHNOLOGY

A

An ethical act rests on the formation of the will; the will that is formed guides the acts that flow from it. Aristotle's conception is well known, namely, that as a result of the force of habit we reach a point where we perform acts in accordance with a proper principle. To the sphere in which acts are guided by pre-arrangement without being continually dependent on the guidance of the formed will belong such institutions as the law, the state, and so forth. The institutions determine ways of conduct, habits, and the directions of acts. The reason for the existence of institutions lies in the fact that such institutions need not continually go back to the source of the deed in the sphere of the individual doer; they need not rely on the will, on the acknowledgment of responsibility with its attendant decisions and similar components that determine the nature of the ethical deed. Institutions guide deeds in what is called the proper direction without relying on the individual doer's acknowledgment of propriety. Thus, for example, in the sphere of law where it is determined by legislation that men of a certain age are eligible for military service, such a law is not based on the personal initiative of the people concerned, or rather not solely on this initiative, nor is it based on the initiative of all the people subject to this law. The arrangement of the institution — in this case law — takes over the guidance of deeds and assures their execution by those to whom the law applies. The comprehensive character of the arrangement is a derivative aspect of institutionality and is arrived at precisely because institutions need not rely on the personal act and decision of each individual affected by the law.

The institution then rises, so to speak, on the border between the orderly *regularity* of conduct and the *formation* of the intention to follow a definite path. The institution is not within the sphere of natural reality, but neither is it within the sphere of the act that flows from the definite decision that leads to a specific deed. The institution may be said to be, if such a comparison is permissible, the musical score of conduct. With respect to a definite kind of institution, as that of the state or the law, we find the component of a pledge or guarantee that conduct will be in the determined direction — that is, the men to whom the compulsory military service law applies will comply with the law. The guarantee for the orderliness of conduct is compulsion or the reliance on compulsion that accompanies a definite kind of institution. Institutions built on guidance by means of compulsion employ physical coercion, such as is exercised by the state, that is, physical punishment or imprisonment. Institutions built on voluntary membership use coercion by expelling a recalcitrant member; in this case compulsion does not enforce a code of behavior within the limits of the institution, but expels a man from its sphere for failing to adhere to the institution's code of conduct after his initial acceptance of that code. It may be said that the minimum behavior required by an institution is the acceptance of the principle of compulsion that is a concomitant of institutional order; the optimal institutional behavior is consent given to the arrangements implicit in the behavorial patterns of the institution. In the instance cited above, for example, the minimal institutional behavior would be to comply with the law and join the army to avoid being compelled to do so by the state; the optimal behavior — optimal from the standpoint of the institution — is the consent of every man to the imperative that enjoins him to enter the armed forces of his country. But even in this optimal instance the element of institutional order is not absent, that is, man does not create the institution of army recruitment by dint of his own decision. At most, man consents to obey the principles imposed by the institution and to adjust himself to its patterns. Thus institutions are manifestations of objectivizations of man's will; without such manifestations of man's will, there would be no institutions that are not within the limits of natural reality, such as the heavenly bodies or the falling of a stone; on the other hand, institutions impose burdens on our will and on the will of those who endeavor to follow the behavorial patterns of these institutions. This union of objectivization and imposition reveals that the imposition, although present in the institution, is not total; if it were not for a definite consent in favor of the institution's existence, we would not be able to adjust to its behavorial patterns. When we speak of consent in this connection, it is possible that we may be referring to a *post factum* consent or to a consent that admits a choice. Consent also exists when I believe that it is not convenient to resist the law of recruitment lest I incur the penalty involved. This is not a voluntary consent but a deliberate consent that considers the alternatives and weighs one consideration over against

another, the relative freedom of the recruit in the army over against
the practically total deprivation of freedom of a prisoner serving a
sentence for not complying with the law. There are other instances
where one may consent to the existence of the state and its principle
of compulsion without necessarily having this consent extend to this
or that particular law; for example, one may not dispute the authority
of the state to tax its citizens and yet disagree with its application in
definite instances, with its rate, distribution, and so forth.

Since institutions are built both on objectivization of the will and
on imposition, they cannot be said to be governed by the will of
certain individuals or be regarded as their product. Even when a law is
enacted by known members of a legislature, the significance of this
institution in serving as a guide to the will and conduct of future
members of society derives its force and validity not from the will of
the legislators but from a mandate that they have been granted by the
people, giving it a representative value that reflects the will of the
people. An institution is always public, and this is true even when a
particular individual initiates the institution's principle of conduct.
The behavior of an individual has its roots in his own will and in
decisions that are valid here and now; but an institution, having its
source in the public domain, regulates the conduct of the individual
from without. Institutions as such are the sum-total of the rules of
conduct imposed on the individual, rules not derived from nature or
matter. Military conscription is a duty defined by the law of the state,
but its force is not comparable to that of a falling stone, the movement of the heavenly bodies, or the alternations of day and night.

What has been said thus far applies to institutions in the sphere of
deeds, the sphere in which are to be found the institutions of the
state, of the law, and indeed all institutions — for it is only within this
sphere that the problem arises concerning public conduct and the
relations of one individual to another. There are no institutions
created in the orbit of intellectual activity since this sphere is based on
discernment, a quality that pertains only to individuals and which,
moreover, has an inner criterion that serves as a guide among things we
desire to understand through discernment or discrimination. The
intellectual sphere is guided by a criterion of 'objectivity' and not
'objectivization' as is the sphere of individual wills and the deeds
directed by these wills including their decisions. The institution regulates the conduct of individuals through codes of behavior that are not
derived from these subjects themselves. From this point of view there
is no room in the sphere of theory for an institution that does not
admit the regulation of conduct by the subjects themselves through

their intentional acts. This may be expressed by saying that in the sphere of theory there is no place for institutions because it makes no room for the various deviations and possibilities of behavior. The status of the object prior to the act of the understanding guides this act, but in the practical sphere of conduct one can object to, for example, conscription for various reasons. Since more than one form of behavior is possible in the practical sphere, institutional regulation has recourse to imposition without the consent or authority of the individual.[1]

A reservation should be made concerning this connection between the institution and the practical sphere in general and the sphere of ethical acts in particular, a reservation that stems from historical circumstance: that there is one institution that has induced a form of behavior clearly related to the sphere of knowledge and not to the volitional or conative sphere, namely, the institution of technology. In dealing with the nature of this institution we must bear in mind the distinction between the technical act discussed in Greek philosophy and technology, which made its appearance much later in the course of human history. This historical circumstance imposes upon philosophy the task of clarifying a problem that was unknown to former generations, for philosophy deals with reality and hence has a legitimate interest in the status of technology as an institution that constitutes a definite part of human reality.

B

The nature of technique or technical knowledge can best be understood in relation to three aspects which will help in clarifying its various components.

1. The first interesting characteristic of technique is its oppostion to nature. Nature is the sum-total of given things and processes; technique is the sum-total of things and processes created by the acts of man. Technique is therefore something artificial, a product of man's intervention and opposed to that which is given and which exists in its own right. The connection between technique and the practical sphere is thus apparent, for acts involve intervention in the course of things. We say of an organism that it is natural and of a machine that it is a technical or artificial production and thus we also speak of natural decay and artificial deterioration that takes place in the organism as a result of human intervention in its natural processes.

2. In dealing with something that is produced and that is not a

natural growth, technique presupposes a prior technical act, that is, an act directed to the production of artificially created things. The term 'technique' or 'technical' then designates the thing produced and the act that produces it.

3. When we speak of the technical act, we refer also to the special skill involved in the act, the ability to initiate acts, dexterity, and similar aspects that emphasize the nature of doing and not only the status of the finished product. Thus we speak of the technique of a pianist with reference to his execution of the musical composition and not to the composition itself; or, in the sphere of skills and workmanship we designate as excellent that which is characterized by a specific expertness in the production of a technical product. Here it is possible to distinguish between the product and the creator, at least it is possible to distinguish these more clearly in the sphere of technical acts than to distinguish between the deed and the doer in the sphere of ethical acts. But in the matter of skills the word 'technique' also refers to the creative ability of the producer himself. In this context we can employ the category of responsibility only in its figurative sense in reference to the responsibility of the creator in producing something in conformity with an end for which it was intended or, more particularly, we can attribute responsibility to the creator of the nuclear bomb and accuse him not of faulty production but of the human consequences of his invention. The introduction of an ethical consideration, the evaluation of the human effects of the production, thus adds another dimension to our discussion beyond that which is only concerned with skilled workmanship and technical perfection. Without this skill on the part of the creator we can have no ethical evaluation of the product. The skill emphasizes the causal status of the creator over against his creation; the determination of the causal relation between the product and the producer is the factual condition for the relation of responsibility that the producer bears to his product.

A skill is a kind of knowledge or ability, but it is not the kind of knowledge that rests on theory that takes into consideration the state of things but rather an operational knowledge. Because of the significance of the element of skill found in the technical act, we see that one of the differences between the technical act and the ethical deed is that whereas the former requires a skill, the latter requires a decision. Even when our decision rests upon former experience in making different decisions, every decision presents us with a new situation and a unique opportunity. This is not the case with respect to a skill which is directed to the production of things in which there is a certain degree of standardization and uniformity.

Skill then involves an element of knowledge that is not theoretical knowledge. To know the qualities of a hammer is not the same as knowing how to use it. Although we distinguish between the knowledge found in theory and that found in skills, we must not underestimate the component of knowledge in the latter. This knowledge is often unformulated, for it is revealed only in the act itself; it is not always the kind of knowledge that can be imparted to someone else, but it can to a certain extent be learned by observation and imitated. A decision, on the other hand, has not this open, visible character and must be deduced from the acts to which it gives rise. This visible aspect of a skill as knowledge often appears to us on the level of technique in connection with the members of the body; the hands, for example, make for manual dexterity, digital manipulation, rapid transfer from one movement to another, and so forth. A skill is also the application of knowledge in assessing a given state of affairs since it is necessary for the artisan to know which tool or movement is suitable in a given situation. A skill, however, is not only application; it is a kind of knowledge incorporated in activity and in the apparatus at its disposal. A skill is knowledge in connection with the members of the body, on the one hand, and the tools used by them on the other, and as such it is also to be regarded as a skill with reference to the musician and the craftsman.

Since a skill remains in the sphere of technique, the technique is in no way separated from the craftsman even though the nature of human activity creates a class of its own different from that of the activity in the sphere of ethical deeds. The status of the doer in the technical sphere and in the sphere of ethics contributes to a certain analogy between the spheres and to the possibility, as we have seen above, of adding a criterion of ethical evaluation to the technical act, that is, to the technical doer of the act. This addition is possible because of the analogy but it is not a logical inner necessity of the technical act; it is a possible addition because we have already in theory combined the status of the doer by regarding him as a total entity, as the bearer of responsibility and ethical value. This aspect of the doer, which characterizes technique in the ethical sense of this concept, is no longer conspicuous in what is called technology.[2]

C

From a cultural-historical point of view it may be said that the transition from technique to technology as an institution is one from

the skilled acts of an individual craftsman to the aggregate of behavorial patterns based on natural science. This does not mean that the
element of skill has disappeared or ceased to exist in the technological
culture. Skill exists as long as there is a need for production, restoration, and repair; it is necessary with respect to electronic computers
and space ships, as well as for pilots suspended in outer space between
heaven and earth employing their complicated instruments. This skill,
however, is different from that of technique in its traditional sense,
for it is not a decisive factor in the relation between man and his tools
or instruments, being subject to the given laws of the exact natural
sciences, of physics or electronics. Skill is an independent element and
yet is absorbed in the sum-total of knowledge at man's disposal. It
could be said that the use of instruments is less dependent on skill
than on science in its methodological sense. Hence, the difference
between technique and technology lies in the fact that science constitutes not only a remote background for acts in the technical sphere
but their immediate and indispensable background. The more complicated a technological act the greater the element of knowledge it
contains, in the theoretical or scientific sense of this concept. The
shift from skill to knowledge is expressed by the fact that in technology the dependence on the craftsman is not as decisive as that
found in technical acts in the traditional sense of this concept. We
might say, to use a concrete illustration, that the craftsmanship of
Stradivarius has been replaced by the assembly line of the modern
factory. Skill is, of course, applied at every stage in the case of the
piece worker who deals with only a fragment of the product, but the
finished product shows little trace of its dependency on a definite
creator.

The individual creator who performs a technical act has in a certain
sense an overall view of the finished product before he begins, and he
himself is part of the pattern in its production. In the sphere of
technology we have instead of this attachment of the creator to his
finished product a general plan of operation that is not dependent
upon any particular individual, as in the operations within a factory or
a laboratory where the worker is attached to a small part of a general
plan that is not of his making. This overall general plan is further
illustrated by the dependence of the technological sphere on knowledge, except that this knowledge is now not that of the creator who
sees the entire finished product at the very outset; the knowledge that
is now required is that of engineering or a technical knowledge necessary to put the plan into effect, a knowledge that involves skill.

The difference between the technical act and the act in the technological sphere as an institution is expressed in the fact that in the latter we not only speak of the production of things but also of the organization of human beings. The organization of work in factories or in offices is within the area of technological performance, for it contains an element of planning and assigning men to different tasks in a common endeavor to accomplish the final work envisaged in the overall plan. The rise of cities and the distribution of their populations in accordance with long-term plans are technological and not technical problems. While the technical act terminates for the most part in a finished product or instrument, the technological act may terminate in such, as a space ship or a computer, or it may not and remain as in a continuous stage of planning. The technical act terminates in a product with a material base, but the technological act has not of necessity such a material component, and it may or may not terminate in a particular product. To the extent that the technological act contains a total product having a material character it is similar to the technical act in the traditional sense of this concept; but concerning the systems of work in the production of products transferred to spheres where things are not produced — such as the organization of work in an office — the technological act is accomplished by removing itself from incorporation in products with a material component.

The fact that these behavorial arrangements are found in the sphere of the production of instruments as well as in the spheres of human organization indicates a definite independence of the technological element, which has become a matter of methods of behavior and is no longer concerned with those distinct modes of individual production that result in the finished product. This removal of the technological element from the material product determines the difference between technology and technique — technology whose regulative principle is the rationality of organization and technique whose regulative principle is the creation of a product by dint of the creator's skill. Rationality is less personal than skill; skill is knowledge in action, but rationality lends itself to a methodical and even mathematical formulation. What technique and technology have in common is an opposition to nature or, at least, a differentiation from nature even when they depend on a material use of nature or on natural laws. What separates technique from technology is the fact that the latter is not concerned with the isolated acts of individuals but with experiments of general organization, whether in the sphere of creation or in the sphere of performance, such as the organization of work. Technology thus organizes patterns of behavior from the standpoint of behavior itself and not only for the sake of producing and perfecting instruments.

D

Separation from skill in the sphere of technology is expressed by the fact that the technological product is not the result of the manual skill of the worker. One technological instrument produces another. As stated, there is room for skill in production but the process of creative productivity is so complicated from the standpoint of its cognitive and material elements that there is no longer room to emphasize the direct relationship between product and producer. This relationship is replaced by a creation that mediates by means of another creation. This is the case with respect to the technological creation embodied in instruments such as computers or space ships and *a fortiori* with respect to the technological creation concerned with the organization of work and with methods of efficiency. Here we witness the almost total disappearance of skill in favor of operational analysis and the formal comparisons of one system with another, such as comparing the system of military operations with that of the organization of work in a factory, entailing methods within methods and combinations of methods, such as a method based on patterns of mathematics, strategy, and so forth. At some point, however, the judgment of the worker is required. This judgment may be regarded as a kind of skill, but it is interwoven in methodological systems which obtrude themselves between the worker and his work. We here have something that may be called a self-contained, closed system of the technological sphere similar to the indirect operations found in institutions where the activities are mediated by the institutional arrangements themselves. This may be illustrated by an example from the field of politics: The participation of the voter in the election of the members of the legislature is a direct, unmediated act; and yet it is not as direct as it appears on first sight, for this participation is itself determined by the laws of the country which grant the right to vote, the order and method of voting, and so on. Voting is a kind of a direct act which is rooted in an institutional circle which is regulated by it as a direct act. Similarly, to continue the analogy, we find in the sphere of technology as an institution operations that are direct and which still have an element of skill and of judgment on the part of the worker and also elements which are rooted in the circle of technology and subject to its inner logic.

The significance of the instruments that serve as mediators for others, or the significance of methods that serve the methodological process, is also evident from another point of view. It is sometimes said that technology is the application of knowledge or of science.

This seems to be true, for without physics, which is concerned with gravitation, it is impossible to construct aeroplanes and without atomic physics it is impossible to make atom bombs. A stricter analysis, however, reveals that knowledge itself, the knowledge prior to definite application, is not possible without technical instruments, just as Galileo's discoveries would have been impossible without a telescope and just as important biological discoveries would have been impossible without a microscope or an electronic microscope. Physical knowledge is inherent in the instrument used which, in turn, facilitates the process of knowledge.[3] Thus, the state of technology is itself the bearer of cognitive significance, for the instruments of technology and the guiding lines of work organization laid down by it impart to the various methodological steps of the sciences their inner conditions. It seems that when we look upon technology as a kind of *application* of knowledge, we can regard it as a kind of *realization* of knowledge both in the instruments and in the patterns of conduct. Scientific progress in the age of technology is not only a transition from hypothesis to application but one cognitive realization that leads to another.

This closed, self-contained nature of the technological sphere is not itself a product of man's ethical decision but a consequence of the character of technology, which shuns contact with man the creator and its dependence upon him. Technology appears as an institution that has developmental tendencies of its own precisely because it is an institution, just as the state as an institution has its own forms of development through its peculiar structure. The state could include contradictory tendencies in its structure, such as those that exist between the legislative and the executive branches, but these are defined within the structure of the state and belong to it with all their ramifications. Similarly, in the institution of technology we find that there could be a tendency to produce large quantities and also small quantities, both being compatible with technological operation. Over against this tendency there can also be arrangements that pertain not to the sphere of small units, but to that of the large corporations which operate on a principle of production of greater compass than even that of large factories, invoking the principle of efficiency and also an inner logic of their own. But to be included in the common sphere of technology does not necessarily make for harmony, just as reliance on the structure of a state does not necessarily produce harmony between the various branches of government. As long as an institution retains an inner logic of its own, it will fail to be in contact with the whole man. Man leads a circumscribed existence within partial institutions — political, legal, or technological institutions —

and he is inclined to judge each institution in accordance with its own inner logic. Philosophical inquiry, one of whose spherical contents is man as a whole, here appears as an external corrective of man's limited views confined to the narrow perspectives of institutions. Man's real orientation is determined by the inner logic of these institutions; he soon becomes deeply imbued with their principles and learns to depend upon their powers and qualities in the formation of his judgment. This seemingly unqualified assurance imparted by institutions is weakened by the contradictions among them, such as the contradiction between technological needs that lead to unemployment and social needs that seek to prevent it. Man adjusts himself to these contradictions and learns to live with them empirically. He becomes sensible of them only when he as man surveys the institutions in their fragmentation, when the immanent-human collides with the external-institutional.

The relatively self-contained, closed nature of the technological sphere, expressed in the fact that one instrument creates another, presents us with an analogy between the sphere of technology and the sphere of knowledge, though we are concerned here with the sphere of deeds and not with that of theory. In the sphere of knowledge we find the course of the inner growth of knowledge in conclusions derived from a hypothesis or when one finding of knowledge leads to another. We come upon a similar analogy in the sphere of technology: Whereas technique, in the traditional sense of the term, is interested in supplying man's wants, technology is concerned with the constant possibility of creating needs which are stimulated, as it were, by the inherent possibilities of this technological sphere itself. Hence, technology does not proceed according to the principle, "these are the most feasible methods for satisfying a given need," but according to the principle, "something can possibly be done, and if it is possible it should be done." We here have no direct path from knowledge to knowledge, for we are already dependent on acts and deeds because without deeds the possibility of creating an atomic bomb, for example, cannot be made into a reality. The transition from possibility to reality is accomplished by deeds. Because of the nature of this transition technology too is a practical sphere. As such it has no principle beyond that of the technological possibility itself. The need for the deed is derived from the possibility of creating this deed. We have here, of course, a relatively self-contained system and were it not for the fact that men existed who, so to speak, evoked this possibility of technological creation and converted it into reality, this possibility would never become a reality. There is no such thing as a technological truth in and of itself as, for example, a mathematical truth which is valid whether it is known by man or not. The relatively closed nature of the institution of technology consists in the fact that man, who evokes the technological possibility, also interprets it as an imperative for a deed. This interpretation is itself a result of the circumstance that man is conditioned by the rhythm of technology and its manifestations. A technological objectivization emerges, parallel to that found in other institutions such as the state or law. The technological institution becomes a guide or regulator of ways of behavior because of this objective character. The empirical expression of this technological guidance of ways of behavior is evident in the fact that the logic of technology creates needs and these are the very needs revealed by the technological possibilities. This is clearly seen in manufacturing, which is part of the technological sphere: Since it is possible to create definite articles made of synthetic fiber, then such articles are manufactured and a need for them appears. An extreme example of the significance of such technological possibilities is evident in the creation of the atomic bomb after its possibility was envisaged to solve certain problems of a strategic nature. This may lead to a state of affairs where various countries will be tempted to create the bomb not primarily because of any strategic need but simply because it is possible: Such a creation bears this acquisition of things not for the satisfaction of a real need but for purposes of prestige was called by Thorstein Veblen "conspicuous consumption."[4] In the course of dictating needs technology itself becomes a factor in the need for consumption with its inevitable concomitant of waste,[5] so that in the end the closed system of technology, from an empirical point of view, encourages waste and technology itself, considered as an institution, becomes a sort of extravagant waste. Technology creates "conspicuous productions." Products become obsolete in order to stimulate a desire for new products, still uncreated but eagerly awaited. The real need for consumption is usurped by a dominant incentive for acquisition and this in turn becomes an invidious standard of the social evaluation of people.

E

From the study of technology as an institution we now turn to a comparison between it and other institutions with traditional modes of behavior, such as those of the state and law, which are characterized by established patterns of conduct and not personal decisions.

A man may decide to be conscripted or not; but a legal institution of the state exempts him from making a decision by prescribing a mode of conduct. The institution thus imposes one burden while removing another.[6] There will always be men who will resist being relieved of this burden involving personal choice and who regard the institution as superfluous or as inimical to man's spontaneity, this being essentially an anarchistic attitude of those who place personal decision above institutional imposition.

The element of alleviation or leisure is also found in the sphere of technique in general and in the sphere of technology in particular. Men have a need to move from place to place; at first this was done on foot, but in the course of time technique was able to provide mechanical transportation beginning with a simple vehicle and terminating in the supersonic aeroplane. Technique made it possible for man to reach the goal he set for himself by reducing his efforts to attain it. The effort involved is due to the need for producing means of trans-portation, but this effort is not exerted by those who use these vehi-cules but by those who are specialized in producing them. We have here a gap between the use of the vehicles, by one man, and their production, which involves the cooperative efforts of many men. Institutions like those of government and law relieve man of the burden of decision; the institution of technology relieves him of the burden of production. The difference between the two is rooted in the difference between the sphere of ethical deeds and the sphere of technical deeds. The aspect they have in common is the tendency to lighten man's burden, a tendency characteristic of every institution. This tendency is in every case expressed in the search for a shorter path to the goal, the goal of behavior in the ethical sphere and the goal of the satisfaction of needs in the technical sphere. In the sphere of technical deeds the goal is limited to man's needs, such as the need to move from place to place; in the sphere of ethical acts the goal is limited by the directions of conduct, with respect to which there are conflicting opinions — whether the direction of conduct is concerned with the realization of man's ultimate goals or with the realization of a general principle that may serve as a guide to man's actions (illustrated from a systematic point of view by the direction of conduct proposed by Aristotle, on the one hand, and that proposed by Kant on the other).

But the element of alleviation or the lightening of burdens in the institution in general and in that of technology in particular also operates in another direction. In the example cited above alleviation is concerned with finding suitable means to reach a goal, locomotion by foot being superseded by that of vehicles. This search for more suitable means also applies to finding means for the proper distribution of food, for the alleviation of hunger and its concomitant evils. Men have been able to create means to satisfy their hunger in addition to those they found at hand in nature without the aid of man's artificial intervention. The technical deed added a dimension of instruments to those supplied by nature, such as public conveyances instead of locomotion by foot (parts of the body are not instruments, of course, but become such from the standpoint of technical operation) or agricultural implements in addition to natural growth. Both examples serve to illustrate the tendency to amelioration — that is, alleviation by way of amelioration.

This tendency to amelioration reveals to us another principle in the sphere of technology. It is impossible to produce tools or instruments without human intervention in the processes of nature. With such intervention man seeks to acquire a mastery over nature. This is not accomplished by dictating laws for it to follow. Nature has its own laws which it does not surrender when man seeks to improve it with the growth of plants or the raising of cattle. Intervention is for the purpose of stimulation, diligence and increased effort on man's part in attaining his goals by using nature as a background or as the arena of his struggles. The mastery over nature is a kind of means for alleviation, while alleviation is the means for the satisfaction of wants. These wants or needs appear as given and the means are created for their sake so that they may be satisfied. The mastery of nature is an instrument in the interest of alleviation of wants. Effort in one direction is needed to alleviate effort in another, a diversion which results in the mastery of nature as explained above.

Before coming to the question of the inner dialectic of the technological sphere we must take another factor into consideration. We have already spoken of the tendency of amelioration as characteristic of technology and of institutions in general. But it is doubtful that one aspect of technology — the esthetic component — is ameliorative or not. In the example of the means of transportation given above it is clear that the basic principle is that of the conservation of effort; this is also the guiding principle in our second example concerning man's intervention in nature in order to increase its productivity by artificial means. But, to take a simple example, it is possible to eat food with one's fingers without knife or fork; moreover, the use of a knife and a fork is not the same as the use of a hammer, which facilitates a difficult piece of work that could otherwise not be accomplished, for the knife and fork are simply substitutes for the direct use of our fingers — they serve to mediate between us and the food. This might be called a hygienic consideration, but it could also be regarded as an esthetic component. Our deportment appears more esthetic when it does not necessitate direct contact between us and the food but employs an implement or utensil as a mediating link. We here have an esthetic factor for tools or implements.

The esthetic component in the technical sphere deserves special consideration because it indicates the distinction between the sphere of technical acts and that of ethical acts. When one jumps into the water to save a drowning man, the manner in which it is done from the standpoint of graceful bodily movements is of no importance. What is of importance is the fact that someone ventured to jump into the water to save a fellowman from drowning. In considering swimming contests, however, the esthetic element — the manner of execution, the grace of movement — is of great importance. Similarly, although perhaps to a lesser degree, this is also true of dress, food, and modes of conveyance. However much an automobile may be judged for its efficient performance in taking us from one place to another, it is also judged for its esthetic contours, its attractive accessories, and similar considerations. The reason for the addition of the esthetic component to the technical sphere is the same as that which we found in the sphere of implements and utensils, namely, our relationship to things in this sphere is dictated not only by their use but by their additional status as material objects. The proper esthetic appreciation of these objects requires that they be removed to a certain extent from their limited practical functions and be regarded for what they are intrinsically apart from their usefulness; our relation to them must be, as Kant states, one of pure disinterestedness. The esthetic relation to technical objects, then, is bound up with an abstraction from their usefulness, even though it was this consideration that brought them into existence. This explains a certain tendency in the technological world to create a situation in which the aspect of utility or function and the aspect of esthetics receive equal consideration with no contradiction arising between them.[7] An additional esthetic dimension is here added to tools and instruments which in their original state were non-esthetic or at least a-esthetic.

F

The presupposition of every act of intervention in the natural course of things is the accessibility of these things to intervention. This supposition is true of every deed, including technical and technological deeds. Deeds of the technological sphere, however, are bound up with additional presuppositions; or the accessibility of things as they are receive some novel features as a result of our technological intervention.

Technology adds level upon level to given nature and it does so, as we have seen above, by using the materials of nature or its laws. Technology does not create its materials *ex nihilo* but finds them already in existence, such as the different kinds of plastic materials which are made of existing substances, nor does technology create its own laws, but uses the law of action and reaction for purposes of flying, and so on. It imposes human purposes and goals on different substances and on the laws that operate among them – the human goal of supplying man's needs or the human goal of beautifying them. The engrafting of this teleological element onto the natural course of things is the presupposition of technology and its essential activity. This explains the connection between science and technology and its essential activity. To the extent that the possibilities of a knowledge of nature become more accessible the opportunites of man's use of nature to serve his purposes are greater. Because of the technological push to use nature and its laws, man seeks new ways to enable him to harness them to his own ends. Cognitive data constitute the theoretical condition for technology, and the continuous pursuit of such data reflects the influence of technology on science which is its theoretical presupposition.

The technical or technological deed is therefore a deed of intervention in the sense that it imposes a teleological rhythm on the order of nature. Since we have here the component of one rhythm imposed on the natural order, the technical and technological deed depend on a knowledge of nature and its laws or on that sphere whereby men attempt to interpret nature, namely, the sphere of the natural sciences. A marked difference emerges here between the technical déed, on the one hand, and the ethical act on the other. To a certain extent the ethical act is also dependent on a knowledge of nature. If we did not know that water could rise and that a man could drown in it, it would not occur to us to jump in to save him; the knowledge implied here is that nature can be inimical to man and this knowledge induces us to attempt an act of rescue. If we did not know that men require food, we would not be concerned with the arrangements that supply them with food. But a knowledge of nature on the level of an ethical act is a kind of elementary knowledge, a knowledge of arrangements found on every hand in daily life. There is no dependence here on natural science in the methodological sense of this term or, at any rate, no close dependence on such science. This is not the case with respect to technology whose very existence depends on a close and continuous dependence on natural science. Without natural science as the interpreter of nature there would be no cognitive background in which human purpose could be combined with nature.

A speculative observation may not be out of place in this connection. It is commonly said that the modern world presented technology with its opportunities because of the emergence of social problems that demanded technological solutions. It is thus said that a need arose for tools and organization of work because there were no longer slaves who did this work in ancient times. There may be some truth to this explanation, but there is also a metaphysical aspect to this transition to technology and to its establishment as an institution. When natural science ceased to be teleological and became causal — that is, when nature was conceived not as a sphere for the realization of ends but as a system of functional arrangements — man could no longer rely on nature to realize his ends by its own unaided processes. Nature's causality was now conceived as a challenge and as an opportunity for the realization of man's ends by means of human intervention in the natural sphere and using the inner laws of that sphere in the process. The course of nature left to itself is simply a causal system and is not designed for the realization of our ends. We might say that when nature was conceived teleologically, it lent itself to man's amelioration; when it was conceived as a causal system it became indifferent to human ends and its place had to be taken by an institution that could function in that capacity, namely, technology. This accounts for the dependence of technology on natural science in modern times, a science that is causal and not teleological.

The system of ends imposed by technology on the lawful order of nature consists of ends concerned with man's needs for food, clothing, transportation. But in the production of its product, in both the operational and esthetic aspects, technology adds a rhythm of its own. This rhythm does not belong to the satisfaction of needs, an additional factor that we have already noted with respect to the reproduction of technology and which we called the relatively closed nature or the self-containment of the institution of technology. This same peculiarity now appears as a teleological rhythm that no longer serves an end in the satisfaction of needs. We here see technology released from its original function. In this connection it is possible to point to the difference between the technical deed which is connected with needs and their satisfaction, and the deeds in the technological sphere which are teleological, but whose teleological nature is an internal characteristic and not connected with the satisfaction of needs outside the sphere of technology itself. With respect to the teleology of the satisfaction of needs, man, who performs the technical deed, retains a relative mastery over against the deed and the product. Man knows the utility of the product from the standpoint of its purpose. With respect to teleology as an independent rhythm man no longer retains control, for technology renews itself by its own inner logic and not by the dictation of man's needs. The common complaint that means are converted to ends is connected with this problem. When teleology frees itself from the technological situation and no longer serves an end outside itself, this situation can be described as the conversion of means to ends. This conversion, however, is rooted in the very status of the technological sphere as a sphere in which teleology is combined with causality and in which this combination keeps occurring with greater and greater frequency. The more we know of causality, the more is it combined with purpose. Purposiveness without purpose is, according to Kant, the criterion of an artistic work. The technological institution thus acquires the status of an artistic work if we accept this Kantian criterion. The esthetic component, which we saw above as an additional component in the technical sphere, is here encountered in the technological sphere from the very outset.[8]

Just as the teleological element freed itself from ends and purposes in the technological sphere, so did the element of the mastery or domination of nature free itself from the element of utility which this mastery is supposed to serve. The mastery of nature became an independent, internal matter of technology beyond its inherent utility. The achievements in space of modern technology is perhaps the best example of this process of the separation of the element of the mastery of nature in technology from the element of utility. It is, of course, always possible to point out a secondary or distant utility, like that of strategic advantages or that of political prestige. But it seems that the achievements connected with the mastery of nature are made for the sake of the scientific development of technology. These achievements acquire a status that was reserved for skill in the technical act, in the traditional meaning of this term. Just as in the sphere of technical acts skill was valued independently for itself, so also is there a tendency in the technological sphere to value an act involving the mastery of nature as an inner, self-contained act of technology and of technology alone. We see the institution of technology, in contradistinction to technical deeds, as having liberated itself from the needs that gave birth to technical deeds and concerning itself with the realization of the principle that man does that which he is able to do. This ability serves man as an independent guide.[9] In all technique there is an element of the mastery of nature; in technology this element becomes conspicuously independent.

G

We have examined the nature of technology as an institution having a logic of its own. The question of the ethical nature of technology now arises, that is, how can we apply to a sphere having a logic of its own the criterion of the sphere of ethical deeds together with its peculiar categories of decision, responsibility, and so forth?

A basic standpoint for an ethical criticism of technology is to be found in the fact that technology as an institution is a sphere based on human acts, acts to which an ethical criterion could be applied. The employment of ethical standards to technology may be compared to the evaluation of a literary work or a work of art which as such is concerned with fashioning matter and not with fashioning the will. The immanent logic of such works, therefore, is to be found beyond the limits of ethical acts. But when such works are produced by man, their effects beyond their original sphere may be evaluated with respect to their influence on-human wills. This was the basis of Plato's criticism of art and of those who have followed him down to the present day, a criticism that culminates in the contradiction between the significance of a work of art from the standpoint of shaping matter and imbuing it with expression, and its ethical effect upon those who come under its influence from the standpoint of shaping their wills. This may also be said for works of technology where we always inquire into their effect on men. It will thus be useful from this point of view to undertake an ethical criticism, or a criticism in accordance with an ethical criterion, of technology as the sum-total of objects and arrangements of life.

A distinction emerges here between the approach of the ethical evaluation directed to works of art and the approach of ethical criticism directed to the institution of technology. We inquire into the effects of a work of art with respect to men's behavior, for such behavior takes place in real time while the work of art as such extends beyond the limits of real time. A statue fashioned out of clay occupies a portion of space as a musical composition or a literary work has a position in time. Hence it is possible to judge the effects of a work of art outside the limits of its proper sphere, that is, within real time. The effects of technology, however, are within its own limits, and here we note another similarity between it and institutions such as government and law where we ask whether they regulate men's behavior in accordance with their proper function. In the case of government we inquire whether it makes for order and stability, for government that leads to anarchy is no government; in the case of legislation we inquire whether it creates fixed patterns of behavior or whether it leaves this to chance, for example, whether it creates a possibility for determining beforehand a penalty for transgression. Similar questions arise with respect to technology: If technology is concerned with alleviating man's condition, then the question is from one point of view an internal one in the sense of comparing achievement with intention in the sphere of technology, and from another point of view ethical in the sense of finding a place for man within the sphere of technology and evaluating man's significance. It has been observed that in alleviating man's physical burden technology has impaired his nervous system and increased his woe.[10] This is an immanent criticism of technology from the standpoint of its reason for existence or it is an ethical criticism for it inquires into man's status in the sphere of technological expression as a partial expression of man and his creative powers directed to the attainment of definite and partial ends.

In summing up we can say that the ethical criticism of technology is based on several fundamental reasons: (*a*) technology insists on the objectivization of deeds; deeds are judged in accordance with an inner criterion, one of which is the ethical criterion; (*b*) technology is evaluated on the basis of its achievement, and this raises the question of whether the alleviation of man's burdens and obligations can be achieved only partially — that is, that for every advance in physical comfort there is a corresponding deterioration in man's psyche; (*c*) over against institutional achievements is man, the total man who is neither technological nor institutional but a spherical entity; man judges all his works from the standpoint of his total status and not as if he were conditioned by some institution, whether government, law, or technology.

We see then that technology is faced with the criticism of its own logic and also with a more extensive criticism, namely, to what extent is achievement compatible with the alleviation of man's condition, since this alleviation has its justification in the ethical principle of man's significance. The criticism directed to technology points to the more extensive content 'man' who is, as we have seen, one of the principal contents of the theoretical approach and not of the practical approach. We have now returned to the total content 'man' in

pointing to lines of criticism of technology. We did not arrive at this
content by discovering an inner relationship of technology to the
contents of theory. This problem leads us to a further inquiry into the
presuppositions of the technological sphere that are not technological.

H

Two presuppositions must be assumed at the very outset with respect
to the technological operations and the institution of technology:

1. From the standpoint of technology as such, no reference is
made to man the creator but only to man who is already within the
institution of technology to a greater or lesser degree, working within
it and in its behalf. Accordingly, man in a given state is part and parcel
of that state, living and working within its limits. Technology, however, is bound up with the presupposition, although not explicit, of
man's relation to the world in its totality. This relationship may be
formulated as man's ability to intervene in the natural course of things
in order to direct it toward those goals that man has set for himself. In
technology man is related not only to a fragment of his work, the
particular segment that happens to be his task for the moment. Even
here we see a continuous expansion of man's technological work both
in scope and intensity, so clearly attested by the modern technological
achievements in space. Man does not achieve full development by con-
fining himself to one particular segment; his mind is as wide as the
world of technology and must be free to roam wherever his technological abilities lead him. It is precisely technology − which may be
called abstract in that it makes use of the laws of nature to attain
human goals − that reveals this aspect of its conscious reliance on
man, which constitutes the explicit or tacit assumption of the technological attitude to the world.

2. A complementary or parallel assumption in contradistinction to
the above is the following: From the standpoint of nature itself or
even from the standpoint of the more comprehensive sphere of the
world there is no hindrance or restriction to man's intervention in
nature or the world, for these have no meaning in themselves and it is
only meaning that could be a guide or a restraint to man's intervention. Nature is not a realization of an idea nor in itself does it hold
a status of theophany; but it is only an aggregate of data. The sole
restraint lies in the lawfulness of nature but this has no regulative,
evaluative meaning, and its only significance is that it serves as a
challenge for man, a barrier for his slow-gathering vitality to over-

come. Technology is bound to a definite interpretation of the world, namely, the conception that the world is nothing more than the sum-total of data and laws. The world offers no hint of meaning. This presupposition of technology defies the characteristic trend of the Platonic or the religious conception. The technological view is that of positivism which holds that there are no indubitable universal axioms with which to confront the tangled maze of experience; the operative principle within experience is always partial, incomplete, and pro-visional. Positivism and technology nourish one another: Positivism supplies technology with an internally consistent system of consilient judgments, and technology presents positivism with its brilliant suc-cesses.

Now that we have examined the presuppositions of technology — presuppositions that imply a world-view — we can take a step further in our inquiry and consider the connections between technology and the various objects of theory which engaged our attention in the early chapters of this study. We must first point out the connection between technology and the content 'time', one of the three spherical contents of theory. It is obvious that the relation to time is implied in every act of production, whether it is a technical deed in the simple sense of this term of whether it is a technological work in the strictly abstract, scientific sense of this concept. In every technical and tech-nological work the creator or the artisan operates by way of antici-pation; man envisages the product or the result of his act beforehand. The relationship to anticipation is expressed in technical acts by a plan of the product or of the final result. But the attitude of anticipation to technology has a wider and more comprehensive significance. Technology as an institution organizes society and regulates the public and private life of its members. Since the incentive of technology is rooted to a greater or lesser degree in the desire for change, the tech-nological worker recognizes the fact that change is not exhausted by his act. The technological act is therefore accompanied by a conscious-ness of the significance of the act within time, the consciousness of the impermanence of the technological achievement, whether it be a product or an organization of work. Since the technological deed is accompanied by a relation to the future as a consciousness of the gap between the act here and now and its extension into the future, there are possibilities of technological works hidden in the future above and beyond the definite work being produced here and now. This brings to our mind the character of technological culture as a culture directed to the future, understanding this future not as the Day of Judgment as it is in the monotheistic religions but as the aggregate or sum-total of unfulfilled possibilities. The relation to the future is not a peculiar property of technological culture; but the interpretation that this culture gives to the future is intimately connected with the inner logic of technology. At any rate, we see the relation of technology to time and the interpretation it gives to this relation.

Time, then, which is represented by the future, is open to man, and herein we again note the distinction between this conception and that of modern existentialism. Technology interprets the future not as having an end but as having inexhaustible possibilities. All the aspects that we have described as representing the act in its totality from the standpoint of its relation to time and the world appear in the character of the technological operation distinctly recognizable. In the act of intervening in the orderly course of nature, man is open to the world and to time. This makes him dependent upon them, for intervention in the world and in time is a result of dependence, a dependence that increases *pari passu* with intervention. This is the part played in technology by the world and time, or the world as represented chiefly by time. We thus see, explicitly or implicitly, the dependence of technology not only on a definite conception of the world but also on the contents 'world' and 'time'.

Technique, in the traditional sense, was closely connected with man's real needs, the need for food, for clothing, and for shelter. These needs exist, to a greater or lesser degree, also in technology despite the fact that they are no longer critical needs in the sense that they are not completely dependent on the technological incentive for change and renewal. But to the extent that there is a connection between technology and needs and to the extent that technology creates these needs out of its own resources, technology is not only connected with man who is always in need of things but also with man who through reflection has insight into these needs and produces things to satisfy them. Therefore the technical act and the entire technological sphere presuppose man having understanding and the power of reflection. We retrace the footsteps of technique from the relatively closed circle that conditions man to man as a reflective being. We return, then, to posit an element of reality, man, and to the determination of the primacy of theory and its content.

Man has the power of reflection in the technological sphere as well as for the sake of that sphere, for if there were no reflection, technology in its relation to needs would not appear in the world. There would in such a case be no technological process with respect to the anticipation of the product. Hence we may say that man as a reflective being exists in and over against technology. The external criterion employed by man in his criticism of technology may be characterized as an ethical criterion. Such criticism is therefore not arbitrary for it can only be made by a being possessing reflection which is an expression of the critical attitude of man over against reality, especially the reality that is based on human acts. By creating distance between subject and object, between man and reality in general, reflection is able to serve man as a guide in finding his way among the diverse behavorial patterns of institutions. Such criticism is the last remnant of reflection and it cannot be eradicated without uprooting the essential character of human existence. Man by himself is powerless to change nature. Yet reflection changes reality since it is peculiar to man alone.

This relation of man as a spherical content of theory is a subject to which we return in the summary of this study. Because of this relation technological culture is not, as is often maintained, self-sufficient. Over against it stands man, a reflective being who is not a part of the technological sphere.

I

We have thus far been occupied with tracing the relationship between technology and theory, whether we conceived theory from the standpoint of its being rooted in reflection or from the standpoint of the spherical meaning which constitutes its primary content. We shall conclude our inquiry with a brief observation concerning the connection between technology and the presuppositions of cognition in the limited sense of this term, that is, cognition as a knowledge of nature and of man's orientation within it.

The dependence of technology on the findings of the natural sciences is obvious and requires no further elucidation except for some remarks concerning several of its aspects. We must first point out the relation that the attitude of anticipation, as an attitude revolving around the theory of time, bears to the definite operational aspects of technology which are a kind of a methodological expression of anticipation as an original attitude. We might say that to the extent that technology is able to envisage its final product or achievement beforehand it can by the same token foresee the place that they would occupy in the social order, the number of their consumers or adherents, their use in the different walks of life, and so forth. Such technological prediction is a matter of common knowledge and requires no further elaboration.

The possibility of classifying and integrating technological achievements in the social order rests in the last analysis on a basic presupposition, namely, that technology presupposes the lawfulness of nature
and utilizes it for its own ends. In presupposing this lawfulness of
nature it also assumes a definite predictability with respect to human
conduct, that is, the assumption that on the appearance of a technological achievement — whether appliances, instruments, machines — it
will be used or adopted by men in general. Technology takes for
granted not only the orderly course of nature but also man's inevitable
use of technological products, a use that it encourages and stimulates.
Here, again, we meet the relatively closed circle of technology — the
attitude of utilization to which technology owes its origin also sets in
motion an attitude of utilization with respect to its own inner processes and productions.

This reliance on the approach of utilization is of importance in
understanding the analogy between the technological and the natural
orders on the one hand, and the difference between the technological
sphere and the sphere of ethical acts on the other hand. Over against
the order of nature we adopt an attitude of conciliation, that is, since
it is impossible for us to change nature we may as well adapt ourselves
to her, in accordance with Seneca's saying, "Fates lead the willing,
drive the unwilling." Nature has a way of enforcing her laws on human
conduct and attitudes. Man's relation to nature is therefore transferred
to his relation to technology, where there is seemingly no way for
opposing its arrangements and productions. This attitude of non-
resistance indicates a kind of an analogy between the order of nature
and the order of technology, an analogy explained by the fact that
technology is based on the utilization of natural laws. Wherever there
is contact with nature we find the element of compulsion that forces
man to submit to her laws. Here we note a marked difference between
the relation to the technological sphere and the relation to the sphere
of ethical acts. Since ethical acts rest on decision, it is assumed that
ethical conduct is not determined by compulsion on the part of nature
and which hence must be complied with willy-nilly. This also explains
the transfer that takes place from the sphere of ethical acts to the
sphere of technology, that is, it is argued that the relation to this
sphere contains an element of decision that cannot be eradicated; we
cannot attribute to it a status of power of the order of nature as is
done by those who believe in the preferential and automatic status of
the technological sphere. We may regard the relationship to the
technological sphere as influenced either by a cognitive relation to
nature and its arrangements or as influenced by an ethical relation to

conduct and behavior; it is in accordance with these two fundamental views that we can determine the status of the technological
sphere. In any case, when we attribute to the sphere of technology a
status of the power of nature, it emphasizes the connection to knowledge in this sphere, which is a characteristic connection to intentionality toward nature. When we attribute to this sphere the status of a
product of human acts and which as such can be used or not, we add
to the technical sphere an ethical relation that involves an element of
choice or a relationship based on choice or on decision.

We may sum up by saying that upon the sphere of technology is
conferred a status belonging to the order of nature. But, despite this,
technology is also evaluated by criteria that are used in evaluating
ethical acts. This double relation of man to technology is a reflection
of the twofold status of technology itself, which is an institution
within nature as well as a human institution. We therefore can no
longer speak of technology, as it appears in the modern world, as
technique along with theory and ethics as we find in the classical
conception. A certain breach is here evident in the classical conception, but this breach does not abolish the relation of technology to
theory or render impossible its relation to ethics. In spite of this
dependence, however, we see the emergence of an independent sphere
with characteristic features of its own. Technology is not to be found
outside of the components of the human intentionalities of the world.
But within the sphere we have to discern the peculiar characteristics of
technology. The discernment of these characteristics represents the
openness of the philosophic discourse vis-à-vis the changes in the order
of reality, the nature of time, and that of history within time.

Philosophical inquiry as inquiry concerned with the structures
within reality also is properly engaged when it turns its attention to a
due appreciation of the bearing of technology on human conduct and
its claim to modern man's allegiance.

NOTES

1 An institution such as a school is no proof of the contrary, for such institutions have the function of imparting didactic related to instruction. They direct
attention to subjects of theory in the sense that they regulate behavior that
desires to follow theory. But these institutions do not regulate the essence of
theory and they do not replace the principle of objectivity. They teach that there
is a principle of objectivity, but they do not govern behavior that is related to this
objectivity itself. Schools function in order to direct the student toward study and
theory. After the student has acquired theory, then theory itself determines his

relationship *in actu*. But with respect to choosing and direction or other aspects the institutions operate in conformity with the basic reason for their institutional existence.

2 Skill is regarded as a special class of knowledge. It is not a non-reflective knowledge (*irréfléchi*) of which Merleau-Ponty speaks. Skill involves a discriminating sense of conditions and instruments, and the most efficient manner of employing these instruments. But it has no insight into these conditions and instruments, for this insight is repressed in giving an account of them. There is, of course, no intentionality here of giving such an account.

3 This question was analyzed by Husserl in *Die Krisis der europäishen Wissenschaften und die transzendentale Phänomenologie*. See Van Breda's edition of Husserl's *Gesammelte Werke* (Husserliana), Vol. VI, edited by W. Biemel (Haag: 1954), pp. 20ff.

4 *The Theory of the Leisure Class*, in *The Portable Veblen*, edited and with an introduction by M. Lerner (New York: 1948) p. 79.

5 *Theory of the Leisure Class*, pp. 126ff.

6 On institutions from the standpoint of their being an alleviation for man, see A. Gehlen, "Mensch und Institutionen," in *Anthropologische Forschung* (Reinbek bei Hamburg: 1961), pp. 69ff.

7 On technology as an institution, see J. Ellul, *The Technological Society*, translated from the French by J. Wilkinson (New York: 1965).

8 Concerning technology as the union of a final order and a causal order, cf. F. Dessauer, *Streit um die Technik* (Freiburg-Basel-Vienna: 1959).

9 I have treated this subject in an essay "Technology as an Order of Reality," included in the Hebrew volume *Zeman u' Mashmaut (Time and Meaning)* (Tel Aviv: 1974).

10 J. Ellul, *The Technological Society*, p. 351. Ellul sees the connection between this question and the primacy of the whole being (p. 350).

INDEX OF NAMES

INDEX OF SUBJECTS

235